MY FAMILY AND OTHER PEOPLE'S CHILDREN

The Care Paradox

AMANDA KNOWLES, MBE

Troubador Publishing Ltd
Unit E2 Airfield Business Park
Harrison Road, Market Harborough
Leicestershire LE16 7UL
Tel: 0116 279 2299
Email: books@troubador.co.uk
Web: www.troubador.co.uk

ISBN 978 1 836283 17 1

British Library Cataloguing in Publication Data.
A catalogue record for this book is available from the British Library.

The manufacturer's authorised representative in the EU for product safety is Authorised Rep Compliance Ltd, 71 Lower Baggot Street, Dublin D02 P593 Ireland (www.arccompliance.com).

Printed and bound in Great Britain by 4edge Limited
Typeset in 11pt Minion Pro by Troubador Publishing Ltd, Leicester, UK

For Stories that Must
Be Told
With love
Amanda x

"Care is not a single story.
The British care system holds many truths.
To improve it all voices must be heard."

'In order to write about life first you must live it.'
— Ernest Hemingway

CONTENTS

Contents

AUTHOR'S NOTE

For five decades, I have had the privilege of working alongside some of society's most vulnerable children and young people – those failed by the very system designed to protect them. Throughout my career in children's social care, I have witnessed not only their extraordinary courage but also the deep systemic flaws that prevent their healing and hinder their future success. I have also been fortunate to work with children who, despite unimaginable odds, have not only survived but thrived, leading lives of remarkable success, resilience, and hope – lives that defy expectations and inspire us all.

My Family and Other People's Children: The Care Paradox is a deeply personal reflection on the challenges of working within a system that often prioritises compliance, bureaucracy, and outdated beliefs over the real needs of children, young people, and the caregivers who support them.

Throughout my career, I have seen firsthand the lasting effects of childhood trauma and its profound impact on the adults these children become. While many have overcome immense obstacles, far too many continue to carry emotional scars that persist into adulthood.

This memoir goes beyond statistics, inspection reports, and policies, offering a glimpse into the human faces and stories often hidden behind the headlines. It invites you to understand what it truly takes to care for children and young people who have experienced hardship and who long for safety, stability, and the support they deserve – far more than a compliance-driven bureaucracy can offer.

It is a call to rethink how we care for the most vulnerable in our society. It challenges the myths and assumptions that often shape public discourse and urges the creation of a system that fosters healing and growth, rather than one that merely enforces compliance to satisfy the agendas of those in power.

Disclaimer

The views expressed in this book are based on my personal experiences and professional observations. While I aim to reflect the realities of children's social care, this is not an exhaustive account of the field. Names and details have been changed to protect privacy. My goal is to provide a thought-provoking perspective on the challenges within the care system and inspire positive change in how we support vulnerable children, young people, and their caregivers.

1

IN THE SHADOW OF INJUSTICE
How Tragedy Shaped Children's Social Care

Over a century after Charles Dickens exposed the cruelty and neglect suffered by poor children in Victorian England, another tragedy gripped the nation – a tragedy that brings to light deep, systemic issues that resonate across generations. This is the story of Dennis O'Neill, a twelve-year-old boy who, like many others, was placed in foster care with the hope of a better life. But instead of care and protection, Dennis faced unimaginable cruelty at the hands of the Gough family, who were meant to care for him and his younger brother, Terry.

Sixty-nine years later, on the day after what would have been his seventy-eighth birthday, his younger brother Terry published *Someone to Love Us*, a memoir that laid bare the horrific reality of their childhood.

Terry had been just nine years old when he and Dennis were sent to live with the Goughs in their remote farmhouse in Hope, Shropshire. Thin and wide-eyed, the brothers clung to each other, trying to make sense of their new life, believing that if they worked hard enough, if they followed the rules, if they stayed out of the way, they might be safe. But it was never enough.

Dennis bore the worst of it. He was beaten for the smallest infractions, left hungry while others ate, and forced to carry out exhausting chores on an empty stomach. The punishments were relentless, each one stripping away another piece of him. Then, one morning, Terry woke up and couldn't wake Dennis. His brother's frail body had finally given out.

Terry was too young to understand what had happened, but the horror of that morning never left him – the stillness of Dennis's body, the silence where his brother's breath should have been, the terrible, unshakable realisation that no one had come to save them.

The case shocked the country. Newspapers carried the horror of Dennis's final days, his thin, battered body covered in bruises, the starvation, the violence, the sheer, merciless cruelty of it all. The public reeled at the idea that this could happen in a system meant to protect children.

The outrage was so intense that even Agatha Christie was drawn to the case, writing a radio play inspired by it that later became *The Mousetrap*, the longest-running play in history. It premiered in London's West End on November 25, 1952. But while the world moved on, reform, as always, moved too slowly. I was born five years and two months later.

Dennis O'Neill's death was not an unavoidable failure. It was the consequence of a system that failed to see children as people, instead treating them as mere cases to be handled, as resources to be shuffled around, as bodies to be placed wherever there was space.

For centuries, society justified cruelty in the name of discipline. It was ingrained in the treatment of charity children in nineteenth-century workhouses, in the cold, impersonal care of pauper homes, in the rigid authority of institutions that claimed to shape 'troubled' youth. But what happened to these children – what had happened to Dennis – was never about discipline. It was about control. Brutal, unrelenting, and unchecked.

In the aftermath of Dennis's death, the government could no longer ignore the rot at the heart of the child welfare system. Herbert Morrison, then Leader of the House of Commons, ordered an inquiry, led by Sir Walter Monckton, into what had gone so catastrophically wrong.

What emerged was a damning picture of a system that didn't check, didn't care, and didn't listen. Dennis and Terry had been placed with the Goughs despite multiple red flags, including previous allegations of mistreatment. Social workers, stretched thin and overworked, had failed to see – or chose not to see – what was happening behind closed doors. This failure to protect children was not unique to Dennis's case, but part of a larger, ongoing problem within the foster care system.

His death led to national outrage and the first major reform of children's services in Britain. It was meant to mark a turning point. But eighty years later, many of the same issues remain. The care system has grown – more staff, more regulation, more policy. And yet, children are still being harmed. In foster homes. In kinship care. In residential settings. The assumption that family-based care is safer continues, despite evidence that it isn't always the case. Some children thrive in foster care. Others find stability in residential homes. Neither model is automatically safe – it all depends on the quality of care and support.

The 2022 MacAlister Review largely reinforced existing approaches: expanding fostering and kinship placements, and calling for more targeted support. But little was said about the depth of relationships or the support needed to sustain them.

Inspections and regulation are now central to the system. Services are rated, protocols followed, but children still get moved without warning, their voices too often unheard. Compliance doesn't always mean care.

Some private providers profit. That's true. But the system as a whole has become a source of income for many – not just private companies, but public bodies, consultants, charities, and self-employed contractors. It's no longer just about protecting children. It's also about sustaining a structure. Focusing solely on providers misses the decisions that shaped this structure – the policy shifts that replaced universal support with targeted intervention, and help with scrutiny. These were choices, not accidents.

When children react to trauma with difficult behaviour, they're often punished for it. The system asks what's wrong with them, but rarely what's happened to them – or what might have helped earlier on.

After fifty years in childcare, one thing stands out: it's not the type of placement that matters most. It's the quality of the parenting – whoever is providing it. Children feel safe when someone sees them, stays with them, and responds with care and consistency. That kind of parenting doesn't just happen. It needs to be supported. And too often, it isn't.

In the 1970s, family support was widely available. It wasn't a mark of failure – it was a shared investment in children's well-being. Today, help arrives only when families are already in crisis. The system waits for things to go wrong, then intervenes with far more cost and disruption. If parenting had been properly supported from the start, many children might not have entered care at all.

Dennis O'Neill's death once sparked a promise that children would be better protected. But that promise remains, in many ways, unfulfilled. What keeps children safe isn't more systems. It's better relationships. It's getting parenting right – from the beginning, and for every child who needs it.

During the trial, Reginald Gough's past came under scrutiny. He had served in World War I, a fact his defence attempted to use to explain his brutality, arguing that he had been shaped by the rigid, punishing discipline of the military. It was a familiar narrative, one used many times before – the war-damaged man, hardened by combat, incapable of tenderness.

It was a convenient explanation, an excuse draped in the language of pity, as though war had stripped him of choice.

But no battlefield, no trench, no command from a superior officer could excuse what he did to Dennis. This was not a man trapped in memories of war, lashing out in fear and confusion. This was a man in full control, who held absolute power over two vulnerable boys and chose to wield it without mercy.

He beat them not in panicked reaction, but in cold calculation. He did not forget to feed them because his mind was lost in some distant battlefield – he deliberately starved them.

Trauma does not turn men into sadists. Soldiers who return from war with Post-Traumatic Stress Disorder (PTSD) do not automatically become abusers. More often, they withdraw. They live with guilt, with nightmares, with an unbearable weight pressing against their chests. Some numb themselves with alcohol. Others struggle to connect with their own families, not because they are cruel, but because war has made them feel like ghosts of the men they once were. They do not, as a rule, become executioners of children.

In the 1940s, PTSD had no name. It was still called shell shock, and the world had little patience for it. Veterans were expected to come home, find work, and reintegrate into normal life as if they hadn't just crawled through mud, watched friends die, or lived through ceaseless bombardment. Some couldn't cope. Some lashed out. Some – far too many – ended their own lives.

But what Gough's defence overlooked was that most men who returned from war, no matter how broken, did not turn to cruelty. There is a difference between a man broken by war and a man who chooses cruelty. Plenty of World War I veterans returned home carrying trauma, but they did not starve, beat, or torment children in their care.

The war might have hardened Gough. But it did not force his hand. He was not an unthinking casualty of circumstance; he was a man who held power and chose to wield it with deliberate brutality. It was easier to blame his past than to face the truth – that nothing in his suffering excused the terror he inflicted on two defenceless boys.

The jury was equally unconvinced. Gough was sentenced to six years in prison, while Esther Gough was given six months for neglect. The public, however, was unsatisfied – six years for the death of a child, six months for the woman who stood by and watched the boy waste away. This wasn't justice; it was a sentence steeped in the same indifference that had allowed Dennis to die in the first place.

In my own family, my great-grandfather's struggles with war-related trauma reflected the broader challenges faced by many returning soldiers and their families. The emotional distance and confusion he experienced had a profound impact on my great-grandmother, who struggled for years to manage the toll of his poor mental health until the situation became unbearable. Despite the social stigma of the time, she made the incredibly difficult decision to divorce him.

Divorce, when chosen by a woman, was once a quiet scandal – whispered about behind closed doors, especially when children were involved. But there was nothing shameful about it. It was an act of courage. She didn't walk away because it was easy; she walked away because it was necessary – to protect herself and her children. They were not sacrificed to a marriage that could no longer offer safety, nor handed over to a system that couldn't be trusted.

Dennis's story is not just one of a child failed by a foster care system – it is part of a larger, historical pattern of failure that spans generations. It is a reminder of the consequences when society ignores the needs of its most vulnerable members, whether they are children in care or veterans returning from war. Dennis O'Neill's death may have occurred more than eighty years ago, but its echoes are still felt today, reminding us that reform, when it comes, often comes too late. The scars left by such neglect can last for generations, shaping the lives of those who came after.

By the time the Monckton Report was published in 1946, the damage had already been done. It exposed a system incapable of protecting its most vulnerable children, laying bare the negligence and failures that had led to Dennis O'Neill's death. Public pressure and growing concern over children's welfare led to the Curtis Report later that year, which in turn paved the way for the 1948 Children Act.

For the first time, local authorities were given legal responsibility for the care and protection of children in need. The Act defined 'children in need,' prioritised fostering over institutions, and introduced family support measures aimed at preventing children from entering care unnecessarily. On paper, it was a significant step forward. But change was slow and the most at risk children remained in danger.

Dennis O'Neill would not be the last child to suffer under the weight of an excuse. For decades to come, history would repeat itself – too often, those in power told the same story: that the past had damaged them, that the system had failed them, that they too were victims. And too often, that story would be enough to convince the world to look away.

The reforms that followed Dennis's death promised protection, yet time and again, children continued to slip through the cracks. The failures that had condemned Dennis did not die with him; they remained hidden behind new policies, new inquiries, new reassurances – while the most vulnerable paid the price.

And yet, out of this horror came the push for reform. The Curtis Report had recommended fostering over institutions, driven by the belief that a home environment was safer than the harsh, impersonal conditions of large residential facilities. Institutions were overcrowded, underfunded, and often cold, sterile places where children received little personal attention. Foster care, by contrast, was held up as the ideal – a place of warmth, stability, and family life.

These recommendations formed the basis of the *1948 Children Act*, which aimed to provide children with the kind of homes they had been denied for so long. But Dennis O'Neill hadn't died in an institution. He had died in a foster home.

This was the great contradiction at the heart of the reforms that followed. The solution had been presented as fostering over institutions, even though it was in a foster home that Dennis had been beaten and starved to death. The idea that a *'home'* was automatically safer than an institution was a dangerous illusion. A home is only as safe as the people inside it.

The Goughs had been entrusted with two vulnerable boys despite clear warning signs that they were unfit foster carers. Social workers, overwhelmed and under-resourced, failed to check on the boys properly, and the system that was supposed to safeguard them instead delivered them straight into harm's way.

By the time I joined the children's workforce in the mid-1970s, sweeping changes were already underway. The 1967 Williams Committee Report – *Care of the People* – had laid bare the realities of the workforce: two-thirds were single women, a third were over fifty, and most lived in the homes they worked in. The introduction of set working hours and formal training programs was meant to professionalise the workforce.

In 1969, the *Children and Young Persons Act* abolished the old, approved *schools* and replaced them with community homes. Then, in 1970, the *Local Authority Social Services Act* merged social care responsibilities under a single department. Change was happening fast – too fast, in some cases. The system struggled to keep up, and vulnerable children slipped through the cracks.

This became tragically clear in 1973, when Maria Colwell, a seven-year-old girl from Brighton, England, was killed by her stepfather, William Henry Kepple, in January 1973. She suffered prolonged abuse and neglect before being fatally beaten by Kepple.

Maria had been placed with her aunt and uncle after her mother, overwhelmed with five children, couldn't cope. Despite her relatives' objections, the newly formed social services department decided to return Maria to her mother.

The result was horrific. She suffered sustained abuse at home, and when she died, the nation erupted in outrage. The press was relentless. The phrase 'social services failure' became a media staple, and the scrutiny has never gone away.

A few years later, another scandal erupted. Staff at a local authority-run assessment centre reported mistreatment, describing a culture of control and punishment rather than care. The Manager had a background in approved schools – institutions where physical punishment had been the norm for generations. Despite warnings, he was reinstated.

Frustrated staff raised their concerns with their MP, who demanded an explanation. The Director of Social Services dismissed the complaints, and that might have been the end of it if the staff hadn't turned to the press.

What followed was a public inquiry that exposed a deeply disturbing reality: the routine use of corporal punishment, the forceful restraint of children trying to leave, and the systematic humiliation of those in care. The inquiry condemned the practices, yet in the end, it justified some forms of control. A police investigation followed. No charges were filed, and nothing really changed. After receiving a formal warning, the Manager was reinstated.

The Director of Social Services defended the decision, citing the officer's background in approved schools – institutions where corporal punishment had been accepted for generations. It was a quiet admission that, for all the reforms, the thinking had not truly changed. The names had changed, the policies rewritten, but the same logic prevailed: discipline over care, control over compassion.

Even in children's homes, where the most vulnerable were meant to be protected, corporal punishment remained legal until 1987 in England and Wales. Little wonder, then, that the abuse scandals of the '70s, '80s, and '90s followed in their wake. These were not isolated incidents but the inevitable result of a system that, while changing its outward appearance, had never truly challenged the deep-seated belief that discipline, and control mattered more than protection and care.

It was clear that renaming Approved Schools as Community Homes had never been enough to dismantle the culture that allowed such abuse to fester. The officer, like so many before him, had been shaped by an environment where punishment was expected, and compassion was not even an afterthought. And so, despite all the promises of reform, those old ways had quietly continued to shape decisions.

There were calls to bring back the old, approved schools, run by charities like Barnardo's and overseen by the Home Office or the Scottish Education Department. Originally intended for juvenile offenders, these institutions had also housed children deemed 'beyond parental control' – many of whom had simply been abandoned.

But the reality was the same, whether in a community home or an institution. These children were still being failed, still facing the same neglect, still growing up in places where punishment was prioritised over protection. Homes were overcrowded, staff were untrained, and children carrying deep emotional wounds were too often met with brutal control instead of compassion.

Two years later, at barely eighteen, I entered the world of children's social care, just as the Equal Pay Act came into force after a hard-fought battle. Women dominated the workforce, yet leadership remained out of reach for most of them. At the time, only a handful of women had risen to the rank of Director of Social Services, their presence in senior positions the exception rather than the norm.

The closure of approved schools had drawn more men into children's social care, attracted by non-residential roles and fixed hours, but senior positions still belonged largely to them. Many climbed the ladder quickly, some with little real understanding of caregiving – decision-makers who had never spent a night comforting a distressed child or de-escalating the quiet rage of one who had learned too soon that trust was dangerous.

Policy decisions were often made without consulting those on the front lines. Worse still, some of the so-called experts steering the system had no place in it at all. Peter Righton, once a respected lecturer on child protection and government adviser, would later be exposed as a child abuser. His arrest in the 1990s revealed not just his crimes but the deep failings of a system that had allowed him to operate unchecked, shaping policies while hiding in plain sight.

By the time I entered children's social care in the mid-1970s, sweeping changes were already in motion. But the real lesson had yet to be learned. The belief that a family setting was always best persisted, even as case after case exposed the harsh truth

– children were still suffering, still being abused behind closed doors.

Foster homes could be places of love and healing, but they could also be places of terror – just like the institutions before them. The problem was never about choosing between institutions and fostering; it was about oversight. It wasn't about where the children lived, it was about whether anyone was really watching.

Hey Miss

Hey Miss, *will you ever notice what's going on, because you come to our house, you're here five minutes then you're gone. You never ask us about our rooms, about our beds or that big bruise. It's all well and good giving smiles; admiring our 'new' toy. But you never asked us any questions before you were straight back out the door. You never asked me if I'm happy or what was my favourite thing or what made me scared of the nighttime...you never asked none of them things.*

Hey Miss, *will you tell me what's on them papers you carry, because I think they're about us...but you're always in and out in a hurry, so I can't ask you, what they were. I need you to say what you mean and mean what you say, if you don't then I get thoughts in my head; I can't make them go away. If I did ask you a question, would you answer... because I can tell when people really don't want to say stuff?*

How am I ever supposed to trust ya to tell you my stuff, if you won't even stay long enough; for me to properly know your name?

Hey Miss, *will you tell me what's going on? I'm scared of all the big people, and it feels like I've done something wrong. I need you to let me know things, even if it won't be ok. I need you to explain the meetings and lots of the things that you say.*

I need you to hear my side. Don't try and shut me up. I have lots of things to tell you and usually start with the safe silly stuff. So, will you give me the time to get around to opening up?

Hey Miss, *will you not talk about me like I'm not there. If you bring me into the conversation, then it's more likely* *that I'll share. I might tell you about the things that are bothering me, my thoughts about my future and where I'd like to be. I might tell you about the things that have played on my mind, made me grumpy and angry; feel awful inside.*

My thoughts and feelings are precious. I don't want them to be dismissed. And if I feel that they are, then I might just call it quits and not try to tell you anything ever again; and would you even remember them anyway.

Hey Miss, *will you remember that I really hate peas, that my best friend is my dog Bandit; that my sister is Emma-Louise.*

Will you remember that I dropped some clues while we were chatting, that I left you some breadcrumbs to follow because I couldn't speak about 'it'; will you remember that tomorrow?

Will you remember the things that are special to me, the things that make me scream? Will you remember the things that make me cross so you can help me blow off steam, in a safe way?

Will you remember all of those things because it shows me that you care, and maybe I can start to trust you a little bit to maybe start to share?

I might tell you my hopes, goals and dreams because I do have all of those things. If only you will be there, be present and try to tune in. Will you ask, notice, listen and remember the little bits, because it's all of them things that will help me put back together the blocks to make positive relationships.

Hey Miss, *will you show me that you kind of understand? Will you appreciate my emotions? Will you try to comprehend where it is that* ***I'M*** *coming from, because I need to know that despite all of this stuff that I'm worth a chance, I'm worth a go!!*

Saira-Jayne Jones

2

FROM MILK BOTTLES TO MILESTONES
Early Lessons in Care

The light was fading fast as I stepped off the bus. Pulling up the collar of my big coat against the icy rain, I walked up the hill to the red-brick house. When I reached the oversized door that separated my future from my past, I hesitated. I was just eighteen. Some of the kids in that house were barely younger than me. My rebellious teenage years weren't far behind, and I wondered – would they take kindly to me?

Gillian Starling, the boss from the office who had interviewed me, had said she was confident I'd get on well with the young people in this home. I wasn't so sure.

Taking a deep breath, I knocked at the door.

The Manager opened it and greeted me, introducing herself as Carol before stepping aside to let me and my borrowed suitcase inside. She was likely in her late twenties, but her weary expression and drab clothes made her seem much older. She lived at the home with her two-year-old son and her husband, who worked at the nearby aircraft factory.

Live-in house parents were not unusual in that era. Her husband received free board and lodging in exchange for spending time with the children and young people in the evenings and on weekends – although I would soon learn that he rarely did.

The family had their own lounge and two bedrooms connected by an adjoining door; a setup typical of family group homes since the 1950s. However, homes run by married couples were being phased out. Old job titles were being replaced: Managers became officers in charge, and working hours were standardised.

These changes created a demand for more staff and opened the door to people like me. I was employed as a residential childcare officer, sometimes referred to as a housemother, and often mistaken for one of the kids. I had not considered working in a children's home until I met Mark, my future husband, who spoke passionately about his own work with children and young people.

After leaving school, I walked straight into a job; having one was simply expected of me. I had already become accustomed to earning my own money delivering newspapers at thirteen and later as a Saturday girl stacking shelves at the local Co-op before leaving school the year after the government raised the school-leaving age. I probably would have stayed there, but it wasn't long before my parents were on the move.

The world was on the brink of a recession, and men like Mark's father and mine were told to relocate if they wanted to find work. Mark was forced to leave his beloved childhood home in the valley, where cotton was no longer king, when his dad faced the stark choice of relocation or redundancy.

My dad confronted the same reality when Royal Doulton announced the closure of one of its three remaining factories in Stoke-on-Trent, making five hundred potters redundant. This was yet another nail in the coffin of a city that had once been at the forefront of the Industrial Revolution. An inability to compete with foreign prices led to successive layoffs, mergers, and factory closures, leaving entire families without work.

Seeing no future in Stoke, my dad took a job at Hornsea Pottery in Lancaster, where he would train others to make pottery. It was his dream job, but my worst nightmare. I had a job and a boyfriend, and leaving either was unthinkable.

My boyfriend's mum offered me a place to stay, but it never truly felt like home. An unspoken pressure weighed on me every day. I felt I had to prove I wasn't lazy or ungrateful, so I made sure I was always the first one home to start preparing tea and the first to jump up from the table to wash the dishes. It wasn't just about helping – it was about not being seen as a burden and constantly trying to please people.

A year later, the relationship was over. I was homeless, with no choice but to follow my family to Lancaster. Letting goes of the life I had envisioned left me feeling uprooted, but I knew that dwelling on it wouldn't change reality.

Living off my mum and dad was not an option. This was 1975, and inflation was squeezing household budgets – I needed a job. Fortunately, I had left school with a handful of GCE qualifications across various subjects, though I likely wouldn't have taken any exams if the government hadn't raised the school-leaving age from fifteen to sixteen in 1974.

That policy change helped me secure a job as a trainee lab technician at the University of Lancaster. Shortly after, I met Mark, who worked on the children's ward at Lancaster Moor Hospital, caring for children and young people with brain conditions like epilepsy, as well as those with mental health challenges and emotional or behavioural difficulties.

Mark loved working with the children – whether it was helping them with schoolwork, taking them on adventures, or engaging them in activities. He found real meaning in those moments of connection. But there were other times, tougher times, when he found himself pleading with them to stay calm, believing that 'the jab,' as both children and staff called it, was more about control than care.

Care-experienced author Nigel Cooper, who was admitted to the unit twice, later wrote about his experience of this practice in '*Boy: A Memoir – One Child's Fight to Survive in the Brutal British Care System.*' Nigel had been admitted to the unit for assessment at just eight years old in 1974, marking the beginning of nearly a decade spent in various institutions. At the time, such placements were seen as necessary for children deemed to need specialist psychiatric care. But for those who lived it, the towering former asylum in Lancashire felt anything but a place of healing.

It was during this time that he experienced the routine use of powerful antipsychotic drugs, often injected without consent. His memoir recounts moments of deep frustration and powerlessness, memories that would stay with him long after he left:

> '*My blood was boiling, but I didn't know what to do to release my inner hatred and anger. So, I grabbed the glass jar of pencils off the table… and threw the glass jar as hard as I could in the direction of his head… He grabbed me and wrestled me to the floor… A minute later, Matron returned with a large syringe. She pulled my pants down and stabbed me in the right buttock. It hurt like hell, and after a short while, my legs started to feel numb.*'

This was Acuphase – an antipsychotic sedative used to subdue distress or perceived disobedience. In theory, it was meant to calm children in crisis; in practice, it became a tool of misguided intentions in the hands of mistakenly legitimised experts. Mark had seen it too. He arrived at the unit as a young man, not yet in his twenties and new to the world of care, and it didn't take long for him to grasp how things really worked.

Like Nigel, he had watched children subdued with medication, their emotions treated as something to be silenced rather than understood. He spent countless hours trying to reassure them, urging them to stay calm – not because he agreed with the system, but because he knew what would happen if they didn't. Though they were on opposite sides of the care journey, both Mark and Nigel bore witness to a system that prioritised control over care – one they were powerless to change.

When the panic alarm sounded, it meant someone was in distress on the locked adult ward. Nurses from other wards were sent to assist. Mark witnessed patients being forcibly restrained and was deeply unsettled by some of the practices he was expected to take part in. At times, when the alarm rang out, he would hide to avoid being sent to C Upper – the secure adult ward – fearing he would be dragged into interventions he was neither trained nor equipped to handle. Unsurprisingly, after these experiences, he abandoned any thoughts of pursuing a career in psychiatric nursing. Fortunately my own early encounters with care were rooted in something much more domestic.

As children, my brother, sister, and I grew up alongside foster children cared for by my mother's lifelong friend, as well as her own. Each year, we were sent home from school with *Sunny Smiles* – a small book of black-and-white photographs of babies and children. We sold these photos to raise funds for the National Children's Society, a Methodist charity that had opened its first home for vulnerable children in London in 1869. A century later, my older sister and I spent the summer collecting clothing and bric-a-brac to sell at a jumble sale, with the proceeds supporting Penkhull Cottage Homes.

Looking back, it's clear how deeply our lives were shaped by the post-war welfare state. From access to affordable housing and stable employment in public services, to the ethos of collective responsibility that shaped our upbringing, the welfare state wasn't just a policy – it was the backdrop to our daily lives.

Some of those around us had come from the Caribbean. They had been invited to Britain to help rebuild the country after the war and worked alongside our parents in hospitals, on the buses, and in public health, helping to keep essential services running. I was born ten years after the first arrivals – when the *Empire Windrush*, carrying 492 passengers from Jamaica and other Caribbean islands, docked at Tilbury in Essex on 22 June 1948.

I remember the district nurse who worked in our community – a Black woman, calm, capable, and respected. It was her uniform that made her stand out to me as a child: dark blue with crisp white cuffs and collar, always immaculate. I can still picture my mum chatting to her when we bumped into her on the street – neighbourly, familiar, part of the everyday.

Health and welfare were woven into the rhythms of daily life – we had a school clinic with its own dentist, and a school nurse we called *Nitty Nora*, who checked our hair for lice with a fine-toothed comb and a practised eye. At school, we were given milk at morning break – those little third-of-a-pint bottles with the foil tops – and if there were any left over, I was always first in the queue for another. I still have a liking for a comforting glass of cold milk to this day.

Their contribution formed part of the same fabric of public service and social duty that shaped our own values and choices as young adults.

I was thankful when Mark and I found jobs in children's homes run by social services. Even more so when I learned that my position came with key worker status, making me eligible for a council flat when I relocated from Lancaster to Oldham. The rent was just £6 a week, including heating from a central boiler, which was a real help. Back then, staff had to declare any meals eaten on duty, with the cost deducted from their wages. After these deductions, my monthly take-home pay for a forty-two-hour week, plus sleep-ins, was roughly £105.

On my first night at the home, I found myself looking after the six children and young people who lived there – along with the couple's own child – while they went out for the evening. The children had no reason to trust me, and I knew I had to earn their respect. Among them were four teenagers: Keith, Pauline, Matthew, and his brother John, as well as the youngest, a brother and sister named Michael and Valarie.

Their dad worked at Swizzels sweet factory in New Mills and, like many single parents at the time, had no choice but to ask social services to care for his children when their mother left. He wasn't the only one.

Years later, I learned that the woman who appointed me had also grown up in care – one of five sisters who were taken into care when their mother walked out, and their father asked for help.

Each week, when he came to visit, their dad arrived like Willy Wonka, with a bag full of sweets. Love Hearts were their absolute favourite – mine too, if I'm honest. But one weekend, as we munched our way through nearly the whole bag during a film, we discovered the perils of bingeing on fizzy sweets.

We were about halfway through *Chitty Chitty Bang Bang* when I realised the bag was nearly empty. I didn't know what a sugar rush was back then. It started with giggling, then cushion rearranging, then tearing around and trying to somersault off the settee like they were auditioning for a Bond film. And if someone had rigged up a turbine, we honestly could have powered a small wind farm. I didn't know then how much I'd come to treasure moments like that.

My days began at two in the afternoon with a quick catch-up with the staff going off duty. Then it was time to prepare the evening meal. During term time, when the children and young people returned from school, they were expected to change out of their school uniforms and complete their homework before tea. However, this didn't always happen, especially with the Keith, who saw little point in homework and had already written off his education.

After tea, the children had chores – including washing up, the least popular task, which often led to squabbles and tantrums. I quickly learned that confrontation only made things worse. Instead, I'd sigh and say, *'I guess it must be my turn again then'* ... A bit of friendly banter and a willingness to muck in always worked better than a battle of wills.

Early on, I learned the importance of trusting my judgment rather than blindly following orders – even from higher-ups.

One unforgettable incident cemented that lesson. I was on duty with a senior staff member who allowed the kids to stay up and watch a horror film. I don't remember the title, but I do remember how frightening it was.

After it ended, thirteen-year-old Matthew took his supper pots into the kitchen. Moments later, he reappeared, holding two knives and moving toward my colleague in a way that immediately set me on edge. With the knives at her throat, instinct left no room for hesitation. I stepped in, speaking calmly, keeping my voice steady. For a brief second, the room felt completely still, the tension thick. Then, after what felt like an eternity, Matthew slowly lowered the knives.

Thankfully no one was hurt, but the weight of what could have happened has never left me. That night, I learned an important lesson – late-night horror films weren't just a bad idea; they had the potential to influence behaviour in ways that hadn't been considered. I also learned that rank does not always get things right.

The hardest part of the job was trying to make sense of the children's lives. One incident stands out. Keith, the eldest, was in his final year of high school when he was caught stealing food from the larder.

Unlike in a typical family home, where food was bought locally, ours arrived weekly in bulk from contracted suppliers. The walk-in larder resembled a small convenience store, and for Keith, the temptation was too much. When he took one too many catering-sized tins of coffee for it to go unnoticed, the police were called. It later emerged that he had been stealing food to sell to the school caretaker for some time. Yet while Keith faced punishment, the caretaker faced none. And there were other moments that, even now, seem more unbelievable.

I vividly recall one involving Pauline, our quiet, fourteen-year-old with big blue eyes. One night, after lights out, she came to me, tears silently streaming down her cheeks. She was in severe pain from a breast abscess, and to my shock, the ambulance crew I had called for assistance told me she was also in the late stages of pregnancy. I hadn't been prepared for this – how could I have been?

A young girl, still a child, carrying the weight of a pregnancy while enduring excruciating pain. Pauline clung to me her body too small, too young for what was happening to it. I called the emergency social work team, hoping they could help. They couldn't. And I couldn't leave the other children alone at the home. There was no choice – Pauline had to go to the hospital with the ambulance crew on her own.

The image of that night stays with me – her pain, her fear, her small frame disappearing through the ambulance doors. A child, in every sense of the word, forced to bear the unbearable alone. And I, too, was alone. Still learning how to navigate my role as a housemother, still figuring out where I fit in a system that so often left us to fend for ourselves. And largely still does.

A few days later, she returned from the hospital – withdrawn and changed. No longer a mother-to-be. No one spoke about it.

The silence hung in the air, heavy with unanswered questions and unspoken pain.

I worried about what she had endured – alone, without the care or support she so desperately needed. But there were no conversations, no follow-ups, no space for her to process what had happened, and no debrief for me. And so, like so many things in that era, it was left unspoken. But not forgotten.

Another issue involved staff sleeping arrangements. When the Manager went to stay with her mother on her days off, her husband remained in the home – but he wasn't responsible for the children. This meant staff had to sleep in a bedroom with a connecting door that couldn't be locked from our side.

At first, it was an uncomfortable inconvenience. Then he started making comments – offhand remarks about the door, always delivered with a smirk, words that lingered just long enough to unsettle. Not outright threats, but laced with innuendo, inappropriate, and impossible to ignore.

Yet instead of addressing the risk – securing the door, relocating staff, or even questioning why he was allowed to stay – we were told to barricade it with a chest of drawers. The logic was simple: if he tried to enter, the noise would wake us. That was the solution. The fact that this measure was even necessary should have been enough, yet it was brushed aside as if we were overreacting.

It was a stark reminder of how easily women's safety was dismissed. In the 1970s, discomfort was ours to endure, unwanted attention was ours to deflect, and risks were ours to navigate. Challenging them was rarely an option. This was avoidant – a crude response that exposed the gaping holes in policy. Those driving the professionalisation of childcare claimed progress, yet time and time again, fundamental issues were ignored, and failures emerged.

As a new kid on the block in the 1970s, I very quickly

learned that the only predictable part of the job was that it was unpredictable.

One morning, while serving breakfast, a sharp knock echoed through the house. As I hurried to answer the door, I placed the milk bottle on the table, ready to refill the jug. To my surprise, it was Gillian Starling, the home's advisor. I wondered why she had arrived so early – barely past eight o'clock – before noticing her disapproving gaze fixed on the milk bottle. Her expression alone delivered the reprimand: *'That should not be on the table.'*

Later, after the children had left for school, Mrs. Starling explained she was conducting an in-depth inquiry into the home's operations. At the time, I hadn't known the reason for her visit, and by the time I eventually saw the inquiry report, the Manager was already gone. Reading the comment that milk jugs should always be used at the table left me with an unexpected pang of shame – I hadn't even explained why that milk bottle had been on the table in the first place.

That small moment has stayed with me over the years, a reminder of how easily we rely on assumptions, how quickly judgments are passed, and how fairness must extend not only to children and young people, but also to those who care for them.

As Christmas 1976 approached, I chose to work on Christmas Day, eager to make it special. I planned to fill pillowcases with presents for the kids, just as my mother had done for me and my siblings. With a tight budget, I drew on her lessons too. She had shown me how to make every penny count – how to stretch even the smallest amount as far as it would go. So, with a list in hand and a careful eye, I made my way to the town's bustling street market. I weaved through the colourful stalls, eyes scanning for treasures, determined to make Christmas as special as it could be.

As I shopped, the stallholders, hearing about my mission, surprised me with donated gifts and generous discounts. Filled with gratitude, I returned to the home, a sense of achievement brimming within me. Carefully, I wrapped each present, hoping to create a Christmas morning they would recall with a smile.

On Christmas Day, six pillowcases overflowed with gifts for six bleary-eyed kids. The room soon awash with wrapping paper. After the last present was unwrapped, we sat down to a traditional breakfast. Later, we listened to the Queen's Speech, pulled crackers, and wore paper hats for dinner.

I knew it wasn't the idyllic family scene from storybooks and films. For some children, it was a painful reminder of the families they missed – the ones they longed to be with, wanting nothing more than to be by their side. Sometimes those families hadn't been safe, but they were familiar. In children's homes and foster homes, they were surrounded by strangers – even if those strangers were kind. And for a child, there can be comfort in what's known, even when it hurts. Because the unknown – the unfamiliar faces, new rules, different smells, the feeling of not belonging – can be its own kind of danger.

And if I'm honest, I'm not sure it ever truly lived up to that perfect picture for anyone. But I hoped that, in that moment, simply wanting to be there with them could offer some comfort and reassurance.

As Christmas and New Year's celebrations faded, the home settled back into its usual rhythm. This was the year of the Queen's Silver Jubilee, punk music was taking root, and Mark and I were planning an early spring wedding.

We married on a wet and blustery March Day, the kind where the wind howls through the streets and the rain feels like it's falling sideways. It wasn't picture-perfect, but it was ours. A quintessential 70s wedding – nothing extravagant, but full of charm. My dress was a simple, affordable find from Debenhams, paired with a blue and white garter, my 'something blue.' Mark, my handsome beau, wore a brown suit, crisp white shirt, and a bow tie that, according to him, looked more like a bat than the finishing touch to his outfit for the big day. Mark, forever the comedian, has always made me laugh – it's saved his bacon on many occasions!

Looking back, it was all wonderfully of its time – imperfect, budget-conscious, and absolutely ours. For the photographs outside the church, there was a brief pause in the rain – just long enough to capture a few hurried shots before the heavens opened again. I stood on mats from the car, gripping my dress to keep it from soaking up rainwater from the ground, while the wind tugged at my veil and blew my hair in every direction.

Mark stood beside me, his brown flared trouser suit speckled with raindrops, his bow tie slightly askew. Guests shifted uncomfortably – some clutching their coats tight against the cold, others huddled under umbrellas that dripped steadily onto their new shoes. The photographer worked quickly, shouting over the wind, while someone – probably my uncle Graham – made the usual joke about rain being lucky.

It's something older people said at weddings, especially when the weather turned. The idea is that rain brings good luck – that it symbolises cleansing, a fresh start, or even that a wet knot is harder to untie. Maybe it's just a way to make everyone feel better when the sky doesn't cooperate.

And in the group photo for the album, Mark's grandma and great aunt stood centre stage, their nylon knitted bags with wooden handles on proud display – a gift from his mum, practical, treasured, and completely out of place in a wedding photo. But it was real, and it was ours.

After a hearty meal and heartfelt speeches, we danced into the night to the sounds of the '60s and '70s – stumbling through the steps of songs we had grown up with, laughing as we went. 'Brown Eyed Girl' had everyone spinning in circles, while 'Dancing Queen' filled the floor with a mix of enthusiasm and questionable footwork. Someone requested 'Sweet Caroline' and the whole room erupted in off-key singing, arms around shoulders. Later, couples slowed to a sway for 'Unchained Melody', as the lights dimmed, and the day drew to a close... Mark's dad had said he would take care of the disco – naively we thought that meant he would pay for it.

We should have known better – after all, it did sound too good to be true. His version was... "I said I would sort it, not pay for it." That was Mark's dad – forgivably tight-fisted to the very end. He once told Mark that if he died with 2/6d in his pocket, he would haunt the person who inherited it. It was his plan to live every day as if it were his last – because one day, it would be. And he most definitely did that.

Mark's dad was another returning veteran carrying scars that never truly healed, only this time from the Second World War. Born in India during the time of the Raj, he enlisted underage at 17 – too young by law to fight overseas, but, like so many others, he lied to serve his country. Eventually, he was captured and held by the Germans as a prisoner of war until the Russian's liberated the camp before the war ended. He rarely spoke about it.

There was just one photograph of him as a young man, marked with his prisoner number, to tell his story. When Mark's sister was small, she would sit on the front step, looking like butter wouldn't melt in her mouth, proudly telling any passerby willing to listen that her daddy had been in prison.

Among his things, hidden in a box, was a letter from the King and an oak leaf medal. He'd been mentioned in dispatches, but it was never shown or spoken about. If All Our Yesterdays was on the television when he came home, he turned it off – it was too close to memories that could never be allowed to surface. Those memories stayed buried, locked away, along with the stories we were never told.

Like my great-grandfather, he came home changed. He

could be funny, charming, and generous – especially over a pint and a game of dominos in the pub with his mates. As a father, he was fiercely protective but distant. He was a product of his upbringing, a generation that learned to survive through emotional restraint and self-preservation. It was his way of managing the trauma of past experiences.

It was a different war, but it mirrored the same silence that shaped generations. The damage wasn't always visible to the naked eye, but it was there. Passed down, reshaped, and inherited. Sometimes it came out as anger. Sometimes as absence. Sometimes as a joke at a wedding no one really laughed at.

Amid the unexpected financial crisis – saved only by the cash from the wedding cards and a whip-round to pay the DJ – my dad took centre stage. He dropped the wedding cake, a gift made by a family friend and iced specially in Wedgwood blue and white, for the girl from Stoke-on-Trent. The icing on the cake, if you'll forgive the pun, was that he'd agreed to be our chauffeur, but the car had one final twist in the tale for us that day when it refused to start.

3

BEHIND CLOSED DOORS
Behind the Façade

So, there we were, in full wedding finery, wedding cake in bits, wedding night on hold, pushing the car down the road in the freezing rain. When we finally arrived at our honeymoon destination, we looked like a couple of drowned rats drenched through and shivering, but somehow still smiling. We had a love to keep us warm. It was like a scene straight out of a comedy sketch – the kind of catastrophe that makes you laugh for years to come, because sometimes, that's all you can do when the universe decides to throw one more twist into the mix. Stick together and keep smiling.

But the day's mishaps weren't the only curveballs thrown our way as we embarked on married life. The financial challenges we faced were equally beyond our control. Prices had risen sharply in just three years. Income tax had increased from 33p to 35p in the pound, and inflation remained stubbornly high in double figures for the fourth consecutive year.

Wages never seemed to stretch far enough, and even the simplest luxuries felt out of reach – not because we couldn't afford the occasional treat, but because every spare penny was going toward saving for a deposit to buy our own house.

The Queen's Silver Jubilee celebrations later that year offered a brief distraction from the economic struggles – bunting-lined streets, Union Jacks waving from windows, and neighbours gathering for street parties – but the challenges remained.

And so, reality set in. There was no grand honeymoon at a romantic getaway, our wedding night was spent at my sister's flat across the road from Morecambe bus station. Nothing extravagant – just the hum of late-night buses pulling in and out of the station. We were back at work on Monday.

For couples like us in the 1970s, buying a starter home was a first step on the property ladder and a chance to put down roots. It was something that had been out of reach for our parents, and we didn't take it for granted. By the time we collected the keys, we knew what it had taken to get there.

It was definitely one thing we could thank Maggie Thatcher for. With ninety-five, even one hundred percent mortgages, and tax relief on the interest, homeownership – once unimaginable for many in our parents' generation – became a real possibility for ordinary couples like us. To us it was a mansion, and it was ours. Above all, we were back in the town that Mark called home – and that meant a lot to him. For me, it was a new beginning.

Mark had secured a job at a local home for teenage boys – many of whom were streetwise, having lived lives far more challenging than our own.

At work, Mark was one of several male staff supporting the boys, offering guidance and discipline when needed, while I took on a role at a nearby family group children's home. Situated on a council estate, the purpose-built facility was designed to feel more like a home than an institution. The goal was to provide the children with an environment as close to ordinary family life as possible, giving them the chance to experience normalcy in a world that had often been anything but.

The children attended local schools, made friends in the neighbourhood, and participated in community activities. They were integrated into the daily rhythms of life, but I soon discovered that not all homes shared this vision. The reality was far more complicated.

The following year, I was asked to move to another home under difficult circumstances. The request came in the wake of an incident that had made national news. A thirteen-year-old boy had handed his social worker a dossier detailing mistreatment. The manager was suspended, and an investigation was launched. However, by the time I arrived, no charges had been filed. The accuser had been moved, and the manager was reinstated, remaining in the role until her retirement a few months later.

From the outside, the home looked like a respectable Edwardian house – solid, familiar, even a little grand. The garden was neat and well-tended by local authority gardeners, and impressive stained-glass windows framed the front door. To the right, a large bay-windowed room – the music room – remained locked, except when the man from the office brought visitors to the home. Behind it was the manager's living room, adjacent to the dining kitchen where the children spent most of their time when not at school – or outside, which is where they were required to be, come rain, hail or shine.

The space was cramped, with barely enough room to navigate between the dining table and chairs. The easy chair, carefully positioned, was reserved for staff. The television was tucked into an alcove between the window and the chimney breast. Beyond that lay the kitchen and the children's bathroom.

What struck me most as I scanned the bare rooms for signs of childhood was the complete absence of toys. Only colouring books and crayons were available to occupy young minds.

Where were the games, the Lego sets, the Barbies? Not even a teddy bear lay waiting to comfort a troubled child. The message that echoed through the barren spaces was clear: Children should be seen and not heard.

Often, they'd spot me from the garden and come running, greeting me at the gate before I'd even reached the path. By the time I got to the front door, I was dripping in kids – clinging to my arms, holding my hands, talking over one another in that lovely, breathless way children do when they're excited to see you. Once inside, the contrast was jarring. There was almost always a list of tasks waiting for me, most of which felt meaningless and unnecessary.

One day, I arrived to find that every curtain in the house had been taken down, washed, dried, and left in a crumpled heap for me to iron and rehang. No explanation, no conversation – just a silent directive waiting on the dining table. There were curtains in every room: heavy fabric, awkward to handle, some with fiddly hooks that refused to cooperate. I stood there for a moment, looking at the pile, knowing full well that by the time I'd finished, there would be no time left to spend with the children.

It felt deliberate – a quiet, well-practised misuse of power. Not loud or confrontational but controlling in the way that chips away at your purpose. A message, unspoken but clear: don't get too close, don't get too comfortable. Keep to your tasks, tick the boxes, stay in your place.

There was something particularly petty about it – an act that served no urgent need but demanded energy and time all the same. And worse still, it came at the expense of what really mattered: connection, consistency, and simply being present with the children who needed it most.

And it wasn't long before curiosity got the better of me. It wasn't in my nature to leave questions unanswered, and I had plenty. Even so, I'm not sure what drew me to the attic at that moment, but whatever it was, I'm glad it did. The cramped, dusty space was filled with forgotten children's toys – relics of years gone by, each one holding its own story – and a massive trunk, overflowing with fireworks.

It was packed to the brim with them, stacked haphazardly on top of one another, their once-bright wrappers now faded. Reds, blues, and greens dulled by age. We'd probably call them "vintage" today, but I recognised the designs from my childhood: rockets, fountains, Roman candles – names that triggered a strange mix of nostalgia and unease.

I stood there for a moment, unsure what to make of it all. No box, no careful storage – just loose fireworks, packed together as though someone had once planned to do something with them, and then… didn't. At first, the sight felt out of place – chaotic, risky, odd. But the longer I stood there, the more I began to wonder.

Maybe they'd been donated – well-meaning, even generous. A plan for a celebration that never came to pass. A bonfire night that was cancelled or forgotten. Maybe the children they were meant for had already left.

And maybe – just maybe – they'd been deliberately set aside. Because fun wasn't encouraged here.

The woman who ran the home wasn't openly cruel, at least not in front of others. But her meanness was threaded through the place – in the way rooms were kept, in the way silence was expected, in the way the children were spoken to when she thought no one was listening. You could see it everywhere: the locked pantry, the absence of comfort, the lists left waiting on the table. You could almost smell it – something stale, heavy in the air, as if the house itself had absorbed the mood and held it in its walls.

There was something quietly sad about it. Like the toys in the attic, the fireworks felt like another promise packed away. A burst of colour, excitement, fun – denied or delayed for reasons no one ever bothered to ask. And downstairs, the crayons waited in their tin.

When I was nine, before we moved, we lived in a quiet cul-de-sac. On Bonfire Night, the whole street would gather in the field behind our house to celebrate. We'd feast on potatoes baked in the fire, treacle toffee, and sticky toffee apples, the air thick with smoke from the fire and the fireworks that only dads and big boys were allowed to go near. The next day, we little kids would rummage through the charred remains, hunting for fireworks that hadn't gone off, as if they were hidden treasure.

That sight in the attic took me straight back to those nights – when fireworks meant excitement, not unease.

It's only as I looked back, that I truly appreciated the dangers we so eagerly ignored, lost in the excitement of the adventure. But as I stared at those fireworks in the trunk, a feeling of unease began to creep in. These were relics of a celebration that, for whatever reason, had never happened. It felt wrong to see them piled up in this forgotten corner. Who would store this much gunpowder in the attic of a children's home – or any home, for that matter – and then simply leave it to gather dust? And now that I'd seen them, I couldn't ignore the potential risk.

I was worried about what the manager would say, but I had no choice – I had to admit that I'd been in the attic. So, I gathered myself and immediately called the children's homes adviser – the person responsible for all the children's homes operated by the local authority. His response was surprisingly matter of fact. He showed no concern, asked no further questions, and made no attempt to dig deeper into why they were up there in the first place.

Part of his job was to accompany local councillors on a monthly visit to each of the homes to ensure everything was in order – or at least appeared to be.

The routine was always the same: the music room, locked between visits, would be opened specially for the occasion, laid out with tea and cake served on the best china, to impress. The children were lined up, presented as proof that everything was in good order while the councillors and officer nodded approvingly, sipping tea and ticking boxes in their heads. But behind the polished presentations were real lives, real stories – many of them filled with pain and uncertainty. When I first started working at the home, I quickly realised that not all children's homes were the same.

The reality was far more complicated. Not every children's home offered the same sense of normality. In some children were treated more like problems to be fixed. The contrast between homes was stark, and it became clear that what we – the next generation – had to offer wasn't always appreciated.

Despite good intentions, the system lacked the resources and vision to provide a truly nurturing environment. There was a clash between old-school thinking and a shift toward something more child centred. Growing up in the 1960s, with the cultural liberation of youth in full swing, and entering my teenage years in the 1970s, I saw things through their eyes, spoke their language – my own rebellious years were not that far behind me. I had not grown up in a world where children should be seen and not heard. The home was family group by name, but definitely not by nature.

The last two children to arrive at the home before it closed had already endured more than their fair share of trauma. At a very young age, their mother fell seriously ill, and with no other family to care for them, they were placed with the same respite foster carers whenever their mother was hospitalised. Tragically, when their mother passed away unexpectedly, they were left to face a world that offered little stability.

Though the foster family had hoped to keep them until a

permanent family was found, overcrowding forced them to let the children go when the search proved more difficult than expected. That was when they were then moved to the children's home where I worked. But the home was scheduled to close due to cost-cutting measures, and once again, the children found themselves facing an uncertain future.

At this time, Mark and I worked for the same local authority. Sometimes, he would take 'the lads,' as we fondly referred to them, to the village where he grew up to earn extra cash haymaking for local farmers or wild camping on land owned by a friend. They might stop by our house for a 'butty and a brew.' Getting time off together wasn't always possible, but we often spent time on duty with each other. This wasn't prohibited then, as it is now, and we had gotten to know the kids in both homes well.

When the Christmas rota came out that year, I was due to work Christmas Eve into Christmas Day. By this time, the manager had retired, and arrangements had been made for all the children, except for the children who had lost their mother, to spend Christmas Day with their families. The enormity of this did not escape me.

Since it would be just the four of us for Christmas dinner, it came as a shock on Christmas Eve when the butcher delivered an enormous turkey. The manager had ordered it before leaving. I couldn't understand why she had ordered such a large turkey, any more than I could fathom who would store a trunk full of gunpowder in a loft.

That night, Mark and I quietly delivered a sack of presents to the foot of each child's bed. At least, we thought we had. In the early hours, they rewarded us for our effort – me with a box of Maltesers, and Mark with a cigar dressed as Father Christmas. The scene felt so much like my own childhood – except here, six excited children tore into wrapping paper, their laughter filling the air as they uncovered their treasures.

After tea and biscuits, we tucked into a hearty cooked breakfast. By then, the turkey had been roasting in the oven for hours, filling the house with its mouth-watering aroma. By late morning only two children remained. With the table set, we settled in for an early movie matinee, watching Christmas classics, the turkey's irresistible aroma making the wait feel even longer. It takes a long time to cook a turkey that size!

When the time finally came to take the turkey out, its sheer size and weight made it a challenge only Mark could tackle. His face – a mix of determination and disbelief – made us laugh; it was like a scene straight out of a sitcom. After three falls, two submissions, and a knockout, he wrestled it free and heaved it onto the worktop, a triumphant victory we had all shared.

Mark and I exchanged a glance, silently agreeing that whatever the reason for this ridiculous amount of food, it would be a Christmas meal we would never forget. With a few final touches, we sat down together, still in fits of laughter, grateful for the simplicity of the moment and the joy of sharing a Christmas none of us had expected.

When the new year began, plans to close the home took priority. Arrangements had been made to move the children back into family or foster care, but for the two who had no family to return to, finding a suitable foster home to take them both was proving difficult. Consequently, the plan was to move them to a large children's home. The reality was that there simply wasn't another option.

The idea of splitting them up or sending them to a home with so many other children with so many different needs was unbearable. Mark and I knew we had to find a way to prevent this from happening. They had already been through far too much.

During the early 1970s, researchers had raised concerns about children and young people drifting in care and the long-term impact on their mental and emotional well-being. In response to these findings, and compounded by the rising costs of residential care, several local authorities and voluntary agencies introduced innovative schemes by the late 1970s to find families for children and young people deemed difficult to place.

However, not all local authorities supported it, with some questioning the idea of paying people to look after other people's children. Fortunately, the local authority we worked for had embraced this new approach. Without the introduction of contract fostering, I would not have been able to leave my job to care for the children until a permanent family was found.

Unlike traditional fostering, where foster carers received only the standard boarding-out payment to cover the cost of looking after children in their care, contract foster carers receive an additional fee. As a young couple with a mortgage to pay, this that made it financially viable for me to step away from work and provide the care they needed at that time.

Our family and friends were incredibly supportive, and the children settled well. They began to enjoy new experiences, make new friends, and create lasting memories. One of their proudest moments came during their final year at primary school when they were both involved in the school play. Mark and I arrived early to secure seats with a good view. As we sat among the other parents, we couldn't help but feel immense pride as we watched them take the stage, knowing just how far they had come.

The show was a fun-filled spectacle, with the stage transforming into a magnificent parade of colourful characters. We couldn't help but laugh with delight and tap our feet to the infectious rhythm of the tunes. A lively array of creatures wearing their homemade costumes made the performance even more special. As I clapped enthusiastically, I wasn't just clapping for myself but also for their mother – she would have been filled with pride to see them on that stage.

The children had already experienced an immeasurable loss, and while we loved them, we knew we couldn't be the permanent carers they needed. In our early twenties, we simply couldn't offer them the lifelong commitment and stability they deserved. Understanding this, the local authority continued its search for a permanent family – one that could provide the commitment and sense of belonging they needed to truly thrive.

That summer, as they prepared to start high school – each at a different school – their social worker said this separation would help them establish their own identities, allowing them to grow as individuals. She encouraged them to reflect on the kind of family they hoped for, giving them a voice in their own future.

We were busy shopping for new school uniforms when we learned that a family had been found who might be a good match for them – a couple with no children of their own. We met them for lunch at a neutral location, hoping it would ease any awkwardness. The meeting went well, and the children quickly progressed to visits and overnight stays with the family. When they eventually moved in, we were instructed to step back so they could settle into their new home. At the time, we didn't question it – that was simply the standard procedure.

We had loved them, cared for them – all the while knowing our role was to be the bridge until they found the permanent family they deserved. When the time came, we knew that letting them go would be the best thing we could do for them. But in our hearts, we never let them go completely. They still hold a special place there.

Decades later, we still think about them – wondering how that sudden separation must have felt, hoping life has been kind to them. We talk about them often; caught between gratitude that they found a family and the quiet pain of not knowing how they made sense of it all. It still haunts us to this day.

If I could go back, knowing what I do now, I wouldn't have

let it happen that way. I would advocate for a gentler transition, for some form of contact, for a way to reassure them that they hadn't been casually abandoned or forgotten. But life doesn't offer second chances – only the wisdom to do better next time.

And now I was about to meet our next foster child, Hannah. Barely a teenager, she had spent two years in a semi-secure institution – without having committed a crime. The house stood hidden from the world at the end of a long drive. I parked the car and walked toward the front door of this unfamiliar place.

The woman who let me in wore a large bunch of keys on a chain attached to her belt. As I listened to the sound of the door locking behind me, I couldn't help but wonder what it must have felt like for an eleven-year-old child. At the time, places like this were still in use, though they would soon be made illegal by the *1989 Children's Act*, which sought to protect vulnerable children from such restrictive, institutional environments. Yet, even now, decades later, the system continues to restrict the liberty of more children than ever before, with rising numbers placed in secure care settings that still limit their freedom.

After signing in, I was escorted in silence past notice boards and lockers to a door at the far end of the wide hallway. My footsteps echoed loudly, despite my best efforts to soften my approach. It seemed to take forever to cross the vast wooden floor and reach the table in the corner of the otherwise empty room. It felt awkward, but my embarrassment and apprehension soon evaporated when I reached the table where Hannah was sitting. We both laughed with relief; I guess I didn't look like her worst nightmare, and she certainly didn't look like mine. The following week, Hannah arrived at our home with her social worker.

The handover was brief and impersonal – more like a delivery than an arrival. She wore the same clothes she had worn when she was admitted two years earlier – shoes two sizes too small, lined with cardboard to cover a hole in the sole, a dress too tight and too short, and a coat that wouldn't keep anyone warm on a cold day.

For much of the 20th century, it had been common practice for institutions to take away a child's own clothes upon arrival, replacing them with standard-issue garments until discharge. Stripping children of their belongings was seen as a way to maintain order, enforce uniformity, and exert control. But for the children themselves, it was a loss of identity – a sign that nothing truly belonged to them anymore. Hannah had been no exception. She had arrived in those clothes two years earlier and still stood in them now. Whether through sheer neglect or a rigid system that saw no reason to provide her with more, she had been left to outgrow the only things she owned.

BIN BAGS

Ah've seen the mounds o' black bin bags,
aw ma life's worth thrown oot like rags,
social workers wi' their distant stares,
tossin' ma stuff wi' nae cares.

Aye, ye think it's just things an' stuff,
but it's ma heart ye've treated rough,
ye bundle ma memories in a sack,
flinging them oot wi' a careless clack.

Foster carers wi' their fleetin' cheer,
gie me a smile then disappear.
ye pack up ma stuff as if it's crap
no seeing the hurt in each lost gap.

Ah've seen aw the bin bags line the street,
wi' ma treasures lost at their feet,
it's no just claes an' toys an' books,
it's ma very soul ye overlooked.

And ah've raged an' roared but who takes heed,
aw ah'm left wi' is a heart that's scarred indeed,
for in each black bag there's a bit o' me,
just tossed aside for aw tae see.

Ao here's tae a system that's let me doon.
an' aw the folk that wear their self-gien croon.
ah'll forge ahead though it's rough an' cauld,
an' reclaim ma spirit, bold an' untold,
ah'll mend ma heart and find ma way
but gonnae just remember, it's no okay!

Sarah Jane Thompson

4

WHEN THE SYSTEM FAILS
Standing Up Letting Go

Nowadays, kids rightly complain about being identified as being in care by the black bin bags used to carry their belongings – Hannah didn't even have a black bin bag. She had only the clothes she stood up in. Nothing else – not even a hairbrush or toothbrush. It's hard to believe, but it still happens today.

That afternoon, we went shopping for clothes and essentials – a simple enough task. But grasping the full extent of the institution's neglect was anything but easy. What disturbed me most, though, was the complicity of her social worker in such overt neglect. She had to earn tokens for good behaviour to pay for a phone call home, some sweets, or a visit to see family. Hannah spoke very little about what happened there; she didn't have to. Trauma and neglect are visible, and what little she did say spoke volumes.

Hannah went to bed that first night wearing her new pyjamas, her dressing gown hanging on the hook at the back of the bedroom door, and fluffy pink slippers neatly placed by her bed. I wanted to believe she fell asleep with comforting thoughts of what outfit she might wear with her new shoes the next day. But I know better than that now.

When social services suggested that Hannah be placed in a special school, I genuinely believed they had underestimated her. Yes, she had educational gaps, but she was intelligent and capable. She deserved better than to be written off. Mark and I fought hard for her right to attend a mainstream school, convinced that with the right support, she would thrive there.

To me, school was never just about academic achievement – it was everything that came with it. It was the friends we make for life, the feeling of being part of something bigger than ourselves, that sense of belonging. It was about leaving school in the time-honoured way, with shared memories and milestones that mark a childhood.

But education wasn't Hannah's only challenge. She was also a witness in a case against a man accused of multiple offences against children on her estate. When the day arrived, we made our way to the Crown Court, hoping for a smoother process, but there was no one there to support us. No private waiting area to shield her from the harsh realities of the legal system. Instead, we were directed to wait in the crowded public area outside the courtroom, exposed to the noise and the tense atmosphere, with no space to process what was happening.

As we walked down the corridor, Hannah suddenly stiffened. Her fingers gripped my arm as she whispered, *'That's him,'* barely audible. I followed her gaze and saw him – the defendant – handcuffed, flanked by two officers, his presence filling the space like a shadow creeping in. My stomach knotted. Instinctively, we slowed our pace, but the damage was done. She had seen him. And worse – he had seen her.

Even then, I thought it was wrong for a child witness to come face to face with the accused before testifying. But justice has a mind of its own – and it seemed there were other priorities. The prosecution barrister was worried that the victims – many of whom were already known to social services – would not be seen as credible witnesses.

In that moment, I realised this wasn't about them; it was about securing a conviction – a win in a courtroom battle.

To ensure that win, the police struck a deal: drop the most serious charges in exchange for a guilty plea on lesser offences.

It may have made the crime figures look better, but this was not justice for his victims.

When we were told we could leave, it should have been a relief. Instead, it felt like a betrayal. The victims had not been consulted, and because the defendant had already spent six months on remand, he walked free. The harm he had caused, the risk he still posed – none of it had been adequately considered.

And soon, we found ourselves back in court – but this time, it was Hannah standing in the dock.

On the advice of her social worker and solicitor, she was appealing a sentence for a minor crime committed under her father's direction while on home leave, months before she came to live with us. Upon his release from prison, he had trained his children to steal, convincing them that any consequences would be lighter for them. The police were well aware of his activities, making frequent visits to their home in search of stolen goods. And yet, now, it was his daughter carrying the blame.

With Manchester Girls' Grammar School in the public gallery on a school visit, the judge took great delight in making a public spectacle of Hannah and me. He threatened to fine the foster parents in a performance that could have earned him a BAFTA from the British Academy of Film and Television Arts.

Months later, I began to wonder whether keeping Hannah in mainstream school had been the right decision. For six long months, I took her to school every day, only for her to leave without permission shortly after arriving. By the time I returned home, the phone would ring with the same message: she had gone again.

Then, one day, the phone stopped ringing. At first, I didn't question it; I was simply glad for the silence, knowing it meant she was staying in school. But soon, I realised that it was all because of one remarkable teacher, whose support and dedication had made all the difference. Mrs. Williams greeted Hannah each morning with a warm smile and a few encouraging words, slowly transforming school from a place of struggle into a place of hope. Rather than scolding her for past absences, she treated each day as a fresh start. In doing so, she became more than just a teacher – she became an ally when Hannah needed one the most.

Soon after Hannah settled into school, we were asked to provide weekend and holiday care for a fourteen-year-old boy who had been placed at a privately run boys' residential school. I accompanied his social worker on a visit to meet him. The headmaster greeted us and took us on a grand tour of the school. I wasn't impressed – by the school or the man. Something felt off. It was one of those moments when instinct detects trouble long before the mind can explain it. But Robert, with his strawberry blond hair and cheeky smile, won me over instantly.

He settled easily into family and village life, loving his weekends and school holidays with us. After returning to school, he would write letters about how much fun he'd had, how he missed everyone at home, and how eagerly he looked forward to his next visit. Yet, despite his cheerful letters, a sense of unease began to take hold. Little things the staff said, offhand comments from Robert – all fed my growing suspicion that something wasn't right.

His first day hadn't been spent in lessons but moving books into the classroom. He said the schoolwork was too easy and, when I asked what the best thing about the place was, he shrugged and said, *'They give me five cigarettes a day.'* His letters sometimes hinted at discomfort: *"At night, when I go to bed, I freeze to death because the window in my bedroom is jammed."* Whenever I called, he was always happy to hear from me, counting down the days until he could come home.

One Friday evening, when Robert arrived, Mark and I were taken aback by his hair – bleached blond and covered in blue splodges. It looked a mess, and we worried that it would make him stand out in the village for all the wrong reasons. When I raised my concerns with the staff at the school, they were arrogantly dismissed.

That was when Mark and I started to think it would be better for Robert to live with us full-time and attend the local high school alongside Hannah and the other kids in the village. It was what he wanted, and securing agreement from social services wasn't difficult. It would be years before I fully understood just how important that decision was.

With both Hannah and Robert settled into the local high school, our house was often filled with a lively bunch of teenagers. When they weren't at home, they could usually be found at the village institute.

Generations of locals had gathered there since it was built at the beginning of the twentieth century. The red-brick building stood at the heart of village life, sharing its grounds with the bowling green, cricket club, tennis courts, children's playground, and park. It was run by a couple who lived on the premises with their four daughters, all close in age to Hannah and Robert. The village kids spent hours there catching up with friends, flirting, buying sweets from the tuck shop, or playing chess.

At home, Hannah and Robert were growing more independent each day. Hannah took pride in her room and appearance – her clothes freshly washed, her paper round later becoming a job waiting tables at the pub. She was discovering the value of earning – and spending – her own money. Robert, meanwhile, had two great passions: fishing and girls. When he wasn't at the institute, you could usually find him at the reservoir, fishing with his mates.

That summer, I found out I was expecting our first child. After months of fertility tests and stress, it was the news we'd been hoping for. We'd planned a short break before school started — a few days at my aunt's caravan in North Wales with Hannah and Robert. But at the last minute, Mark had to cancel. I ended up taking the children on my own with a friend.

The manager — I'll call him Tim — had recently left to take a senior role elsewhere. You'd think things might have settled after that, but instead, it showed just how much had been allowed to slide while he was there. Mark had been coming home with stories for a while, but now they started to take on a different weight.

Staff said they'd seen bottles of whisky in his overnight bag. He sent younger lads out to place bets at the bookies or pick up more drink. After arguments at home, he'd turn up drunk, looking for somewhere to sleep. One evening, Mark found him passed out over the steering wheel of his car, the horn barring. Another time, he was face down on the lawn.

Then there were smaller things that pointed to bigger problems. One morning, the cleaner waved Mark over, clearly upset. She was dealing with dirty bedding left behind by a staff member on the sleep-in shift. *'I'm not paid to deal with this,'* she said. Mark sorted it out, but the whole thing unsettled him. If the people responsible for caring for vulnerable young people couldn't manage their own basic responsibilities, what would happen in an emergency? What if there was a fire? Who would get the boys out? That worry stayed with us. We couldn't shake it.

Then there was missing money. A staff member, Mrs. Forshaw, discovered twenty pounds gone from her wage packet.

Mark had locked the envelopes away himself — only one had been touched, and there was no sign of forced entry. It was a lot of money at the time. He offered to replace it, but she refused. She trusted him completely — and didn't believe for a second that he or the lads had taken it.

Still, it was another sign that things weren't right. So he raised it with the person in charge. He thought they'd at least listen. Instead, he was told flatly: *'Unless you've got proof, and you're prepared to stand up in court and say it, keep your mouth shut.'*

That was the moment it really hit home. He'd tried to raise concerns before, and nothing changed. Now it was clear: without undeniable proof, there'd be no action — and if he kept pushing, he'd be the one at risk.

That stayed with both of us. The message was obvious: speak up, and you lose. Not just your job — maybe more. When the system's focus is on protecting itself, doing the right thing becomes nearly impossible.

With a baby on the way and his job security on the line, he knew he had to tread carefully. The weight of the situation pressed down on him, and the fear of losing his job silenced him – much like those who went before him and those who would undoubtedly follow.

We had waited a long time for this baby, enduring years of frustration, fertility tests, and disappointment. When Mark's dad read *'keep the sample warm on the journey'* in the letter from the hospital, he thought someone was pulling his leg. My mother quipped, *'If that baby isn't born fourteen years old, you won't know what to do with it.'* It was meant as a joke, but after seven years of caring for other people's children, her words weren't far from the truth.

Becoming a mum changed everything. The weight of that responsibility pressed heavily on me, yet there was an overwhelming joy that Mark and I shared. I remember that cold

January morning in 1983 – Hannah and Robert had stayed up all night, eagerly awaiting news of the baby's arrival. Later that day, Mark returned from the hospital carrying a bouquet of flowers and matching cards – one for me and one for Emma, our beautiful baby girl, who was sleeping peacefully by my side. As we gazed at her, tears rolling down our cheeks, the full reality of our new, shared responsibility sank in – my mother's words echoing in my head.

When we finally returned home from the hospital, the log burning stove was roaring, casting a warm glow across the room. Hannah and Robert were there, grinning like it was Christmas morning all over again as they greeted me with big, welcoming hugs. While I was away, Hannah had run the house like a seasoned general – we still laugh about it now, picturing Mark tiptoeing around under her no-nonsense command.

Parenting two teenagers and a newborn was a delicate balancing act – one I never imagined would lead us to reconsider fostering. As the months passed, the arrival of our baby reshaped our world in ways we hadn't predicted, revealing the perfectly normal conflicting demands of a newborn and teenagers.

But we were novice parents, and as our responsibilities shifted, we made the difficult decision to step back from fostering. It wasn't just about managing the everyday demands of parenting; it was about giving our baby a chance to grow up without the constant intrusion of social workers in our family home and the loss of privacy that fostering inevitably brings.

At the time, I had no entitlement to maternity leave – it simply didn't exist for me. Foster parents were not employed, so things like maternity leave weren't even on the table. Paternity leave wasn't part of the conversation at all. And to be honest, it didn't even cross our minds.

It was a five-day stay in hospital – which I hated – and then straight back to it.

There was no recognition of the physical or emotional toll of becoming a new mother, let alone one already caring for other children. These things weren't thought about back then. The expectation was simple: you had a baby, and you got on with it.

Thankfully, through it all, we managed to hold onto each other, keeping our connection strong despite the pressures of new parenthood.

Looking back now, with what we know about postnatal recovery and mental health, it's easy to see how much of that time was shaped by circumstance – and how little support there really was. The pressure was enormous. And the truth is, society still struggles to fully recognise that even today.

The government spends public money on free childcare yet fails to provide real financial support for parents who want to stay home with their children during those crucial early years. In many ways, the system pushes families into the workforce and children into out-of-home care, while offering little to those who wish to focus on home life. It's a contradiction that erodes choice, leaving families to decide between financial stability and the opportunity to raise their children as they see fit.

Given these pressures, I returned to work, taking a job at an Intermediate Treatment Centre. There, we helped young offenders get on track through rehabilitation instead of traditional custody – offering them a fresh start and a path toward reintegration.

Yet the centre still bore the marks of its past as an approved school for boys. A rigid hierarchy persisted, with teachers higher up the pecking order than the care staff. Every morning, we escorted the young offenders to the school assembly presided over by the headmaster.

One morning, just as I was about to leave the hall, a teacher stopped me for a chat. I tried to excuse myself, but as I turned, I saw the headmaster signalling impatiently for me to leave. His gesture cut through the room like a sharp command, and a hush fell as all eyes turned to me – the weight of their attention almost unbearable.

In that moment, I felt belittled, humiliated, shamed – even though it wasn't my shame to bear. The respect I had worked so hard to earn in this male-dominated environment vanished in an instant. His dismissive gesture wasn't just an accusation; it was a public command, a reminder of my place. Embarrassment surged through me, quickly giving way to anger and frustration.

I was, a young woman working with young male offenders in a setting where respect for women was already scarce, and now I was being publicly dismissed and reduced to nothing more than a minion. As I walked back to the cramped office assigned to care staff – a space that felt more like a concession than a real workplace – I knew I couldn't let this go without challenge.

After regaining my composure, I waited for the assembly to end before heading to the headmaster's office. I doubted he even knew my name before that moment. When we finally stood face to face, he brushed off his behaviour with a casual excuse – he'd had a bad day. Then, almost offhandedly, he muttered an apology.

'Accepted,' I said, meeting his gaze before turning to walk away. As I left his office, I felt the familiar fire stir inside me – that same defiance I'd felt as a child whenever I saw or experienced those in power abusing their position.

At school, my biggest struggle wasn't foreign languages or advanced mathematics – it was injustice. Unfair treatment – whether directed at me or someone else – sparked something deep within me. And it was never just about me; I always stood up for others. I'd been this way since primary school when I led a playground strike – a rebellion that, unsurprisingly, ended with my mum being called into school to sort me out.

Even now, I can still hear my mother's voice if I'm about to do something she wouldn't approve of. It doesn't have to be a crime or a sin – just a choice that she wouldn't approve of, or something that doesn't sit right. That voice, whether in my head or in my heart, always brings me back. It's not just about rules – it's about the care that shaped my decisions. That voice has the power to stop me in my tracks, reminding me of who I am and what I stand for. Sometimes, I can even hear her words coming out of my own mouth.

I hadn't expected my next job to be at a place with so much history. Known locally as *'the homes,'* the residential school had cared for vulnerable children for over a century. It was a place built on the ideals of rescue and refuge – but as I would soon learn, not all children found safety within its walls.

The mission of the organisation was to rescue children in need, providing them with a safe home away from the negative influences of the city, where they could access fresh air and develop new skills for a better future. During both world wars, many children were sent to this home due to the loss of fathers and the struggles their mothers faced in raising large families.

After the war, the home continued to cater to children and young people with special educational needs. School routines remained traditional for decades, including special meals, chapel services, and an annual reunion for former residents to reconnect with their past.

In May 1985, during the annual reunion, I was expecting my second child. My pregnancy came as a surprise – one I hadn't expected so soon after the challenges we faced conceiving our first child.

It wasn't until I developed an insatiable craving for fruit – buying it in bulk at the local shop – that an older colleague at work asked me if I thought I might be pregnant, which finally led me to acknowledge the possibility.

Our baby was due at the end of October. She arrived on the 30th, just before Halloween – a day often associated with playful mischief, but now it holds an even more special meaning for us. It's the day we welcomed our second daughter, adding a touch of magic and wonder to this already mystical time of year. We named her Sarah, meaning *'princess,'* after the mother of our close friend Gareth, who has always been like family to us. From the start, she was curious, always ready for a little adventure, and never deterred – her spirit as lively as the day she was born.

With Mark's parents in Lancaster and mine in Scotland, having *'Nana Sal'* close by was a blessing. Gareth had moved to America with his wife, Julia, a few years before Sarah was born. He worked in IT, and by the time Sarah arrived, they already had two girls. Unlike Julia, I couldn't afford to be a stay-at-home mum. We had a mortgage to pay, and both our salaries were necessary to make ends meet. Returning to work once my statutory maternity pay ran out wasn't a choice – it was a necessity.

Gareth and I were the same age, and I remember teachers telling us that IT was the future. But I'd taken a different path – one that suited me better, even if it came with its own challenges. I had chosen work I cared deeply about, even though it meant juggling bills, balancing childcare, and putting in long hours. Unlike Gareth, my life didn't come with the same financial security or comfort, but it was the right choice for me.

Still, there were days when I couldn't help but wonder what life might have been like if I'd listened to my teachers – especially in 1985, when everything seemed to be falling apart. Interest rates were in double figures, the miners were on strike, and a fire at *Bradford City* killed fifty-six people. The *Heysel Stadium* disaster in Brussels left thirty-nine dead, and English clubs were banned from European competitions. Riots erupted at the FA Cup quarter-final between *Luton* and *Millwall*. Even *Live Aid*

– which raised over £50 million for famine relief in Ethiopia – couldn't fully lift the sense of doom and gloom.

At home, there was little sign of things getting better. The House of Lords had just ruled that a child aged sixteen or under might be competent to consent to medical treatment without parental permission or knowledge – a decision that became known as *Gillick competency*. While some hailed it as progress, others debated its ethical implications for years to come.

Around the same time, civil unrest flared across the UK. In Birmingham, fewer than five percent of Black pupils who left school that summer had found employment. Despite this, MPs in Parliament insisted that unemployment was no excuse for the riots. The tension in the air was impossible to ignore.

It was against this backdrop that Sarah was born. When she was just three months old, I returned to work – apparently becoming the first woman at the homes to do so after maternity leave. The man who ran the central food, equipment, and clothing stores believed women of childbearing age had no place in the workforce – an attitude that, at the time, was far from uncommon. Even my own mother still believed a woman's place was at home, raising her children.

The head of childcare came from the same era. She was one of eighteen women who had dedicated their lives to caring for other people's children. Having never married or had children, she devoted her life to the organisation and its work.

5

SOME WOUNDS DON'T HEAL
A Doll, A Baby, and a Bruised Heart

The *Sisterhood* had begun a century earlier. Young women who wished to join were expected to have a good general education and complete a trial appointment of at least three months at one of the homes. If, at the end of this period, the governor or sister in charge approved, the applicant would be accepted as a candidate for the *Sisterhood*. Training at the organisation's college in London, followed by a satisfactory probationary period of up to two years, would then lead to ordination. In 1979, the *Sisterhood* was disbanded, but its members were allowed to retain their titles, a quiet recognition of the lives they had devoted to the organisation.

Due to the limitations of maternity leave and financial pressures, I returned to work – an experience many women shared in that era, many like me still breastfeeding.

Not long after, the headmaster called me into his office to discuss developing a fifty-two-week care unit at the school. Over the past decade, demand for places had declined, and many of the children referred could not return home during school holidays. With my background in local authority-run children's homes, he felt I was the right person for the job.

Excited by the opportunity, I immediately set to work on plans for the new service. My experience had taught me that caring for children and young people with special educational needs, as well as mental and emotional challenges, required an extra level of parenting. I knew that relationships were the golden thread; play and activities were important, and keeping children and young people constructively occupied helped them stay out of mischief. With this in mind, I set up a playroom, filling it with toys and craft materials, and sourced play therapy training for myself and the team.

The day Jessica arrived, I wasn't scheduled to work, but with no one else to cover the shift, my line manager suggested I bring my children in with me – an arrangement that wasn't unusual. At the time, many staff lived on-site and raised their own children alongside the young people they cared for, it wasn't uncommon.

What was uncommon was that I was the first non-resident group leader – another break with convention that didn't sit well with everyone.

Sister Ivy had managed the referral and agreed to the admission, so I knew very little about Jessica – except that she looked bewildered and was clutching a life-size baby doll.

Using the doll to connect, I chatted with Jessica about her baby and mentioned that she would meet my baby later that day. The social worker said nothing. When he announced it was time for him to leave, the panic and fear in Jessica's eyes were impossible to miss. I could only imagine what she must have been feeling as I tried to reassure her that everything would be alright. There were no tears, just pools of sadness in her big blue eyes.

The next morning, something told me to leave Sarah in her cot with the bedroom door closed while I helped the children and young people with their morning routine. She'd been unsettled at bedtime the night before – crying more than usual.

It could have been anything: teething, tiredness, or just one of those nights. Mark stayed with her until she settled.

At the time, I didn't give it too much weight. What happened the next day was completely beyond my experience – nothing I could have imagined, let alone prepared for without warning.

With six children in the house, a well-organised start to the day was essential. But today was Saturday, so there was time for some playful fun as they made their beds and got ready. Just as I was about to head downstairs to serve breakfast, one of the children called me from the bedroom. He was looking through the open door where I had left my youngest daughter.

'Miss… Jessica is hitting the baby.'

For a split second, my body refused to move – my brain rejecting what I had just heard. Then, as if waking from a nightmare, the horror crashed in, and I ran. My feet pounded the floor, my breath caught in my throat. When I reached the bedroom, my heart stopped. Sarah lay there – silent, wide-eyed, her tiny body frozen in shock. My stomach twisted as I saw the bruises, dark against her delicate skin. A wave of nausea rose in my throat. This was a moment I would never forget – a moment I would never, ever be able to unsee.

Panic threatened to consume me as I lifted my baby into my arms, confronting the unthinkable. I was caught between my despair and my responsibility for the other children. I paced the landing, my baby clutched to my sobbing chest, followed by a parade of confused children. I don't know how long it took for my senses to return or for me to call for help, but thankfully, my good friend and colleague, Katy, arrived in what felt like an instant. We had worked together previously, and I trusted her to take control.

The journey to the hospital was a nightmare. Every red light felt like a merciless accomplice. When we finally arrived, I blurted out what had happened, and we were seen immediately by a doctor. I explained that I hadn't witnessed Jessica hitting my baby but had seen the injuries – and the look of terror on Jessica's face as I entered the room.

The doctor confirmed there were no severe injuries. The fingertip bruising on my baby's left cheek and the larger bruise on her forehead aligned with the story. But I was overwhelmed with shame, caught between self-blame and the relief that my child had survived. Later, I learned that the hospital and senior managers had decided against a child protection investigation. Even though I knew violent behaviour doesn't come from nowhere, I was left to process it on my own.

What Jessica had done was devastating, but I couldn't bring myself to blame her – and thankfully, Sarah wasn't seriously injured. Raising the cot side had protected her from the full force of the attack. What haunted me was learning that the social worker had known Jessica was being locked in her bedroom overnight because she was considered a risk to the foster parents' baby. I have never been able to work out why he didn't tell me. Without that knowledge, I couldn't protect either of them.

What I hadn't fully understood at the time was that Jessica didn't just see my baby as another child – she saw her as a threat. A symbol of what could happen to her again. In her mind, getting rid of my baby meant getting rid of the threat. It wasn't malice. It was fear. It was survival. It was a symptom of the trauma she carried – the deep, unresolved fear that love was limited and always conditional, and that she could be replaced at any moment.

That realisation stayed with me. It didn't just change how I saw that night – it changed how I understood the children I was working with. Jessica was dangerous, like others I would go on to care for in later years. But she wasn't beyond help – she was a child in deep distress, shaped by layers of trauma and neglect.

Children like Jessica don't become dangerous on their own. They are crafted by circumstance – and by failure.

Over the years, I saw this pattern repeat itself more times than I care to remember. Children labelled as *'challenging'* or *'unmanageable'* were often the ones who had been most profoundly failed.

I knew Jessica needed to trust me before she could begin to understand what she had done, and why it was so wrong. I also knew that children often express what they can't put into words through play. So, I spent time with her in the playroom, letting her take the lead.

I needed her to know that the grown-ups had let us both down – and that I wasn't angry with her. Instead, I wanted to understand why she had reacted this way – for her sake as well as mine.

I knew little about her life before she and her sister were fostered – and even less about what had happened to her since – but I did know that children who have experienced severe neglect and abuse often exhibit signs like withdrawal, aggression, and difficulties with empathy.

Slowly, as she began to trust me, her stories started to take shape. As Jessica began to feel safer, I saw more than just fear of rejection in her behaviour. There was something else beneath the surface – something darker that hadn't yet been named. Bit by bit, through her drawings and the way she played, she allowed me to see what she had been holding inside. She had been sexually abused by her foster father's father. To her, he was her foster grandfather – a figure who should have been safe. But he wasn't. And that was later proven in court.

Looking back now, I realise how many of Jessica's behaviours had been misinterpreted – or ignored altogether – because no one had taken the time to truly listen. The system responded to her risk, but not to her pain. She was managed, not understood.

Jessica's learning difficulties gave adults a way to explain away her struggles, which is likely why she was placed in a residential special school. But the attack on Sarah suggested that her challenges went far beyond cognitive delay. Her behaviours pointed to something deeper, something rooted in her earliest experiences – something the system had either overlooked or failed to address.

There was no therapeutic framework around her, no consistent relationship to help her make sense of her experiences. She was placed, labelled, and moved – as though safety could be achieved by logistics alone.

Jessica's story wasn't an anomaly. Over the years, I saw how children who had been abused, neglected, or dismissed were often the same children described as "aggressive," "manipulative," or "too complex to place." But those behaviours weren't the problem – they were the message. The problem was that too few adults knew how to read it.

Although attachment theory had been around since the 1950s, it only began to reach mainstream thinking in the 1980s – the same decade that also raised awareness of child sexual abuse and its devastating consequences. Yet even as professionals were beginning to acknowledge the long-term effects of trauma, many children were still being failed.

At the time, awareness of attachment disorders was limited. Children who had experienced severe neglect or abuse often exhibited extreme behaviours, though understanding of why was still developing. Knowing that Jessica had been kept in her bedroom with the door locked at night for safety in her previous foster home, I wanted her to understand that she would not be punished or confined here.

It wasn't until five years later that I first watched *Child of Rage*, a documentary that introduced many people to Reactive Attachment Disorder. Seeing Beth Thomas's story not only brought back memories of Jessica – it also deepened my understanding of the children I had cared for in the past, and those I would go on to care for in the future.

The film told the story of a young girl who had suffered severe neglect and abuse in early childhood, and the behavioural challenges that followed. Her mother had passed away when she was an infant, and she and her younger brother, Jonathan, were left in the care of their father, who neglected them both and abused Beth. By the time they were adopted, the effects of that trauma were already showing.

Beth's adoptive parents were unprepared for what they encountered. She exhibited behaviours that were deeply concerning – she was aggressive toward her brother and struggled to form connections with others. In the documentary, she openly admitted to having violent thoughts toward her family. Eventually, she was diagnosed with Reactive Attachment Disorder (RAD), a condition that affects children who have experienced significant neglect or disruptions in caregiving.

RAD makes it difficult for children to form secure relationships, often leading to challenges with trust, emotional regulation, and behaviour. It is commonly seen in children who have been in multiple foster placements, orphanages, or unstable home environments. Studies show that attachment difficulties can have long-term consequences, with research suggesting that a high percentage of juvenile offenders have some form of attachment disorder.

But Beth's story wasn't just about trauma – it also demonstrated the power of intervention. With the right support, healing was possible. Through intensive therapy and structured care, she was able to rebuild trust and develop healthy relationships. Today, she works in the medical field and advocates for others who have experienced similar challenges. Her journey reinforced what I had always known but had now seen with my own eyes: trauma changes children, but it does not have to define them. With patience, support, and the right interventions, they can heal. They can thrive. And they can rewrite their own stories – just as I had seen so many of them do.

The attack on Sarah had been a turning point for us. It had shaken everything I thought I knew about safety, stability, and the systems we worked within. The emotional toll it took on all of us was profound. In the midst of everything, my instinct took over. I swaddled Sarah, just like I had when she was born. It wasn't for warmth – it was to make her feel safe, as if she were still in the womb. A *'let's try again'* moment. It felt like the right thing to do – a physical expression of care, amidst the trauma. Sarah had us. Jessica had no one. And that truth sat with me long after the bruises faded, and the routines returned – although the memory never has.

Arriving at Gower House felt like the beginning of a new chapter – a fresh start, full of potential. Mark was stepping into the responsibility of leading a new residential education service for young people with learning difficulties. This role promised not only professional fulfilment but also the chance to make a real difference in the lives of those who needed it most. The decision to live on-site was a significant one, offering the opportunity to immerse ourselves in the community while still maintaining a balance between our family life and our careers.

Gower House provided a transformative stepping stone for young people who had completed their education at a residential special school and were preparing to live independently in the community at 18. The program combined practical learning – budgeting, cooking, and daily responsibilities – with the development of confidence and self-sufficiency. Staff guided each young person in exploring employment opportunities, further education, and supported housing, empowering them to shape their future in ways they had not imagined.

It wasn't just another program; Gower House was a visionary space, truly ahead of its time. The teacher, a deeply inspiring man with an impressive list of credentials, approached education with a passion that ignited the students' imaginations. He didn't just teach; he encouraged them to think big, to dream beyond the boundaries of their daily lives.

Under his guidance, the students embarked on extraordinary projects that pushed them to new heights. One of their most ambitious endeavours was the construction of a flight simulator, a hands-on project that brought learning to life in an entirely new way. Upon completion, the simulator was moved to Manchester University, a testament to the success and innovation of the project.

The classroom itself was a reflection of the team's innovative approach – a wall map was the heart of their planning, marking out weekend walks and youth hostel stays as part of their social learning experiences. This wasn't just about textbooks; it was about living and learning in the real world, gaining confidence and independence through practical experience.

The program didn't stop there. The students were also given the chance to expand their horizons through exchange trips with a children's home in the Netherlands. These trips weren't just about travel; they were designed to give the students a glimpse of life beyond their familiar surroundings, to expose them to different cultures, and to build a deeper sense of self-awareness and global perspective. This was a place where young minds were nurtured, where education went beyond traditional classroom walls and into the realm of real-world exploration and personal growth.

One trip was indeed a true test of their growing independence. The students were late meeting up at the agreed rendezvous point, and when Mark arrived for the handover, the teacher was in a panic, unsure how to handle the situation. Mark, stepped in. When he returned with the missing students in tow minutes later, the visibly relieved teacher gasped, *'Where on earth did you find them?'* The question hung in the air for a moment until Mark, with a wry smile, replied, *'Where do you think?... we're in Amsterdam!!'* Only then did the penny drop.

It was from here that Mark purchased Kinder Klomper's for the girls – those iconic wooden shoes that can be found in every souvenir shop. Back at Gower House, two little girls, full of excitement, eagerly awaited their daddy's return. The shoes were too big, clunky even, but that didn't stop them from *'klomping'* around the house, strutting proudly in their wooden shoes.

In the grand scheme of things, those clogs were far more than just a gift – they became a special memory, a symbol of their childhood that lived on long after they had outgrown them. Eventually, they found their final resting place in the dressing-up box, tucked away with the fox fur collar complete with eyes and snout that once belonged to my great-grandmother, along with other forgotten treasures. But their legacy remained – a reminder of the boldness and joy of childhood, and the adventures they had, one klomp at a time.

Gower House stood on a spacious site in what had once been an affluent area of Salford, not far from Manchester United's old training ground. In the early 1800s, the area had been a beacon of prosperity, with grand houses overlooking the River Irwell. It was one of the earliest suburbs, offering a tranquil refuge for professionals and merchants commuting to Manchester and Salford. By the time we arrived, however, many of these homes had been subdivided into multiple-occupancy dwellings, and the area's prosperity had long since faded.

Constructed in the 1960s, the purpose-built facility featured a quadrangle design with two flats at either end, connected by classrooms, offices, living rooms, and bedrooms, all surrounded by gardens overlooked by an impressive, detached house. The building had more accommodation than anticipated demand, creating a need for suitable uses for the surplus space. Renting rooms to local college students not only addressed economic necessities but also proved mutually beneficial.

Most of these students were training to become chiropodists and physiotherapists in the NHS and were experiencing their first time away from home. This made them excellent role models for young people transitioning to adult life, fostering a supportive community that benefited everyone involved.

It was during this time, a few months after we left the village, that Esther Rantzen, the BBC presenter of 'That's Life', launched Childwatch, a programme raising awareness about child protection. Her initiative was sparked by the tragic death of four-year-old Kimberley Carlile in Greenwich earlier that year. Convinced there had to be a better way to identify children at risk, she invited viewers who had experienced cruelty in childhood to participate in a survey detailing their experiences. Over three thousand people responded – most of them women who had never spoken about their experiences before.

The results were undeniable. Childline, a helpline offering free, confidential support to children and young people, was launched on Sarah's first birthday. The response was staggering. On its opening night, over fifty thousand calls flooded in – an overwhelming testament to how many children had been suffering in silence. It was a moment of reckoning – not just for the public, but for those of us working in children's social care. By the end of my first decade in the field, it became clearer than ever how many voices had gone unheard and how much work remained to be done.

As I entered my second decade in children's social care, I had seen what I believed to be both the very best and the very worst of the system. I had also felt the silencing power of authority – from senior staff and managers who clung tightly to their own views and, when challenged, pulled rank rather than listen. Alternative perspectives weren't welcomed. They were shut down.

The final humiliation came when I was denied the right to sign my own written work. The headmaster told me I wasn't qualified – despite having completed all the training available to me at the time, including day-release courses and the Open University's in-service study scheme for residential care staff. I had nearly ten years of experience caring for children, and I had become a mother myself. Still, it wasn't enough – in his eyes. In that era, teachers pulled rank, and experience counted for little.

In that moment of deflation, I knew I could wait no longer. The very next day, I sent a late application to UCAS (Universities and Colleges Admissions Service) for a place on the CQSW (Certificate of Qualification in Social Work) – a course introduced in 1972 alongside the creation of social services departments and the shift towards generic social work.

I had hoped for employer-funded training, but with residential care and education in steady decline, it was rarely – if ever – seen as a priority.

Field social workers, eager to establish their profession as fully recognised rather than semi-professional, successfully redirected focus, funding, and resources. In the 1970s, the Children's Act 1974 marked a significant shift towards family care and support for children in their own homes, signalling that residential care should only be used as a last resort for children at risk. Social workers and probation officers, whose work centred on keeping families together or placing children in foster care, aligned with the prevailing narrative of reform. This allowed them to secure more attention and funding, while residential care was increasingly sidelined.

As the policy shifted toward preventive measures, prioritising keeping children at home and offering support, when necessary, many residential schools closed. Residential care became increasingly viewed as an obsolete part of the system – the forgotten stepchild of social work left behind in the push to establish social work as a fully recognised profession. For those of us working in residential care, it was clear we were not a priority. The headmaster's attitude merely reinforced this – without a formal qualification, my role, no matter how much training or experience I had, was considered inferior – I was just the babysitter.

Given this, I decided it was time to move on, regardless of how my application turned out. I applied for an assistant social worker position to cover a maternity leave, and to my delight, I was offered the job. The timing couldn't have been better – it was a six-month role, it was a bit risky, but I knew that even if I wasn't accepted onto the course, the experience would be invaluable and open new doors further down the line. As it turned out, I was offered a place on two courses and began my social work training in 1987, just as Sarah turned two.

After becoming Mark's wife and a mother, being a student was one of the most rewarding experiences of my life. Not to forget, of course, passing my driving test on the first try (which I'm still rather pleased about, especially since Mark doubted I would). On a more serious note, I truly valued the academic investment. The chance to connect theory with professional and personal experiences, and refine my skills under the guidance of memorable role models, was something I embraced fully.

I completed placements at a maternity unit, a community mental health team, and a local authority family placement team. Each of these placements opened my eyes to different facets of social care, but it was the family placement team that really left a lasting impression on me.

At the maternity unit, I witnessed the highs and lows of new life – the joy of welcoming a child into the world, and the heart-wrenching weight of stillbirths, premature births, and the agonising decisions families face, such as the termination of a pregnancy for health or social reasons. These experiences made me reflect deeply on what it means to be a parent and how vulnerable families can be when life takes an unexpected and tragic turn.

In the mental health team, I began to grasp just how complex mental health issues can be, especially when they intersect with social care. Families struggling with mental health often find themselves trapped in a vicious cycle: the strain it puts on relationships, the impact on children, and the overwhelming sense of being caught in a system that often doesn't provide enough support.

Sally, my first practice teacher, also volunteered for SAFA (Soldiers', Sailors', and Airmen's Families Association). Having cared for the children of service personnel myself, I understood some of the challenges these families faced, which made her work resonate with me even more. She had also raised funds to build a memorial garden at the hospital for families of stillborn children. The significance of the memorial garden struck a chord with me, reminding me of the long wait for my first child and the lasting impact of Sarah's experience. It was a quiet space made from grief and love, and in it, I saw how care could take many forms – some spoken, some silent, all of them needed.

My final placement was with the family placement team, where I assisted prospective foster parents in deciding whether fostering was the right choice for them. I was involved in evaluating applicants' suitability, providing training for new foster parents, and offering support to carers with children in placement. I also volunteered to answer calls during the first Find a Family programme, a nationwide initiative designed to find homes for children.

The programme aired short videos during the advert breaks, showcasing children who needed a home, alongside the weekly results of the phone-in campaign. Local authorities were desperately seeking more foster parents at the time – just as they are now. But after that first experience, I chose not to take part again.

Advertising children didn't sit right with me. It reduced vulnerable kids to a commodity – a cause for public sympathy, perhaps, but at the cost of their dignity and privacy.

That experience stayed with me. Over time, it came to reflect a growing concern in my work: the increasingly blurred line between raising awareness and exploiting vulnerability.

Today, personal stories – especially those involving children or marginalised groups – are often shared on social media to attract engagement or promote services. But in the rush to be seen, liked, or funded, the ethical implications are too often overlooked.

Stories that should be handled with care are broadcast without context or consent. Pain becomes content. And the children at the centre of these stories – the ones we claim to protect – are too easily reduced to images or narratives that serve someone else's purpose.

With the commodification of children's social care and the rise of digital platforms, these concerns have only deepened. What was once a private act – like delivering Christmas presents or Easter eggs – has become a public spectacle, curated for posts and photo opportunities.

The distinction between sharing a story to raise awareness and using it for personal or organisational gain is critical. It becomes harmful when those stories are used to boost a profile, attract funding, or signal virtue. Even when faces aren't shown, details like location, background, or context can still reveal a child's identity – exposing them to risk, attention they didn't ask for, or emotional harm.

Technology has created new ways to share and spread stories, but it has also opened opportunities for individuals and organisations to capitalise on others' vulnerabilities. The constant drive for likes, shares, and visibility often overshadows the real-world consequences, and in the process, the very people these stories are meant to help are too often exploited in the name of good intentions or self-promotion.

Despite the challenges of navigating a world where privacy and ethical boundaries are often blurred, I thrived during my time as a student. It was a profoundly positive and rewarding experience, where I felt truly invested. The opportunity to learn from experts in the field and practice alongside experienced professionals gave me invaluable insights. This sense of support shaped my approach to the field and reinforced my commitment to making a difference.

The year after I completed my training, we left Gower House and moved back to the village. It was a very different setting – quiet and peaceful, with green spaces around us and a sense of freedom. It was the kind of environment where our girls wouldn't have to face the challenges that so often came with inner-city life. A place where our children could play outside without fear, explore their surroundings, and experience a simpler, more carefree childhood, far removed from the pressures and struggles of the city.

Emma, then seven, started juniors that September, while Sarah joined the same school as a first-year infant, having completed reception before we moved. Looking back, those years were filled with transition, growth, and new beginnings – both for our family and for me professionally. They were challenging but rewarding, shaping the path ahead in ways I could never have predicted.

But there is one regret from that decision that still haunts me. A teacher told Mark Sarah had an *'attitude problem.'* At just five years old, Sarah was labelled – and that label followed her throughout her entire statutory education. Although I was troubled by this at the time, and said so, dyslexia wasn't even considered. It was a disputed diagnosis back then, and the prevailing belief was that children who struggled with reading were simply lazy or not trying hard enough. The damage was done.

6

THE CINDERELLA OF SOCIAL WORK
Fighting for Respect and Recognition

My first job as a qualified social worker was with a local authority intake team based at the town hall, alongside housing and various other departments.

I was sent to reception, where a teenage girl was moving restlessly, her voice growing louder with frustration, drawing stares from those patiently waiting in the queue. The receptionist, clearly irritated, shot her a disapproving glare, which only risked escalating the situation. I didn't hesitate – I knew I needed to get her out of there before the situation got any worse. But with the interview room occupied, there was no choice but to take her to the staff room.

Once inside, she told me she had been kicked out, was sleeping in her car, and needed money for food. Since I didn't have the authority to provide financial assistance, I relayed her story to the team manager. When I returned without the money, it wasn't the answer she wanted. In her desperation, she refused to leave without it.

When I explained there was nothing more I could do, she became aggressive, blocking the door and refusing to let me leave. I tried to reason with her, but it was futile, and no one came – not even to make a brew. I was trapped between a rock and a hard place. While I understood her situation, desperate people do desperate things, and I couldn't ignore the need to protect myself – especially with two little girls waiting for mummy to come home.

The room was filled with tension, and I was stuck in that small space with her blocking the door. I glanced around, hoping someone would intervene, but the office was eerily quiet, and the usual hustle and bustle of the workplace felt miles away. No one was coming. I was on my own, and in that moment, I realised I had no choice. Without another word, in a fleeting moment of distraction, I saw my chance. I opened the door to the corridor, which felt like my only escape. She grabbed my hair, trying to stop me, but I quickly slipped past her and into the hall.

In the commotion that followed, the police were called. Thankfully, I wasn't badly hurt, but the incident raised serious concerns that the union wouldn't let it go. As a result, a decision was made to create additional interview rooms, specifically designed with personal safety in mind. Even now, on the rare occasions when I pass that way, that building stands as a reminder of that eventful day – a near miss, you could say.

On another occasion, the partner of a woman struggling with alcoholism threatened me, convinced that intimidation would make social services back off and help him persuade the court to return the children to their mother's care. He was wrong.

The children were twin babies, just six months old when I became their social worker. They were living with foster parents but were still the size of newborns. Once a week, I took them to a contact centre for visits with their mother, where I observed their interactions from behind a one-way mirror.

I felt deeply for the mother – perhaps because I was a young mother myself. Sadly, she could not see her real battle was with alcohol not social services. The weight of losing her children, of knowing every moment with them was scrutinised, must have been unbearable. But none of that mattered. Under *The Children Act 1989*, despite its focus on the welfare of the child and supporting families, the judge's focus was solely on the risks her drinking posed if the children were returned to her care.

After the court granted social services the authority to place the children for adoption, against the mothers wishes, she expressed a desire to have them christened. Despite her struggles, I had no doubt about her love for them. I believed this was the right thing to do for her children and sought the necessary permissions for it to take place.

The christening was meticulously planned, much like any special family occasion. Guests arrived smartly dressed, proud parents beamed with joy, photographs were taken for posterity, and a traditional buffet was served. Yet beneath this facade, the heartbreaking reality remained as I observed from a discreet distance. Before long, it was time to take the children back to their foster home.

The next contact would be their last before they returned to their foster parents, where they would wait for adoption. The thought of them waiting for a family weighed heavily on me. Finding adoptive parents willing to take on the uncertainty of twins diagnosed with Foetal Alcohol Syndrome (FAS) would be no easy task. Many prospective parents might feel hesitant about the unknowns surrounding their development, as the full impact of FAS often remains unclear until later in life.

While FAS had been identified in this case, its long-term effects were uncertain. Its physical signs – such as a thin upper lip, smaller eye openings, and a smooth or absent philtrum (the vertical groove between the nose and upper lip) – can be subtle, but the greatest challenges lie in its impact on brain development, affecting learning, memory, and emotional regulation. Children with FAS may struggle in school or act out, but the underlying cause is often misunderstood.

It wasn't just about finding the twins a home – it was about finding the right home, one that would understand their needs and the struggles they faced. The system was overstretched, and the most vulnerable children often fell through the cracks. Adoption wasn't just a matter of ticking boxes – it was about creating a safe space where they could heal, grow, and be loved for who they were. They deserved a family who would truly understand and care for them unconditionally.

Years later, I learned that after a long wait the twins had been adopted. They had found their family. It was a relief to know they hadn't been separated or passed from one foster home to another, as so many children in care experience. They finally had what every child deserves – a home, a future, and the chance to grow up together. And knowing that was enough.

Another child on my new caseload was Melissa, who had been left in the sole care of her drug-addicted mother.Melissa was in her last year of primary school, and her teachers had repeatedly raised concerns about her behaviour. This was hardly surprising, given the chaos of life in a drug den, growing up in the midst of drug wars where violence and danger were everyday occurrences – a reality that still affects too many children.

Imagine the terror of being jolted awake by the sounds of adults fighting, desperately seeking safety in the arms of an absent parent who was out working the streets, only to stumble sleepily into the bathroom and find a stranger bleeding profusely from a head wound.

In the court proceedings, a supervision order was granted. Melissa was placed with her maternal grandmother while her mother entered a residential drug rehabilitation unit. The court recognised that Melissa's safety was paramount but also saw the potential for her mother's recovery. While it wasn't the perfect solution, it was a step toward stability for Melissa. The supervision order meant that social services would continue to monitor the situation, ensuring Melissa's well-being during this uncertain time. Though the road ahead was still fraught with challenges, there was hope.

But for me, court days always carried an emotional toll. I would often wake up with an upset stomach, eventually realising it was the anxiety about what lay ahead. The adversarial nature of care proceedings unsettled me. It felt like a war – win or lose – with the right outcome never guaranteed and the stakes impossibly high. Some social workers seemed to relish the courtroom drama, treating it as a battle of wits rather than a serious pursuit of the child's welfare. I often wondered if the true focus was on the child's best interests or if it was about professionals trying to outwit each other.

I began questioning whether field social work was truly the right path for me. I wanted to make a difference, but too often, the system seemed to fail the very children it was meant to help. The focus of the system often appeared to be more on navigating legal procedures than on addressing the children's needs. This disconnect between my aspiration to make a difference, and the limitations of the system left me feeling disillusioned.

Looking back now, I see how deeply the impact of growing up amid drug wars has affected generations of children. What seemed like chaos at the time has only worsened, with County Lines now pulling vulnerable kids into criminal networks. It's almost like a pandemic that's taken hold in ways that were not anticipated. And it's not only children who once endured neglect and violence that are being manipulated and exploited, trapped in a cycle of criminality. The toll it is taking on young lives is immeasurable, and it's clear that without decisive intervention, this cycle will only deepen.

When an opportunity arose to work for the NSPCC, it felt like a chance to step away from statutory social work and engage more directly with children and their families. It was an opportunity to focus on their needs, free from the complexities of legal procedures and the adversarial nature of the system.

Unlike social services, which had the legal responsibility and authority to remove children who had suffered or were at risk of suffering significant harm and initiate care proceedings, the NSPCC could only investigate concerns and refer cases to local authorities. The final decision on whether a child should be removed rested with the local authority. Although, with the introduction of the Children Act 1989, a new power was granted, allowing the NSPCC to apply for an Emergency Protection Order (EPO) if a child was in immediate danger.

This gave them the ability to act in urgent cases without relying on social services, though their involvement remained limited to crisis intervention rather than long-term care decisions.

When I joined the charity, I was fortunate to work in the same office as Ann Bannister, a pioneering psychotherapist in child protection. Her expertise in therapy and training, combined with her unwavering commitment to giving children a voice, made for an invaluable learning experience. Being exposed to her work not only deepened my commitment to child-centred practice but also profoundly shaped my approach to supporting vulnerable children.

One day, while on duty, a mother came into the office seeking help with her son's behaviour. As I listened, a painful story of generational trauma unfolded. Since childhood, she had endured a lifetime of sexual abuse and, like many children in incestuous families, she had believed she was sacrificing herself to protect her younger sister – a misguided act of bravery that often arises in such toxic circumstances.

Now, as a mother herself, she was struggling to protect her child from her own father. His abuse had extended far beyond them, affecting her sister, her children, and others in the community. When he was finally brought to justice, he was sentenced to five years in prison – an amount that, given the immense harm he had caused, seemed woefully inadequate.

At the time, sentencing laws meant many offenders served only half their sentence – or even less with good behaviour. A five-year term could often translate to just two and a half years in prison, and in some cases, offenders were released after only two years. Worse still, prison offered no meaningful rehabilitation. Offenders would walk free, unchanged, with distorted thought processes intact, facing little oversight or restrictions.

There was no Sex Offenders Register – no monitoring, no safeguards to warn future victims. The offender could be free before the victim's childhood had even ended. It wasn't until the Sex Offenders Act of 1997 that convicted offenders were required to register with the police, although gaps in enforcement remained. The system was later strengthened by the Sexual Offences Act of 2003, but at that time, these protections didn't exist.

For those of us working to protect children, the legal system provided little confidence that predators would be held accountable, or that the damage they caused would ever truly be addressed. This case, along with Ann Bannister's influence, led me to question the criminal justice system's approach to offenders – and in many ways, I still do. Many convicted abusers served their time but received no meaningful rehabilitation.

Released back into the community, they often reoffended, while the psychological and physical wounds they inflicted on their victims were left to fester. Worse still, many perpetrators were never brought to justice at all. Cases were dismissed due to lack of evidence, victims were disbelieved, or they were too afraid to speak out. Some secrets were buried under shame, fear, or misplaced loyalty, and never shared.

It was years later that the justice system began to evolve in response to these failures – and still does. The introduction of video link testimony, for example, allowed vulnerable witnesses, such as children and those traumatised by the experience, to give evidence without having to face the defendant. While this was a step in the right direction, it exposed how much more still needed to be done to create a system that could truly support and protect those who had already suffered so much.

The legal system had failed those it was meant to protect, leaving survivors to carry their trauma in silence. Witnessing this made it clear to me that safeguarding children required more than just prosecution. It wasn't enough to remove a child from danger; the trauma they had endured had to be addressed. Real protection meant a systemic shift in how both survivors and perpetrators were treated.

Ann believed in giving children a voice – using creative therapies, storytelling, and play to help them express experiences too painful or confusing to articulate. Her approach was radically different from the clinical, detached methods common at the time. It wasn't just about documenting the abuse – it was about helping children make sense of their experiences and rebuild a sense of self.

At a time when many professionals were reluctant to acknowledge the extent of sexual abuse, Ann's work was unapologetically direct. She didn't shy away from difficult truths, and she pushed for better support – not just for children, but for those working with them. Her influence reinforced what I had already believed: safeguarding was about more than just removing the abuser from a child's life. Without proper intervention, trauma didn't fade away – untreated wounds too often led to lasting health problems that shaped the rest of their lives, without any redress.

It was this mindset that guided me when I visited another family on my caseload. I was horrified to find two children, already known to social services, living in appalling conditions. Their bedroom door had no handle on the inside, and the light fitting was bare, with no bulb. It was hard to comprehend. How had they been left in this state for so long without intervention? In a home like this, the children learned what they lived. There was no furniture, no toys – nothing to bring them even the smallest comfort. It was hard to see how any sense of normalcy could evolve, but it likely wasn't difficult to predict the future.

After sharing my concerns with the team manager, social services concluded that the case didn't meet the threshold for care proceedings. The decision left me stunned. I couldn't understand how they could overlook such clear neglect, but I was powerless to change it. I began questioning whether social work was truly the right path for me.

Being forced to collude with decisions like this left me feeling frustrated and conflicted. I had entered social work with the belief that the system existed to protect vulnerable children, but in cases like this, it felt as though the system was failing them. Reconciling my duty to the children with a system that didn't prioritise their well-being became increasingly difficult.

At that time, the rationing of services was becoming more and more apparent. In the 1990s, resources were scarce due to budget cuts and increasing pressure on social services, driven by factors like high unemployment and high interest rates. These economic challenges strained public finances, making it harder to allocate sufficient resources to support vulnerable children and families.

I found myself witnessing firsthand the impact of a system that was trying to manage these constraints while still addressing the real needs of vulnerable children. The bureaucratic process became the focus, not the children themselves. Thresholds were set, and services were only available to those deemed the most urgent cases. In many situations, like this one, children who were suffering emotional neglect or more complex forms of abuse, including sexual abuse, didn't meet those thresholds.

Families were left without the support they needed, and children were left to suffer in silence. It was hard to reconcile this with my commitment to social justice, knowing that the system, under the pressure of limited resources, was struggling to provide the care these children truly needed. It all seemed penny wise and pound foolish to me – these cuts would cost far more in both hard cash and human suffering in the long run.

A weekly visit to check if there was food in the cupboards was inadequate. This wasn't just about physical abuse – it was about emotional neglect, a much deeper, insidious harm. A full cupboard meant nothing when children lacked the emotional support and stability they needed to thrive. The system was focused on the basics – food, shelter, and safety – but it overlooked the deeper needs of emotional security, connection, and reassurance that someone cared.

Children grow up facing challenges that can't be solved by ticking boxes. They need the unspoken things – attention, kindness, and a consistent presence. These children were growing up in an environment where their emotional needs weren't met, isolated from the love and connection they desperately needed. The system failed to see this bigger picture, focusing on what was measurable, while the real damage – the unseen emotional scars – remained unaddressed.

It was hard not to feel complicit in something that contradicted everything I stood for by accepting these decisions. Every time a case didn't meet the threshold for intervention, it seemed like the very thing that brought me to social work – protecting those who can't protect themselves – was being ignored. This wasn't just about policy; it was personal. My values were being compromised, leaving me to question whether any real difference was being made.

As time passed, it became increasingly clear that the bureaucracy and adversarial nature of field social work were not where I belonged. The constant rationing of services, thresholds and strict rules, away from what really mattered – actually helping children and families. After a year or so in the job, I saw a vacancy for a children's resource centre manager. It felt like the opportunity I needed, so I applied, hoping it would be my chance to truly make a difference.

I carried the image of that bedroom with me – two young brothers confined in a space devoid of comfort. It still brings to mind *Flowers in the Attic* by Virginia Andrews, whose portrayal of extreme isolation and neglect struck a deep chord with me.

Some cases stay with you long after your involvement ends. I still wonder about those children – how they turned out, whether things ever improved for them. That haunting memory remains etched in my mind and that is what nurtures my compassion – a reminder of why I do this work.

Stepping into my new role felt like a homecoming, though not everyone welcomed my arrival. My years in residential care and children and families social work had prepared me for the challenges ahead, yet nothing could have fully equipped me for the systemic failings I uncovered – that left vulnerable children without the support they so desperately needed.

The children's centre served a defined area of the city, providing targeted support to children identified as being in need, while also offering specialist services for the broader community. Housed in a Victorian building that had once been a children's home, it shared its site with the youth justice team, an education unit, and a sixteen-plus service for young people preparing to leave care.

I took up the role in 1991, shortly after my predecessor transitioned to the newly established arms-length inspection unit, created in response to public inquiries like the Pindown Inquiry, which had exposed widespread abuse and neglect in children's homes. The unit was designed to provide independent oversight of both local authority and private care homes, ensuring impartial scrutiny of issues such as mismanagement and abuse, free from conflicts of interest.

On my first day, I was shown to my predecessor's office – empty, since they had already moved on. The office, tucked away in the attic, felt isolated from the day-to-day business of running children's services, so I decided to relocate to a small office closer to the admin team. I wanted to be more visible, more connected to the daily rhythm of things. It didn't take long to get a feel for how things operated around there.

The manager and deputy of the sixteen-plus unit were indifferent, neither had sufficient length of service to benefit from early retirement schemes, and age was against them when it came to finding another job with the same benefits. The 1990s were marked by economic challenges, with a recession and widespread downsizing. As the job market shifted, particularly towards the private sector, older workers struggled to find comparable roles, especially with the same pay and benefits. There was no real motivation to drive change.

This disengagement reflected a larger shift happening in the public sector at the time. The 1980s and 90s saw a push to downsize government-run services, driven by the belief that privatisation would make things more efficient and cost-effective. To reduce spending, experienced workers were often offered early retirement or laid off, and services were handed over to charities and the private sector.

The focus was on cutting costs, but it came at the expense of losing skilled professionals and reducing the quality of services.

The young people, caught in the middle of this shift, were left without the support they needed to thrive.

During one of our first meetings, I learned that a young person had been relying on a weekly food parcel for 18 months. The parcels provided only the basics, and there was no fresh produce included. Nobody had noticed – not the manager, nor the child's own social worker. It was a stark reminder of how deep the gaps in support were and how the system failed to see the real needs of these young people. When I proposed reinstating his weekly allowance, seeing how the current approach was clearly not working, the deputy reacted with anger, slamming his fist on the desk in opposition.

This response highlighted a bigger issue for me: the widespread belief that punishment changes behaviours. Even though we've known for a long time that punishment alone doesn't work, it still persists. It fails to address the trauma and underlying causes of behaviour, and instead of fostering real change, it often breeds resentment. If punishment were the solution, UK prisons wouldn't be overcrowded, and reoffending rates wouldn't be so high.

The office, with its smoke-filled air and overflowing ashtray, said it all – no one moved far from it, and nobody cared. It was a warehouse – a place where goods are stored until someone decides to move them on. The young people, like products on a shelf, were left to stagnate in an environment that lacked the necessary conditions for growth.

What these kids needed was a greenhouse – a place where warmth, light, and care help plants grow strong and ready for the outside world. But that wasn't happening here. This wasn't a nurturing environment where growth was guided, and skills were developed to prepare young people for adult life. The staff were disengaged, the atmosphere stagnant, and resources too limited to offer the support they needed. Instead of growing, the young people were left to wither, their potential untapped and unrealised.

But they weren't the only ones who made it clear that my arrival wasn't welcomed. The deputy centre manager, who had also applied for my position, wasted no time in showing his discontent. His cold reception signalled the start of the resistance I would face as I worked to establish myself in the role and take people along with the changes needed to improve services.

He oversaw the youth justice and community support team, which worked to prevent children from being criminalised and reduce the number entering care. Yet, whenever I requested a meeting, he was always unavailable. The more he avoided me, the more determined I became to understand the work being done. When I finally managed to secure a meeting, he called in sick on the day.

In his absence, the manager of the admin support team took charge of ensuring the youth justice and community support team had access to the necessary funds. When the bank statement arrived, she opened it and discovered a large payment to a cleaning company that raised her suspicions. She brought it to my attention, and together, we went into his office to look for an explanation.

7

THROUGH THE CRACKS

How Systems Fail the Most Vulnerable

A t first, I thought my eyes were deceiving me as I scanned the documents – bank statements stacked haphazardly on the desk each one showing unusual transactions. Multiple payments to the same account, along with letters from debt collectors and county court summonses stuffed in filing cabinet drawers. This wasn't just a mistake. It was a pattern. A cover-up. And it had been going on for a long time. Fortunately, it was Friday, and the regular lunch meeting with the senior management team was already planned.

I drove to our meeting place, taking deep breaths as my mind raced and I tried to collect my thoughts. Upon arrival, I stepped out of the car, clutching the small sample of evidence I had brought with me. I had no doubt something was seriously wrong and was relieved to hand over the evidence to the assistant director, who assured me she would handle it. A few days later, police officers arrived to seize the contents of the filing cabinets and his abandoned computer.

Months later, the investigation confirmed what had been suspected all along: he had exploited his trusted public sector position to siphon off funds, diverting them straight into his own business account. The police estimated that he had stolen nearly half a million pounds in today's money – money that never reached the children it was meant to support.

As the investigation dug deeper, more troubling details came to light. He had applied for grants from charities, claiming the funds would be used to buy outdoor equipment and support youth development programmes. But the money was misappropriated, and no one had been tracking where it was going. The lack of proper oversight allowed him to operate unchecked, quietly diverting public and charitable funds to his own business account under the guise of community support.

When officers examined his abandoned computer, they found letters he'd written to adult contact magazines, adding another potentially disturbing layer to the case. The scale of his deception – both financial and personal – painted the picture of a man who had long manipulated the system, hiding in plain sight while exploiting the very people he was supposed to support and protect.

From our very first encounter, I doubted everything about him. He didn't speak the language of the qualified social worker he claimed to be – everything about him felt inherently fake. Six weeks later, he was gone, taking his questionable credentials with him.

It took months for the police to conclude their investigation, and when they finally went to arrest him, I accompanied them. As we approached his house, the silence was unsettling. The curtains were drawn, the doors locked, and the entire place seemed frozen in time. Inside, dust covered the furniture, and papers were scattered, as though someone had left in a hurry.

The place had clearly been abandoned for months. While we didn't know where he was, one thing became painfully clear – he had planned his escape long before we caught up with him.

Eventually, he was traced to another country, where he had fled to avoid prosecution.

But this wasn't the first time I had witnessed such a devastating breach of trust – or the last. It was a stark reminder of how easily power can be misused, and how vulnerable the systems designed to protect children truly are.

Around the same time, Ralph Morris, the principal of Castle Hill Independent Special School in Ludlow, was convicted and sentenced to 12 years for sexually abusing pupils in his care.

I had met Morris during a visit to the school, when I was introduced to Robert before he came to live with us. I couldn't have foreseen what would come to light, but something about his manner left me uneasy. Polite and professional, yes – but I walked away with a discomfort I couldn't quite place.

I was working quietly in my relocated office when I read the news. At first, the headline barely registered. Then I saw his name – Ralph Morris – and everything came flooding back. The tour, the charm, that lingering discomfort. Now, it all felt horribly clear.

Between 1984 and 1989, when Castle Hill was finally shut down, Morris sexually abused 43 boys in his care. Another 50 suffered physical abuse. He had falsified qualifications, overstated capacity, and tampered with pupil records. Despite multiple allegations, no action was taken for years – the boys' concerns dismissed, labelled as 'maladjusted' and unreliable.

Robert had been there when the school opened. Thankfully, he wasn't among the abused. But others he knew were not so fortunate.

Castle Hill wasn't unique. The Pindown Inquiry in Staffordshire exposed abusive disciplinary practices in children's homes. Social worker Alison Taylor lost her job for raising concerns in North Wales – concerns later validated. Christian Wolmar's *Forgotten Children* documented widespread abuse in care over two decades. The scale was undeniable.

The fallout from Castle Hill was a wake-up call. I was relieved we had removed Robert when we did – but the sense of a near miss stayed with me. It reinforced what I had come to believe: vigilance is not optional. It's essential – for the safety of children, and for the credibility of the systems meant to protect them.

In the years that followed, historic abuse inquiries – known as "trawling operations" – began. The intention was just: to give survivors a voice and pursue overdue justice. But over time, the methods drew criticism. Investigations grew less focused, more sweeping. Allegations were sometimes pursued with more urgency than care. Pressure to uncover wrongdoing began to eclipse due process.

Investigations by *The Guardian* and *The Independent* revealed troubling flaws. Former residents spoke of being encouraged to shape or exaggerate memories. Some felt manipulated. Others, who came forward willingly, later regretted it – their accounts twisted to fit a narrative. In some cases, convictions were overturned when courts found evidence had been mishandled.

The fallout was far-reaching. Ethical questions were raised about retraumatising survivors, and about the impact on those wrongfully accused. The drive for justice had, in some instances, undermined the very principles it set out to uphold.

At the same time, the media's appetite for scandal fuelled a wave of sensationalism. Institutional abuse became headline news, and trust in residential care plummeted. For those of us still working in the field, the consequences were real – suspicion, fear, and the slow erosion of public confidence.

When I spoke to Robert about Castle Hill, he remembered Morris – his manner, the way he interacted with certain boys. Even at the time, something felt off. Looking back, he recognised those moments for what they were.

Over the years, he'd stayed in contact with some of the boys. He saw how trauma lived on – in broken trust, troubled relationships, and quiet self-doubt. The scars weren't always visible. But they were there, carried into adulthood by boys who had once simply needed protection.

In the years that followed, children's homes began to close. Officially, it was reform – a shift toward community-based care. But to many of us, it looked like cost-cutting. Residential care was expensive and politically unpopular. Councils, under pressure to reduce budgets, targeted it first.

By the time Tony Blair's government came to power, the language had softened, but the message remained. Early intervention and fostering were prioritised. Residential care was quietly pushed to the margins.

But the infrastructure wasn't there to support this shift. Community-based alternatives were cheaper, although not always better. Behind the rhetoric of reform lay the reality of austerity. Homes closed. Children were moved. Promises of improvement often masked financial motivations.

And it didn't escape anyone's notice that the land those homes sat on was valuable. Redevelopment followed quickly. What was lost wasn't just buildings – it was a system of care, supervision, and stability. What replaced it was patchy, underfunded, and increasingly privatised.

Closing homes reduced scrutiny and helped decision-makers distance themselves from the reality of what vulnerable children actually needed.

For politicians, it offered the opportunity to claim reform, efficiency, and accountability – quick wins with public appeal, gift-wrapped as progress, and rewarded in votes. Instead of investing in what could be improved, the emphasis turned to cost avoidance and political point scoring. Yes, too many children were harmed – but not all. Some homes offered care, safety, and stability. But in the rush to dismantle the system, little distinction was made. The focus was on failure, not on learning from it.

It was in this era that Danesford, a residential children's home in Congleton, closed. The news struck a chord. Danesford had been a steady presence a familiar name in residential care circles. At the time, there were quiet rumours – unspoken concerns that never made it into formal reports but seemed to linger just beneath the surface. Whether those concerns played any role in its closure, no one said aloud.

The focus had shifted. It was no longer about improving what we had, risk became a reason to retreat, not a call to act. And so, bit by bit, the fabric of residential care was pulled apart not through bold reform, but through quiet withdrawal and the avoidance of accountability.

A young person was moved from Danesford to Gower House in the early 1990s, around the same time Ralph Morris was convicted, and an investigation was launched into allegations involving former staff. One name surfaced: Richard Burrows, a former housemaster. In 1997, he was arrested and charged with multiple serious offences dating back to the late 1960s. But before he could face trial, he vanished. For decades, nothing more was said.

This wasn't just about one home. It was part of a wider pattern we were starting to see across residential care. Institutions closed quietly. Children were moved on. Stories were buried. The closure of homes like Danesford was framed as progress – but for those of us working in the field, it looked very different. You could say it was driven less by meaningful reform, and more by cost-cutting, risk management, and the quiet erasure of long-standing provision – with no clear plan for what would take its place.

It wasn't until 2023 that Burrows was finally located in Thailand, extradited to the UK, and brought to trial. In 2025, he was convicted of 54 serious offences, including indecent assault and buggery. The crimes spanned nearly three decades.

What shocked me most wasn't just the scale of the abuse. It was how long it had taken for the truth to be acknowledged. There had been no inquiry. No public reckoning. Just silence. It felt like a familiar strategy – one I'd seen before. A way to protect reputations, avoid scrutiny, and limit liability. Whether driven by insurers, internal policy, or institutional self-preservation, the result was the same: delay, denial, and a failure to do the right thing by those who had already been failed.

This was never just about one man, one home, or one conviction. It was part of something much wider – a system that too often buried concerns and quietly shut its doors. The children were moved on. The buildings were sold. But the damage remained. By the time the conviction finally came, Danesford had long since disappeared, its buildings replaced by private housing. The children, and the adults they became, were the ones who lived with the consequences. The system made the decisions. They lived with the outcome.

When Gower House closed in the mid-nineties due to a fall in demand, Mark took a job at a privately owned residential school for children with learning difficulties. But it didn't take long for him to see that the school's approach to supervision was seriously outdated. He was expected to monitor the boys in the toilets and showers, even though there was increasing awareness around child protection and policies were beginning to evolve.

The school was stuck in the past, and the owner ran the place with a top-down, rigid approach, leaving no space for real discussion or change. Staff concerns were dismissed. Procedures were outdated. And the children – already vulnerable – were left in a system that was lagging behind the times.

At the same time, our own family was adjusting to new routines. We had moved house, and the girls had started at a new school, when the cracks in the plan began to show. With limited after-school clubs available, they had to spend time in someone else's home after school – an arrangement that unsettled them more than we expected. On reflection, it was perfectly understandable. Before the move, Mark or I would collect them from school and bring them straight home. We coped for a while, but it chipped away at us – and as Mark's dissatisfaction with his job grew, the strain became more difficult to manage.

When we found out that one of the local pubs was for sale, it seemed like the answer. Mark could leave the job that was causing him so much angst, take over the school run, and I could finally ease the guilt I felt about leaving the girls in after-school care – something they'd never really adjusted to.

At the time the pressures of balancing family life, work, and the need for a dual income to stay afloat in the early 1990s made it feel like a *'no brainer'*.

Not long after Mark left his role and we took over the pub, I transferred to a resource centre serving another area of the city, with responsibility for a regional secure unit. Housed in an Edwardian manor, the unit offered placements for children who were either in serious trouble with the law or considered too vulnerable to be left in the community without secure supervision. Some had committed offences; others were there purely on welfare grounds. They weren't criminals – they were children at risk.

Only a few months into the role, news broke of a local murder that deeply shocked the community. A 16-year-old girl had been found with severe burns. Early reports suggested it may have been self-inflicted, possibly following a dispute with a boyfriend. But when a man walking his dog discovered her, she was still alive and she lived just long enough to name her attackers.

Her story stayed with me. She had spent time in local authority care and later returned to live with her sister and stepfather. By the time she was 14, her behaviour had begun to deteriorate. Teachers noted the change and attributed it to the company she was keeping. She started spending more time at the home of a family acquaintance – unaware that it had become a dangerous and chaotic environment.

What unfolded was horrific. She was subjected to prolonged abuse over several days before being set alight. Her attackers included a 16-year-old boy and five adults. Despite the horrific nature of the crime, the public response was strangely muted. Her death – just two months before the murder of James Bulger – did not dominate the headlines. There was no national outpouring of grief, no emergency parliamentary debates. For me, it raised uncomfortable questions about who we notice – and who we don't.

By contrast, James Bulger's murder in February 1993 shook the country and dominated public conversation. The fact that two ten-year-old boys, were responsible caused widespread outrage and forced a reckoning with the justice system. But both tragedies revealed, in different ways, what happens when vulnerable children fall through the cracks – whether as victims or as perpetrators.

A year or so later, a similar case in Belgium involving two boys under the age of 14 took a very different turn. Rather than being prosecuted, they were placed on a residential therapeutic rehabilitation programme. The setting was secure, but its purpose was entirely different from what we were seeing in the UK. The emphasis wasn't on punishment, but on understanding – the emotional and developmental factors that had shaped their actions. A multidisciplinary team of psychologists, social workers, and educators worked together to support the boys' emotional growth and reintegration into society.

It stood in stark contrast to the UK's increasingly punitive approach, where the focus was shifting toward containment, deterrence, and public reassurance. In Belgium, they had chosen to treat the children as children – complex, damaged, but not beyond help. The comparison stayed with me, highlighting what was possible when the goal wasn't simply to punish, but to understand and to heal.

At that point, English law still recognised *doli incapax* – a centuries-old principle that protected children under 14 from criminal responsibility unless it could be proven they understood their actions were seriously wrong. This was not even a consideration for the 16-year-old. He was tried as an adult, as were the ten-year old boys who murdered James Bulger, after the prosecution successfully demonstrated that both boys understood right from wrong.

But that safeguard was under pressure. By 1999, it was removed under the *Youth Justice and Criminal Evidence Act*. Children as young as ten could now be prosecuted without any need to assess their developmental understanding. This shift came despite mounting evidence from neuroscience and psychology that children's brains – especially the parts responsible for decision-making, impulse control, and empathy – do not fully mature until their mid-twenties.

A child might understand the difference between right and wrong but still lack the capacity to foresee consequences or regulate behaviour. Yet the law was increasingly treating them as miniature adults.

In the wake of the Bulger case, conversations about crime and punishment intensified. Pressure was building to increase the number of secure beds. But those of us working on the ground knew that locking children away wasn't the answer. Most of the young people we saw didn't need punishment – they needed support, therapy, education, and a real chance to change.

Politically, though, the tone had already shifted. In 1993, following the Bulger murder and the resulting public outcry, Tony Blair – then Shadow Home Secretary – delivered a now-infamous line: 'Tough on crime, tough on the causes of crime.'

It struck a chord. To many, it promised both justice and social reform. But in practice, the focus leaned heavily toward control and containment.

By the time Blair became Prime Minister in 1997, that slogan had become central to Labour's platform. It helped rebrand the party as capable of tackling crime without abandoning its social justice roots. But for professionals in youth justice and social care, the reality was more complex. The message reassured voters – but it didn't always translate into early intervention or child-centred reform. In fact, it meant more punitive measures, expanded secure accommodation, and lower thresholds for criminal responsibility.

What won political favour wasn't always what worked best for vulnerable children. The system became increasingly risk-averse, focused on public protection and managing behaviour, often at the expense of rehabilitation. The rhetoric may have won votes – but it came at a cost we saw every day in the lives of the young people in our care.

The secure children's home attached to the resource centre I managed was small – just seven beds. At its core, it was a children's home and a school with locks on the doors. But it never felt like a prison. The focus was always on care and education, not punishment; on relationships, not control.

Many of the children arrived carrying deep trauma, loss, and unmet need. Some were angry, others withdrawn – but none were beyond reach. The staff offered structure, therapeutic support, and consistent routines. They knew that safety wasn't about locked doors – it was about trust, clear boundaries, and a sense of stability.

They couldn't undo what had happened in these children's lives. But they could show them something better. And they did – quietly, patiently, and every single day.

In my role, I was directly involved in the development of a

new secure facility for children and young people. The site had a long history of providing secure accommodation – originally as an extension of an adjoining education facility – but by the early 1990s, it was clear that the existing provision no longer reflected the standards – or the values – needed for modern secure care.

The vision for the new facility was ambitious. What emerged would become one of the first purpose-built juvenile secure facilities designed in line with the principles later formalised in the Design Guide 2000. This wasn't just a construction project – it was a chance to rethink what secure care could, and should, be.

I was invited onto the design team when funding was approved and took on the role of site manager. It was an extraordinary opportunity – not just to help shape a building, but to contribute to a new philosophy about how we support children in crisis. We weren't interested in replicating the past. The new unit would be secure, yes – but it also had to be humane. The goal was to create a space where safety and rehabilitation could truly coexist.

The design reflected that intention. The final build provided fully purpose-built accommodation for twelve young people, with integrated educational and sports facilities, and a complete internal upgrade of the existing secure provision. Every element was shaped by the needs of the young people who would live there, and by the insight of the staff who worked with them. Even the security systems were reimagined: fixed panic buttons were replaced with portable handsets that staff could carry – tracking location in real time and improving both safety and accountability.

Though I moved on before the building officially opened, being part of that project remains one of the most formative experiences of my career. It reaffirmed what I had come to believe so strongly: that if we want to protect society, we can't rely on containment alone. We have to offer something more –

opportunities for young people to understand their behaviour, to reflect, to grow, and to heal.

Because no matter how serious the offence, a child is still a child. And if the systems around them can't offer a path forward, then the failure isn't theirs alone. It never was.

Being part of that development gave me the rare chance to help shape a new direction – one rooted not just in safety, but in possibility. It reminded me that the spaces we create, both physical and emotional, matter. And it strengthened my conviction that the justice system must be capable of both accountability and compassion.

8

BEHIND THE BAR
Lessons in Business, Community, and Care

Running a pub was never part of the plan, but at the time, it felt like the best way forward. Childcare was scarce, after-school clubs were limited, and Emma and Sarah wanted to come home each day. They didn't want to be looked after by someone else – they wanted us. And we wanted to be there. So, we took the plunge. We swapped our house for a lease, and Mark traded the job he no longer wanted, exchanging worries about childcare for the challenges of running a business.

As a working mum, I knew the emotional weight of leaving your children in someone else's care – not because you wanted to, but because you had no choice. So, when Mark took on the pub, it gave us a way around that. I stayed at work, the girls were able to come straight home after school, and I didn't have to worry. It made going to work almost guilt-free for me and for the first few years, it worked really well.

Mark and I weren't seasoned businesspeople when we took on the pub. We were just young parents with aspirations – aspirations shared by most parents – balancing family life with earning a living to give our children a good life. We didn't know all the ins and outs of the business, but we learned quickly – we had no choice.

The pub was always full of life, and despite the challenges, there were plenty of good times too. Many of our regulars were friends, and those who weren't at first often became them. We got to know people by name, shared laughs, and built a real sense of community.

To keep up with the changing times, we adapted – adding a bistro and even bed and breakfast to attract more customers. But despite our efforts, there were so many demands on the money that came in before we took a penny – made worse by one or two staff who thought it was okay to help themselves.

Most of our team were honest and loyal, but there was the odd one who thought helping themselves a free drink or taking a fiver from the till wouldn't be noticed. It wasn't just about the money – it was the betrayal, and the doubt it cast on everyone. And the financial pressures didn't stop there. The brewery, business rates, music licenses, machine rental, repairs and renewals, maintenance – the list went on. Each of these costs took a chunk of what we earned.

Balancing the books was like a work of fine art, sometimes keeping me up into the early hours. The introduction of all-day opening hours meant even more work, and with rising beer duties, the cost of a pint crept up too. We kept trying to diversify – offering after-match chip butties to the local football team, hosting quiz nights, and creating a welcoming atmosphere – but the rewards never seemed to match the effort that went in.

Finding a good chef became like looking for a needle in a haystack. The shortage of skilled kitchen staff pushed wages up, and we simply couldn't compete with the big pub companies entering the market. Some pubs closed altogether. Others were bought out by larger chains. A few were repurposed – some even became children's homes. The landscape shifted.

I stepped in to run the food side of the business. Learning to run a commercial kitchen was another steep learning curve, but it was one I genuinely enjoyed – even though it was hard work for little return. The long hours, the missed weekends, the constant demands – it all added up. We poured so much of ourselves into that place, sometimes with very little left for each other. Looking back, I can see how much it took from us, as well as what it gave.

Running a pub and restaurant with letting rooms meant training staff, maintaining the property, and keeping customers happy. Like working in children's homes, evenings, weekends, and bank holidays weren't optional – but here, the risk of failure wasn't shared. It was entirely ours.

Mark was the face of the place – the host, breakfast chef, and the person everyone expected to see behind the bar morning, noon, and night. Together, we organised quiz nights, karaoke evenings, and celebrations for weddings, christenings, and wakes. The pub was busy and well-loved, but it was a hard way to make a living. The brewery took the lion's share of the profits, and staffing challenges compounded the difficulties.

For some, it was more than just their local – it was where they celebrated, mourned, caught up on gossip, or simply felt a sense of belonging. That kind of connection is hard to measure, but you feel its absence when it's gone.

Saturdays during football season were buzzing, with post-match gatherings in the afternoon and live music in the evening. Sundays revolved around Sky Sports football, roast dinners, and karaoke. Now and then, Big Sam and his wife, Lynne, would pop in to join the fun. Lynne often shared stories about their early years when Sam had been a youth player earning just £4 a week – a time when making ends meet had been a constant struggle.

I liked Lynne a lot; she was down-to-earth and had no interest in the glitzy WAG lifestyle. Instead, she liked to reminisce about the challenges they'd faced together. We used to joke about writing our memoirs – hers, she said, would be called '*Bread and Butter Football*'.

As the end of the millennium drew near, we'd been at the pub for seven years. That year, the festive season felt extra special, with the world gearing up to celebrate the year 2000, and we made it a night to remember. With food fit for royalty, live music, and a piper in full regalia playing the pipes to usher in the New Millennium, the atmosphere was electric. As *Auld Lang Syne* faded, handshakes, hugs, and toasts filled the pub, and we danced into the early hours. By New Year's Day, I was more than a little relieved to settle back into the quieter routine that followed the holiday madness.

But even as things returned to normal, there was excitement in the air. One family who joined us every week for Sunday dinner and karaoke had an especially thrilling year ahead. Fifteen-year-old Vicky and her younger brother Danny had made it to the final of BBC One's *Steps to the Stars* – a children's version of *Opportunity Knocks*, the popular TV talent show that ran in the 1960s and 70s, and *years later* would be resurrected as *Britain's Got Talent*, *The X Factor*, and *The Voice*. Every time I heard Vicky sing *Baby Think Twice*, it gave me goosebumps, so when they asked to do a live gig at the pub to prepare for the final, we were more than happy to support them.

When Danny went on to become one of McFly's lead singers and guitarists, we were thrilled for him. Later, when he became a judge on the children's version of *The Voice*, and then the adult version, I couldn't help but feel a tiny sense of pride, as if we'd been a small part of his journey. Watching him and Tom Fletcher, his bandmate, share the first-ever double chair on *The Voice UK* was a special moment. Seeing Danny hit those milestones has been a real privilege.

Emma and Sarah grew into teenagers during the pub years, attending the same high school as our foster children – and Mark before them. Emma went on to sixth form, but Sarah wasn't interested in staying in education she took a job as a trainee hairdresser in a local salon.

By the time Sarah finished school, we were ready to move on. The dream of owning our own business hadn't paid off as we'd hoped, despite all the promises and effort we'd invested, and buying a house close by the pub was out of our reach. For me, leaving wasn't as difficult as it was for Mark and the girls. I wasn't from the area to begin with, and I was ready to bring this chapter to a close.

The pub taught us a lot – about people, pressure, and perseverance. It wasn't where our future lay, but it was a chapter that shaped what came next.

What once felt like a close-knit community had changed. The warmth and familiarity had faded, and the personal connections that had once made it feel like home had been disrupted. The area had become a magnet for city dwellers seeking a quieter life. The local train station made the Manchester commute easy, and good schools added to the appeal.

It was a familiar story across the country – rising property prices and an influx of newcomers slowly pushing out long-time residents, changing the landscape of the place we once called home.

But it wasn't just the community that had shifted – the pub trade had changed, too. We faced rising costs, corporate pressures, and changing consumer habits, with more people opting to drink at home rather than in pubs.

We left the pub just days before Sarah turned sixteen at the end of October, with little more than a new mortgage to pay. The shame of having to sign on weighed heavily on me. For someone who had always prided themselves on their independence, it felt like a personal defeat. Emma, who had just graduated from university, was struggling too. The experience of signing on was particularly humiliating for her, leaving her distraught and uncertain about her next steps. It was heartbreaking to watch my daughter, who had so much to give, feel lost and unsure of her place in the world.

Sarah had already secured a job as a trainee in a small hair salon, but it was clear that we were all struggling to find our footing during this difficult time. We were a family in transition, facing challenges we hadn't anticipated, each of us trying to navigate a new reality in unfamiliar territory.

Meanwhile, Mark knew he had to find work – fast. When he told his friend we'd left the pub and desperately needed a job, his friend didn't hesitate. *'How does tomorrow sound?'* he said. Mark didn't miss a beat. The next morning, he was ready and waiting. His friend arrived at 7, drove him to work, and brought him home at the end of the day. He ran a small engineering firm. The work was repetitive, and the pay wasn't great – but it was enough to keep the wolves at bay until better times returned.

It's at times like these that the true value of friendship becomes clear. His friend didn't just offer him a job; he threw us a lifeline, a way to keep going when it felt like everything else had fallen apart. The simple act of stepping in, without question, was something that would stay with us forever. For that, I'll always be grateful.

Looking back, I can see that I was defeated. The decision to take on the pub felt like a personal failure. I gave it my all, but in doing so, I lost sight of who I was – my qualifications, my experience, my sense of self-worth. The demands of the business, and the way it ended, took their toll. It wasn't just the stress of running a business – it was the people and the politics that came with it.

An affair between a customer and an employee – it could have been the backstory to a primetime drama. The customer, his wife, and the barmaid. But this wasn't fiction. This was real life, and it tore through everything we'd worked for.

The fallout didn't just hurt the business – it ended friendships, split loyalties, and shook the foundations of the life we'd created. It changed my relationship with the community I had once called home. For ever.

It took time, but eventually, I regained a sense of direction. I signed up with a social work recruitment agency and took my first assignment with a social work team at a nearby hospital. The work was challenging but grounding, helping me reconnect with my professional identity. From there, I moved to a children and families intake team, and later, to a long-term team, working with young people transitioning from a large local authority establishment to independent children's homes – a shift that was becoming increasingly common in the sector.

Fylde Farm first opened its doors in 1905 as a rehabilitation centre for juvenile offenders. By 1933, it had transformed into an approved school, later under The Children and Young Persons Act 1969 it became a community home with education (CHE). It offered boys who had made mistakes a chance at a better life – teaching them trades, building their confidence, and treating them as students, not criminals. For decades, it served its purpose, and it was easy to believe this was a place where real change could happen. But by the late 20th century, everything began to shift.

In the 1980s, government policies focused on reducing public spending and increasing privatisation, slowly reshaping the landscape of children's care. By the 1990s, the shift was undeniable – vulnerable young people were increasingly seen through an economic lens rather than a welfare-based one.

Against this backdrop, the Quality Protects initiative was introduced by Tony Blair's Labour government. It promised better services and improved outcomes for children in care. But even as the policy language became more aspirational, the reality on the ground told a different story. Questions were already being asked: could spending millions on just fifty-five boys really be justified? Yet beyond the figures on a spreadsheet, the needs of the boys themselves were too often lost.

The decision to close 'The Fylde', as it was known, was made behind closed doors at a council meeting. No public debate, no transparency – just a quiet decision, taken at the same time planning permission was sought to convert a nearby former nursing home into a home for sixteen boys.

Dales House had opened in 1996 on the same site as The Fylde, designed as part of a new generation of purpose-built secure homes for young people convicted of serious offences – arson, armed robbery, even murder. It was intended to offer more than containment: a blend of education, therapy, and structured support. In 2000, just two years before its closure, the unit underwent a £2 million refurbishment. Then, in 2002, it was gone. No headlines. No consultation. Just silence.

By 2016, the consequences had become hard to ignore. Only 13 secure children's homes remained in England – nine fewer than before. At any given moment, around 25 children were waiting for a secure bed that no longer existed. The need hadn't gone away. Only the capacity to meet it.

The Howard League for Penal Reform described secure homes as offering 'the highest standards of care and rehabilitation' for children who, for a time, couldn't safely be anywhere else. Yet even these homes, they said, 'became the victim of a decade of closures,' with decisions made 'on the basis of short-term cost savings, with little consideration given to the needs of children – or the long-term costs of failure.'

That's exactly what it felt like: not reform, not progress – just systemic failure and a blatant misuse of public funds.

This wasn't just about economics. It was political. The 1980s and 90s saw high-profile abuse scandals in children's homes that rightly demanded reform. But they also handed power to those eager to shrink public services. Residential care was rebranded as unsafe and outdated, while more 'cost-effective' models were ushered in. Public trust eroded – and so did political will. Soon, decisions about children's futures were being made behind closed doors, with little public accountability.

As local authorities stepped back, private providers stepped in. Companies like Northern Care, Advanced Childcare, and CareTech quickly filled the vacuum left by the state. It wasn't just that services were changing – the entire infrastructure of care was being quietly rebuilt around a different set of priorities.

And now, we find ourselves in reverse. New funding is being pledged to reintroduce secure places. There is talk of semi-secure units, innovation, bridging gaps. But those of us who remember the semi-secure units of the 1980s – like the one Hannah was placed in before she came to live with us – know that language can obscure reality.

Worse still, research from Cardiff University's CASCADE centre shows that in the years since, two in five children referred to secure homes have been turned away – placed instead in unregulated, inappropriate settings, with untrained staff and little oversight.

So, when government ministers speak of rebuilding, it's not progress – it's repair. The public is being asked to fund – again – what was already paid for, shut down, and left to rot.

This isn't about drawing neat lines between public and private, good and bad. It's about accountability. When purpose-built homes are closed, abandoned, and left to decay – and nobody asks why – that's not reform. That's negligence. And as always, it's children who pay the price.

Fostering was promoted as a more *'family-centred'* and *'cost-effective'* alternative – a cheaper solution, easier to sell politically than the infrastructure and staffing required for residential care. In an era of austerity, it quickly became the default option for those holding the purse strings.

But with hindsight, it's clear that the political spotlight on care scandals did more than expose failings – it helped drive an agenda of cost-cutting disguised as reform. The shift toward fostering and private provision, while helpful for some, was built more on budget logic than on what children with complex needs actually required. And those children – the ones who needed the most – were too often left behind.

It's not hard to see the ghosts from the past in the present. On paper, it looked like progress – investment in a system that had been allowed to unravel. But for those of us who witnessed the dismantling of secure care facilities in the 1990s and early 2000s, the irony was hard to miss. Millions are now being spent to restore what had already been built, only to be scrapped without explanation.

The closure of many secure homes and the shift towards fostering and community-based care began well before the Labour government took office in 1997. Under Thatcher's Conservative government, cuts to public spending were made across all sectors, including children's services, and these trends continued into the Major years. Yet, it was under Tony Blair's Labour government, particularly in the late 1990s and early 2000s, that the closure of secure units accelerated. Budget pressures, the desire to cut costs, and the focus on reducing public sector spending led to a marked reduction in the capacity of state-run secure homes, despite their documented role in providing care and rehabilitation for vulnerable children.

What's clear is that the political environment of both the

Conservative and Labour governments contributed to the steady reduction of secure care facilities. The prioritisation of fostering, which was viewed as cheaper and more 'family-centred,' made sense in financial terms, but it often overlooked the complexity of care that the most vulnerable children needed. These decisions, driven by short-term cost-saving measures, came at a long-term cost – to the children, the workforce, and the very fabric of the care system.

And now, years later, we find ourselves in a cycle of 'repair.' The current government has pledged new funding to expand capacity in secure homes, but it feels like a reaction to problems that were created by the very same kinds of cost-cutting decisions that have plagued the sector for decades. The public purse is now being asked to pay again for something that had already been invested in, only to be dismantled through political mismanagement.

This is where the irony becomes glaring: a Labour government, having overseen significant cuts to residential care facilities, now pledges funds to rebuild what was erased. It's hard not to view it as an attempt to reframe past failures as present-day solutions.

However, this isn't just about the politics of the past. The question that remains unanswered is: what happened to the children who needed these places during the years they were closed down? If that's not a glaring policy failure, I don't know what is.

When I returned to children's social care in the early years of the new millennium, partnership working had been a longstanding goal. The idea was for agencies to collaborate, all working towards the same outcome: a holistic response to the complex needs of children in care and care leavers. But in practice, achieving real collaboration proved far harder than anyone had anticipated.

By then, influencers from the world of business had already begun to reshape public services. They brought with them a new language – one of performance management, measurable outcomes, targets, and efficiency savings. Concepts like *'value for money'* and *'return on investment'* became central, and public services were increasingly expected to function like competitive businesses. In theory, this was about raising standards and driving improvement. But in reality, it often led to fragmented priorities, where care was measured in metrics, and relationships – the foundation of good care – became harder to value.

During this period, the number of independently run children's homes was on the rise, and I eventually joined a company that operated small homes in the private sector, where I strived to hold onto the primacy of mutually rewarding, authentic relationships. While education, healthcare, housing, the police, and the courts were all supposed to be working towards the same goal, each was now regulated, inspected, and rated separately – each with its own standards, pressures, and priorities.

This fragmentation made alignment incredibly difficult. At the same time, budget cuts and growing demand placed immense pressure on already stretched services, making meaningful partnership work harder still.

A growing divide between public and private services only intensified the problem. This isn't about saying public is good and private is bad – I don't believe it's that simple. But the systems had stopped talking to each other in the way they needed to.

Each agency became more focused on hitting its own targets and defending its budget and blaming each other when things went wrong. The result was a loss of coordination across the system – just when children needed it most. On paper, everyone had clear objectives: schools were judged on academic outcomes, the police on crime rates, health services on waiting times, and social care on protection plans. But when a child needed help from all of them at once, the cracks appeared. Data protection laws added another layer of complexity, making it even harder to share information and coordinate care.

In theory, the concept of the corporate parent was meant to cut through this fragmentation. It was intended to ensure that every agency involved in a child's life would take collective responsibility, acting with the same care, attention, and urgency that any good parent would offer their own child. It sounded right. It was the right idea. But in practice, it rarely lived up to that promise.

The reality was that no one person – or agency – held the whole picture. Each service saw a different slice of the child's life, and each was accountable to a different regulator, budget holder, or political agenda. The result? No one truly held onto the whole child. And without that shared sense of ownership, the role of the corporate parent became more symbolic than practical.

I sat in meetings where professionals spoke passionately about outcomes and improvement plans, but too often, the child's voice got lost in layers of process. The intentions were good, but when push came to shove, competing priorities and stretched resources meant decisions were too often driven by risk avoidance or cost-efficiency – not by what mattered most to the child.

What should have been a united front too often resembled a relay race – with different professionals passing the baton, each doing their part, but rarely running alongside one another. And the child? They were left trying to make sense of the system, rather than being held safely within it.

It's easy to write corporate parenting into policy. It's much harder to embed it in practice – because that takes time, trust, continuity, and a willingness to work across boundaries. It takes a shared mindset that says: *this child is not someone else's problem. They are ours.*

And for all the rhetoric around partnership and joined-up working, the structures we built didn't always support that mindset. Too often, they got in the way.

9

PREDATORS AT THE DOOR
Lessons in Courage and Advocacy

She was fifteen when she arrived – bruised, silent, already slipping through the cracks of a system that should have protected her. At first, she ran away at night, disappearing into the streets and returning in the early hours. But it soon became clear she wasn't just running. Someone was pulling her back.

Despite our best efforts to keep her safe, she would leave the house late at night. Staff followed, trying to intervene, but she always managed to slip away – only to return the next morning. The pattern repeated itself. This wasn't defiance. It was something more insidious. Someone was exerting control over her, and whatever hold they had, it was stronger than anything we could offer.

When she turned sixteen, she moved to a semi-independent living service that had been established by Mark and me before I took the job. I believed relocating her would break the cycle. I was wrong. Within days, a man arrived, claiming to be her cousin. It was an obvious lie, but one she was willing to go along with.

Soon, reports surfaced of them being seen together late at night. Despite warnings, she kept going missing. One night, I received a frantic call: she was being held against her will. Without an exact address, the police couldn't act. Mark and I searched for hours but couldn't find her. By morning, she had returned – bruised and withdraw – denying the call had ever happened.

On another occasion, I combed the streets with a police officer, checking late-night venues and pool halls where men gathered. No one helped. But the most harrowing moment came in A&E. Her arms – layered with scars and fresh wounds – told the story of years of pain. That night, I learned she had first been exploited at just twelve years old.

Days later, the man posing as her cousin came to the door. Fortunately, she wasn't home. I called the police immediately and opened the door, trying to stay calm. He stood there, confident, smirking – as if he owned the place. *'She home?'* he asked, casually – like we both knew the answer.

Every instinct told me to slam the door, but I had to keep him talking. My pulse thundered in my throat. The police were on their way. I just had to stall him. Then something changed. His smirk faded. He turned. Realisation hit him like a slap. *"You called the police,"* he spat. I met his glare. *"I told you – you're not welcome here."*

Fear came later – because now, he knew where I lived. Any courage I'd mustered in that moment vanished in the quiet that followed. The officer reassured me later that he wouldn't risk further exposure – his actions had already caused shame in his community. He never came back. But I knew he wasn't the only one.

And he wasn't. It felt like predators were everywhere, waiting to exploit the vulnerable, ready to strike at any moment. They picked up girls from the front door of children's homes, trapping them with gifts, alcohol, and drugs. Mobile phones became tools of control, keeping victims tethered. Moving them from one placement to another didn't help. Even secure placements couldn't guarantee safety. Some girls left with more numbers to call than when they arrived.

Too often, victims weren't seen as victims at all. They were labelled *'troublesome'* or *'promiscuous'* – as if a twelve-year-old girl could choose to be trafficked. Blame was passed around like a game of pass the parcel. Parents were shamed for not keeping them safe. Social workers were accused of doing nothing. Care staff were accused of not being able to do their job.

Locks on doors became a source of debate – were they about safety, or a restriction of liberty? Instead, staff stood guard on landings, followed children when they left, making futile attempts to persuade them to return. But in truth, that was never really the issue. This was a battle about whether we truly believed these children were worth protecting, even when they didn't – or couldn't – act like victims.

Meanwhile, the men who exploited them walked free – because the system was too slow, too blind, or too afraid to confront the real issue. The young people we were trying to protect weren't the problem. They had been groomed and broken by those who should have been stopped. The fight to protect them wasn't just about individual cases. It was about challenging a system that refused to see what was happening in plain sight.

The failures weren't limited to one area. Many of the men were mobile, dangerous, and sometimes armed, while those trying to intervene were left at risk – forced to navigate policing boundaries without backup. On one occasion, staff received chilling messages from the girls: *"Go back, there's a gun on the back seat."* When police were called, they said they couldn't assist – the vehicle would cross into another jurisdiction before they could respond.

These invisible lines of duty made effective intervention almost impossible. Bureaucratic red tape gave authorities an excuse to look the other way. Victims were left at the mercy of their abusers, not because help wasn't possible – but because no one accepted responsibility.

Child protection was in crisis, and the rise of organised grooming gangs was just one stark example of the danger children faced. These gangs operated openly, systematically preying on vulnerable children – many already known to social services – yet the system failed to act. Despite multiple agencies bearing responsibility, the cracks between them were widening. Social services, police, healthcare, and local authorities all had roles to play – yet too often, no one did.

In 2000, the horrific case of Victoria Climbié exposed catastrophic failures in child protection, prompting a major public inquiry and countless government pledges of reform. Yet, seven years later, what had really changed? Organised gangs were still thriving in the very gaps the system had promised to close.

Rather than strengthening frontline support, multi-agency collaboration, or early intervention, the government doubled down on centralised control and regulatory oversight. In April 2007, responsibility for inspecting children's social care was transferred to Ofsted – an inspectorate with expertise in schools, not in safeguarding vulnerable children. This was meant to introduce greater accountability. In practice, it created a system obsessed with compliance over care.

Just four months later, public confidence was shattered again. Peter Connelly – known as Baby P – died in August 2007, despite being on the radar of social services. His death laid bare a devastating truth: seven years after Victoria Climbié, the system was still failing children in the most tragic ways. Once again, the response was more rules, more inspections, more red tape – but not the urgent, practical support children desperately needed.

Despite being on the child protection register, despite being seen by medics and professional's multiple times, Peter endured prolonged abuse and died at just 17 months old. His death didn't just provoke public outrage – it shook those of us working in the sector. It cast serious doubt on the effectiveness of the very systems meant to protect children.

In the aftermath, Ofsted's role came under scrutiny, but the regulator largely escaped blame. Instead, attention turned to Haringey Council. Sharon Shoesmith's high-profile dismissal became a symbolic gesture – a politically expedient response to public anger. Her sacking may have satisfied the call for accountability, but it did nothing to fix the systemic failures that had allowed Peter to die.

By December 2008, Haringey's children's services rating was downgraded to 'Inadequate,' prompting urgent reforms. But the fallout had already begun. More children were taken into care, but the system wasn't ready. Foster placements were scarce, children's homes overstretched, and care-leaver accommodations couldn't meet demand. A system already on the brink was now buckling under the weight of its own failure.

In the wake of intense media scrutiny, public outcry, and mounting political pressure, my then-employer Pete and I became business partners. We established a new care-leaver service under a separate company – determined to build something better.

We converted a former public house into six self-contained flats with communal space, specifically designed for young people transitioning out of care. Five flats were occupied by young people, while one was designated for staff providing 24/7 support. The service also supported young people living independently in the community. We had also taken over the management of a group of children's homes in another region, hoping to expand our reach. Yet, even as we worked to create something better, the challenges within the system were never far behind.

With growing scrutiny from the media, regulatory bodies, and public concern over standards in private children's homes, the transition proved far harder than expected.

Some staff turnover isn't unusual after a takeover – you expect a bit of change. But in our case, posts were vacated early on. The training manager was made redundant because the post just wasn't affordable, and not long after, the care manager left the organisation. In the months that followed, concerns began to surface – things like poor management practices in the homes and school, issues around physical restraint, and serious safeguarding failures.

One young person told their social worker they had been assaulted during an incident involving restraint that hadn't been recorded. Safeguarding checks hadn't been completed on an adult who had befriended the young person, and another unvetted adult had reportedly stayed overnight at the home. When Pete became aware of these issues, he notified the regulator as required, suspending the registered manager without prejudice while a child protection investigation began.

The timing couldn't have been worse. I was on holiday when the concerns emerged – stuck abroad, delayed by the Ash Cloud. By the time I returned, it was clear something had gone seriously wrong. I contacted the Ofsted inspector responsible for the home, but my call went unanswered. Instead, the inspector contacted Pete, claiming I had refused to make a notification without speaking to him first.

This was untrue but attempts to rectify the misunderstanding were ignored. The next day, the inspector arrived at the home unannounced.

With the registered manager suspended, an assistant manager from another region took over the operations. The inspector, described by staff as formal and direct, rejected the suggestion to speak with me. Before leaving, the inspector briefly met with the young person who had made the allegation, and was gone by the time the other children returned from school.

On arrival, the youngest child told staff they'd been restrained at school. No one at the home had been informed – not even the staff member who had done the school run. The child was complaining of back pain and hadn't seen a doctor. I told staff to take them to the hospital immediately.

At the hospital, the doctor asked what had happened, then turned to staff. They explained that the incident had taken place at school, but no report had been shared with the home. The staff were unable to validate the child's account – and in that moment, it was clear the child wasn't believed. The doctor discharged them without a physical examination. That alone should have raised serious concerns, but it wasn't even mentioned at the safeguarding meeting that eventually followed.

The next day, the child was still in pain. When staff checked, they found significant bruising and abrasions. I immediately sent them back to the hospital to request a re-examination and proper documentation. It wasn't until this second visit that a safeguarding concern was officially raised, triggering a formal meeting.

Given everything, we had learned from past child protection failures – particularly the Baby P case – it was deeply concerning that these injuries had been overlooked. The initial examination had been cursory at best. I planned to address this, along with the school's failure to inform us and the involvement of untrained staff in the restraint. But I only discovered the meeting was taking place by chance.

While visiting the homes with Pete, we happened to be present when staff received a call requesting the interim manager's attendance the next day. We hadn't planned to stay overnight, but there was too much at stake to leave this in unfamiliar hands. I didn't even have an overnight bag with me – no change of clothes, no toothbrush – so it was a trip to the supermarket for essentials. There was no question we were staying.

The next morning, we arrived early, but it was a long wait before we were eventually ushered into the meeting room – well past the scheduled start time. The social worker chairing the meeting, the school manager, and the inspector were already seated. The atmosphere was tense.

What followed was even more unsettling. The meeting went ahead without the hospital report, the looked-after children's nurse, or the child's social worker. Their absence was irregular – and unexplained. Even more unusual was the lack of inquiry into what had actually happened: no one questioned why untrained staff, including the maintenance man, had been involved in the restraint; no one sought medical advice; and no one notified the home. It all seemed highly irregular to me.

During my time as a field social worker, it was often said that the real decisions were made before the meeting even started – and that's exactly what this felt like. This was especially evident in the outcome: the only agreed action was for all school staff to complete physical intervention training. Discussion about the incident itself was quickly steered towards concerns raised during the recent inspection.

The inspector said there were concerns about the safety of children in the home, based on a conversation he'd had with the child who had made the complaint. When we asked why this hadn't been shared with us at the time, there was no answer.

That silence was troubling enough. But it was made worse when we were asked what steps we'd taken to manage a risk we hadn't even known existed.

As we got up to leave, we were reminded that any consequences for failing to do so would be ours alone. The inspector remarked that we were *'on a journey,'* and that it remained to be seen whether Ofsted were on that journey with us.

It sounded more like a threat than an observation – one we didn't fully understand until years later.

Meanwhile, I was still waiting on a response to my complaint about the inspection, while working through a long list of requirements outlined in a letter from the inspector. No report, just tasks to complete by a set deadline.

Shortly after the meeting, further concerns about physical intervention were raised during refresher training. The instructor revealed that staff had been taught unauthorised techniques and that the procedures for reporting prone restraint were not being followed.

A review of the logbooks confirmed: unauthorised methods, excessive use of restraint – some lasting for hours – and missed opportunities for medical care.

When we raised them as safeguarding concerns, no meaningful action was taken. And it wasn't until five months later that I learned my complaint had not been upheld.

What troubled me most was that, despite the well-documented risks of restraint – and the deaths of 15-year-old Collin Day and 14-year-old Adam Rickwood – both of whom died in secure facilities there appeared to be no urgency from the wider system. Public inquiries had warned about prone restraint and stressed the importance of qualified oversight. Yet when I raised these concerns, no investigation was launched.

Complaints became our only way to communicate with Ofsted. In the past, an investigating inspector would speak directly with the complainant. That kind of conversation allowed for nuance. But by the time we were dealing with these issues, Ofsted had shifted to a formal, paper-based process that made real dialogue almost impossible.

What had once been a human exchange had been reduced

to a paper exercise. Despite exhausting every available option within the process – and then some – none of our concerns were upheld. Still convinced they merited further scrutiny; we escalated the matter to the Independent Adjudicator.

Meanwhile, delays in inspection and re-registration put the homes at risk of closure. Most local authorities had adopted policies preventing children from being placed in homes rated below 'Good.'

Under re-registration rules, all previous inspection reports were removed from public view. Even if homes had suitable vacancies, placing authorities could not progress and offer without a current report. This meant that beds sat empty – not because there weren't children in urgent need of care, but because the system's own rules made them invisible. Bureaucracy had tied its own hands.

And that wasn't the only flaw in the system. It was only after growing concerns about potential conflicts of interest that Ofsted eventually tightened the rules around inspectors working as consultants.

Looking back, what stands out most sharply is not a single failure, but the pattern that emerged – a pattern of silencing, deflection, institutional paralysis, and, at times, bullying. Others have named it too, and it's not hard to see why. Sometimes, it was individuals. But more often, it was the system – so preoccupied with self-preservation, so entangled in its own processes, that it lost sight of its purpose.

We stepped into this work with a clear intention: to do better. We wanted to build a service grounded in care, transparency, and accountability. But even with experience, integrity, and commitment on our side, we found ourselves in a system that actively resisted the very principles it claimed to uphold. What we encountered was not just bureaucratic inefficiency – it was a culture of defensiveness and delay. When things went wrong, the instinct wasn't to listen or learn, but to protect reputations and avoid liability.

When we tried to raise genuine concerns – about restraint, safeguarding, or inspection failures – we were met with silence or fob-off letters. The young people at the centre of those concerns – some injured, some re-traumatised – became almost incidental to the process.

Even more troubling was how information was fragmented across agencies. Key players – school staff, health professionals, social workers – were often missing from meetings. Medical reports were overlooked, injuries went unexamined. There was no shared urgency, no coordinated responsibility. Everyone had a piece of the jigsaw, but no one had the whole picture. And in the gaps between roles, between jurisdictions, between institutions, children disappeared.

When we pointed to clear evidence of harm – restraint logs, staff testimonies, bruises, and outcomes – it wasn't so much challenged as ignored. Some children were deeply affected. Some even ended up on secure mental health wards.

What haunts me most is that these failures weren't caused by apathy. They stemmed from a system that believed in its own myth of protection. It's a system that treats procedure as care, inspection as safeguarding, and punishment as accountability. Meanwhile, children continue to be harmed – not because no one knows, but because knowing doesn't always lead to action.

There is a particular kind of grief that comes from being complicit in a system you struggle to believe in. We did our best – and yet it wasn't enough. Not because we didn't care, but because care alone cannot overcome structural dysfunction.

I carry that weight. I carry the faces of the children whose trust we tried to earn, whose safety we fought for, and whose pain was too often disregarded or minimised.

10

WHEN THE SYSTEM LOOKS AWAY
Unchecked Power and Silent Dissent

The anniversary of my thirty-five years in childcare was no cause for celebration. Instead, I found myself staring at a report that answered none of the questions we had raised. The adjudicator's response was clear: our concerns about safeguarding and regulatory failures were 'outside their remit.' No investigation. No accountability. Another door slammed shut in our faces.

The adjudicator was limited to assessing whether Ofsted had followed its own procedures – which, of course, it had. The real issues – safety concerns and systemic failures – were outside the scope of their review. As far as I could see, this left the key matters surrounding safeguarding and inspection practices unresolved, and I was left with more questions than answers.

When I approached the Ombudsman, on the advice of the Children's Commissioner, I ran into yet another limitation: complaints couldn't be made on behalf of children. Children were expected to recognise that they'd been wronged and then pursue a complaint themselves – a standard most children simply couldn't meet. And when it came to vulnerable children, the idea that they would even know where to start was way beyond unrealistic.

I was stunned. From my perspective, the system closed ranks. No meaningful action was taken, leaving both the children and the company with no recourse.

By then, David Cameron was nearing the end of his first year as Prime Minister, leading the coalition government with the Liberal Democrats. One of his early actions in 2010 was to rename the Department for Children, Schools and Families as the Department for Education – signalling a shift away from *Every Child Matter's* initiative and its holistic approach to child welfare. The focus was now on academic achievement, rebranded as *Helping Children and Young People Achieve More.*

At the same time, the age of austerity and nudge politics had arrived. Local authorities began slashing essential services, from youth programmes to libraries. Child benefit was frozen for three years, housing benefits were restructured, and life support systems were eroded. Although this shift was presented as community empowerment, it effectively placed the burden of government cutbacks on individuals and charities, with society as a whole bearing the consequences.

The Nudge Unit still exists today. Originally designed to apply behavioural science to public policy, it has since become an independent social purpose company, advising governments worldwide on issues ranging from health and education to crime and social behaviour. But while policymakers were focused on influencing everyday behaviours, we were dealing with something far more urgent – children's lives caught in a system that failed to protect them.

By 2011, we had spent years trying to protect girls from exploitation – only to be met with indifference, inaction, and blame. According to the response police we came into contact with it was a lifestyle choice. Then, *The Times* broke the story.

Andrew Norfolk's investigation exposed what we had known all along: vulnerable girls had been trafficked, abused, and abandoned by a system that refused to listen.

We had seen it firsthand – girls disappearing at night, returning bruised and silent, police unwilling to intervene because the perpetrators would '*cross jurisdictional boundaries*.' And now, the world finally knew.

His reporting led directly to the Jay Report in 2014, authored by Professor Alexis Jay. The report found that around 1,400 children had been sexually exploited in Rotherham between 1997 and 2013, exposing shocking levels of neglect by social services, law enforcement, and local government. But this wasn't news. People had been raising concerns for more than twenty years.

We had cared for girls who had been sexually exploited and supported others at risk long before the headlines. By the time the story broke, I had already been a member of police-led working groups set up to tackle the issue. Yet, time and again, efforts to confront the perpetrators were derailed – buried under bureaucracy, stalled by inaction, and twisted by misplaced blame.

Our mostly female staff went to great lengths to protect these girls. They documented suspicious activity, recorded vehicle registrations, and even followed cars picking up young people from the front doors of children's homes. None of these efforts made the headlines. The media was far more interested in scandal than in exposing the quiet, difficult work being done to protect vulnerable children.

In response to public outrage, MPs branded the childcare system as '*not fit for purpose*.' New policies were introduced – restrictions on out-of-borough placements, increased tracking of missing children, and a requirement for Ofsted inspectors to report on missing children during inspections. Yet, these measures failed to address the complexity of organised child exploitation.

Caregivers were blamed by the police for failing to keep

children safe, while the media fixated on private children's homes. The fact that most victims were still living at home when the abuse began was largely overlooked. And despite clear evidence of systemic failings across various settings, the strongest criticism was directed at the private sector.

Listening to the news on the radio during my drive to work became a painful experience. The condemnation of caregivers wasn't just injustice – it was a gut punch to those of us who showed up every day and tried to do the right thing, often against the odds. Sometimes, I'd find myself yelling at the radio, *'You've had your say. Try listening to the other side of the story for a change. Or better still, try walking in our shoes.'* But the urge to retaliate faded fast – lost in another one of those *'why bother'* moments. And there have been plenty of those over the years. The truth often falls on deaf ears. Decades of mistrust had seen to that.

But that mistrust didn't come from nowhere. It was built on a string of tragedies that became front-page news and shorthand for systemic failure. The media ran with it, turning complex stories into simple blame. Headlines rarely waited for facts. Politicians responded with inquiries, policies, and promises to never let it happen again – but rarely by listening to those doing the work. Instead, more rules were added, more oversight layered on, and more suspicion cast on the people expected to care.

It cannot be denied that crimes were committed – but the backlash didn't just target the guilty. It created a culture of fear and suspicion that punished everyone, including those doing the job with love and integrity.

In the aftermath of Rotherham and Rochdale, the media needed villains – and private children's homes became a convenient scapegoat. The real story, of course, was far more complex: failures across police, councils, and safeguarding partnerships – some rooted in denial, some in fear, and some in plain exhaustion.

But nuance doesn't sell papers, and it doesn't win votes. So instead of asking how we'd built a system that left children invisible, attention turned to where profit was being made, not where vast amounts of public money had been wasted. Suddenly, the assumption was that if you were running a children's home as a business, you must be part of the problem. That was never the whole truth.

But it stuck – and became ammunition in the ongoing struggle between public and private sector ideologies. The media and political narratives had their own agenda, and it was easier to use the private sector as the punch bag than to acknowledge the deeper, systemic failures across the board.

Over time, fear crept into the work itself. The space for warmth, for humanity, grew smaller. What should have been natural became rehearsed. What emerged was the era of side hugs and handshakes. Bathrooms fitted with tinfoil mirrors, just in case a child might self-harm, and melamine plates, safer and less prone to breakage, replaced real crockery. These decisions weren't made to meet the real needs of the children but to comply with an increasingly rigid system that demanded control at the expense of genuine care.

Eventually, something had to give. The constant pressure, emotional toll, and sense that we were being set up to fail – locked in a battle we never chose – wore us down. When Pete decided to sell the business, it was the inevitable result of a system that made authentic care nearly impossible.

We had been left to carry the weight of past failures in a system that refused to place responsibility where it belonged, and the harsh reality was that there was nothing we could do about it. A legal fight with Ofsted was not something the business could afford.

Walking away entirely wasn't an immediate option for me. The government had raised the state pension age for women, which meant I now faced seven more years of work I hadn't planned for – a future reshaped by yet another sudden decision. After the sale, I stayed with the company for another two years, until it no longer felt like a place I wanted to be.

As a WASPI woman – someone who had spent her life looking after other people's children – I found myself denied the entitlement I had earned. Forced to work longer because of the government's decision to accelerate the equalisation of the pension age, I was part of a generation caught in a policy shift that gave no time to prepare. This denial of entitlements to women who had paid into the system for decades was yet another example of how governments – regardless of political affiliation – have repeatedly ignored the rights of the very people they're meant to serve.

But that was the reality. So, let's not pretend the reduction in public sector jobs, including those in children's homes, was anything other than a deliberate government strategy to reduce the burden on the public purse. Children's homes didn't drift into the private sector by accident – they were placed there, because that's where the government wanted them. It was a clear and calculated move: shift responsibility, reduce costs, and hand services over to private companies – removing them from public control and scrutiny.

Many individuals from the care sector – people like me, who had spent our working lives supporting vulnerable children – invested our own time, effort and money to open homes in the private sector. Not out of ambition or greed, but because we were encouraged to do so. It was part of the government's own plan. But when the market changed, and larger corporate or equity-backed providers began to dominate, no protections were offered to the individuals who had built these services from the ground up.

The result was predictable: people who had dedicated their lives to care were left exposed, unsupported, and pushed aside – another casualty of a system that claimed to value children, but too often prioritised vested interest instead. Speaking of government betrayal, I couldn't help but reflect on another instance of political neglect: when Keir Starmer had the opportunity to right the wrongs done to WASPI women, he chose not to act, refusing to implement the compensation that had been recommended. His decision was a stark reminder that governments, regardless of party, can disregard the law and its consequences without facing any real accountability. Governments can make life-changing decisions and leave the consequences to ordinary people – without hesitation, without consequence.

Claiming the country couldn't afford it overlooks the reality that many women were not only forced to work longer but were also cheated out of a considerable amount of money – money they were rightfully due through their pension contributions. Those without the benefit of generous early retirement schemes available to public sector workers, civil servants, and politicians had no option.

It wasn't a choice – it was, quite simply, an insult to injury. And while many women faced this unfair and forced delay in their retirement, I couldn't help but reflect on the stark contrast. Those in more protected public sector roles had security and benefits most of us could only dream of. It wasn't about envy – it was about fairness. About who gets to step away with dignity, and who has to run until empty.

Starmer's refusal to act exposed a troubling reality: governments can make decisions that devastate lives, and walk away without consequence.

The ombudsman's recommendation, which carried real weight, called for action. But it was ignored. And so, the wrongs remain unaddressed, and those responsible remain untouched.

It was a painful reminder of how the gap between those in power and the people they are supposed to represent had grown ever wider. I realised just how disconnected those in power had become from the lives of ordinary citizens – and how easily rights and recommendations could be disregarded.

That same disconnect was painfully clear in my work. I had worked tirelessly to help Pete realise his vision for the children's homes, and in recognition of my commitment, he rewarded me with a share option scheme. This meant that if I remained with the company when it was sold, I would receive the value of my shares – my retirement plan. However, with the sale of the business, the value of that plan was now drastically reduced, leaving my future uncertain in a way neither of us had anticipated.

While we chose to sell the children's homes, we decided to retain the supported accommodation for care leavers. This service was not subject to the same regulatory framework and operated in a different region, where we had developed relationships with local authorities based on trust and mutual respect. Social care had always been regulated – ever since I joined the children's workforce, that oversight had been a given, and rightly so. But regulation should enable good practice, not create barriers to it or destroy people in the process.

That said, the absence of regulation in supported accommodation should not be confused with the absence of responsibility. Laws were in place that set standards for rented accommodation, the 2009 ruling on homeless teenagers had established legal precedence, and the Leaving Care Act had made clear what care leavers were entitled to. The problem was that these laws were ignored, and those responsible for enforcing them failed in their duties.

If these basic standards had been enforced, it's hard to see how anyone could have thought it acceptable to place children under 16, or even care leavers for that matter, in the appalling conditions exposed in The Times investigation in 2020. If the system had truly looked beyond the paperwork, it might have seen that there were people running supported accommodation who shouldn't have been anywhere near vulnerable young people.

They passed their DBS checks because they had no convictions, but that didn't mean they were safe. That's where the DBS system falls short. It tells you if someone has a criminal record, but it doesn't tell you how they behave behind closed doors – how they treat children, or how they use their power. It doesn't tell you who will commit the next crime. And this was all happening against the backdrop of broader changes in the sector.

During this period, the Charterhouse Group of therapeutic children's homes merged with Adult Therapeutic Communities to form the Consortium of Therapeutic Communities (TCTC), and I joined the board as both a trustee and director. At the same time, Sir Michael Wilshaw replaced Christine Gilbert as Her Majesty's Chief Inspector, marking a new era in the oversight of children's social care.

Wilshaw's ties to Ark, a government-backed charity closely aligned with the political and educational reforms of the time, raised questions about the influence of private interests on public policy and oversight. In Westminster, it's often said that it isn't what you know, but who you know that shapes policy. Apparently, knowing the right people is a handy shortcut to the top.

Meanwhile, on the ground, the consequences of these policy decisions were playing out in real time. Too many care leavers were being placed in unsafe, unsuitable accommodation, left to navigate adulthood with little support. The sector was full of contradictions – a growing emphasis on corporate efficiency and regulatory compliance on one hand, and a stark lack of meaningful oversight in the areas that truly mattered on the other.

On 19 January 2012, Children's Minister Tim Loughton visited Brighter Futures. The visit was arranged by Janet Rich, founder of The Care Leavers Foundation, who was also instrumental in the organisation of 'Care Leavers Week' and 'The Care Leavers Charter' launched by new children's minister Edward Simpson during care leavers week 24th-30th October 2012. Janet wanted the minister to see firsthand a service providing supportive alternatives for care leavers, particularly those being placed in unsuitable accommodation at just sixteen or seventeen years old. Inspired by Brighter Futures' success, Pete and I had replicated the model, eventually establishing two more services in the Midlands.

During his visit, Tim engaged with the young people we were supporting. They spoke openly with him about their experiences in the care system. Some shared their struggles, others their triumphs, but all of them painted a vivid picture of what life in care was like and how different it could be with the right kind of support. The Minister seemed genuinely moved by what he heard, particularly by the stories of young people who had found a sense of hope and purpose through the service we provided.

Two weeks later, on 3 February 2012, I attended the first Ofsted seminar in London. When I returned, a letter from Tim Loughton was waiting for me, thanking us for our hospitality. He praised the young people for their openness in sharing their experiences of the care system and their aspirations for the future. He had added a handwritten note that read: 'Please tell Patrick I have passed on his letter to David Cameron. It may take a while to get a reply.' Patrick is now in his thirties – and still waiting.

Motivated by Tim's words and the insights I had gained from the seminar, I decided to write once more to Sir Michael Wilshaw, urging him to reconsider my request for an investigation into the safeguarding failures I had uncovered. When his response arrived, once again declining my request, I was reminded of the numerous child abuse scandals that had emerged in the 1980s and 90s, as well as the high-profile cases like the BBC's Jimmy Savile scandals in the 2010s.

All of these cases shared a common thread: power. The power to silence victims, suppress evidence, and shield those responsible from accountability. The pattern was all too familiar – one I now saw repeating itself in our own struggles to make real change. The same fear, the same system of denial, the same refusal to confront uncomfortable truths.

The creation of an independent regulator was meant to prevent such failures, yet Ofsted seemed more concerned with shielding itself from scrutiny than addressing serious concerns that had been raised.

Later that year, the ITV documentary '*The Other Side of Jimmy Savile*' aired, featuring testimonies from several women who revealed they had been abused by Savile as teenagers. Following the programme, hundreds more victims came forward. The scandal triggered widespread investigations into how institutions – including the BBC, the police, the Crown Prosecution Service, the NHS, and Children's Homes – had failed to protect those in their care.

What stood out to me was how these organisations distanced themselves from responsibility. Institutions that should have safeguarded the vulnerable appeared more concerned with protecting their own reputation.

CARE LEAVERS' CHARTER

A Charter is a set of principles and promises. This Charter sets out promises care leavers want the central and local government to make. Promises and principles help in decision making and do not replace laws; they give guidance to show how laws are designed to be interpreted.

The key principles in this Charter will remain constant through any changes in Legislation, Regulation and Guidance. Care leavers urge local authorities to use these principles when they make decisions about young people's lives. The Charter for Care Leavers is designed to raise expectation, aspiration and understanding of what care leavers need and what the government and local authorities should do to be good Corporate Parents.

We Promise:

To respect and honour your identity

We will support you to discover and to be who you are and honour your unique identity. We will help you develop your own personal beliefs and values and accept your culture and heritage. We will celebrate your identity as an individual, as a member of identity groups and as a valued member of your community. We will value and support important relationships, and help you manage changing relationships or come to terms with loss, trauma, or other significant life events. We will support you to express your identity positively to others.

To believe in you

We will value your strengths, gifts, and talents and encourage your aspirations. We will hold a belief in your potential and a vision for your future even if you have lost sight of these yourself. We will help you push aside limiting barriers and encourage and support you to pursue your goals in whatever ways we can. We will believe in you, celebrate you, and affirm you.

To listen to you

We will take time to listen to you, respect, and strive to understand your point of view. We will place your needs, thoughts, and feelings at the heart of all decisions about you, negotiate with you, and show how we have taken these into account. If we don't agree with you, we will fully explain why. We will provide easy access to complaint and appeals processes and promote and encourage access to independent advocacy whenever you need it.

To inform you

We will give you information that you need at every point in your journey, from care to adulthood, presented in a way that you want including information on legal entitlements and the service you can expect to receive from us at different stages in the journey. We will keep information up to date and accurate. We will ensure you know where to get current information once you are no longer in regular touch with leaving care services. We will make clear to you the information about yourself and your time in care you are entitled to see. We will support you to access this when you want it, to manage any feelings that you might have about the information, and to put on record any disagreement with factual content.

To support you

We will provide any support set out in current Regulations and Guidance and will not unreasonably withhold advice when you are no longer legally entitled to this service. As well as information, advice, practical, and financial help we will provide emotional support. We will make sure you do not have to fight for support you are entitled to, and we will fight for you if other agencies let you down. We will not punish you if you change your mind about what you want to do. We will continue to care about you even when we are no longer caring for you. We will make it our responsibility to understand your needs. If we can't meet those needs, we will try and help you find a service that can. We will help you learn from your mistakes; we will not judge you and we will be here for you no matter how many times you come back for support.

To find you a home

We will work alongside you to prepare you for your move into independent living only when you are ready. We will help you think about the choices available and to find accommodation that is right for you. We will do everything we can to ensure you are happy and feel safe when you move to independent living. We recognise that at different times you may need to take a step back and start over again. We will do our best to support you until you are settled in your independent life; we will not judge you for your mistakes or refuse to advise you because you did not listen to us before. We will work proactively with other agencies to help you sustain your home.

To be a lifelong champion

We will do our best to help you break down barriers encountered when dealing with other agencies. We will work together with the services you need, including housing, benefits, colleges and universities, employment providers, and health services to help you establish yourself as an independent individual. We will treat you with courtesy and humanity whatever your age when you return to us for advice or support. We will help you to be the driver of your life and not the passenger. We will point you in a positive direction and journey alongside you at your pace. We will trust and respect you. We will not forget about you. We will remain your supporters in whatever way we can, even when our formal relationship with you has ended.

11

REGULATED TO FAIL
Systemic Blind Spots in Child Protection

Ayear or so later, a court case came to light involving three care leavers known to me through my work. Each alleged they had been in an intimate relationship with the defendant while underage and still in care. As the trial unfolded, I followed the proceedings from the public gallery. What I witnessed left me deeply troubled.

The defence relied heavily on the accused's *'impeccable'* employment record – a familiar strategy used to cast doubt on allegations. Meanwhile, the prosecution left key aspects unchallenged, making me wonder whether the police investigation had overlooked crucial evidence – personnel files, school registers – documents that could have clarified whether the two girls had attended the same school at the same time and whether the defendant's work history was as flawless as claimed.

Though never stated outright, the possibility of collusion loomed in the absence of that evidence. And possibilities, I knew, had a way of planting seeds of doubt – especially when those in question had been in care. Concerned by this, I informed the barristers that official records could provide clarity and offered to testify, but the idea was politely dismissed. I was told that new evidence *could not be introduced once a trial was in progress.'* I didn't believe that was entirely true, but I wasn't in a position of influence. I was merely a spectator.

Exceptions were made when it mattered – when the evidence served to strengthen a case, not complicate it. But these were care leavers, and the willingness to scrutinise their words did not extend to scrutinising the facts. The narrative had been set, and seemingly inconvenient truths had no place in it.

There are procedural rules for introducing new evidence, and courts can allow it under certain circumstances. While the process is complex, stating outright that it was not possible was, at best, an oversimplification.

And so, the trial unfolded as expected – shaped not just by the evidence presented, but also by what was missing. The accused's professional record remained untarnished in the eyes of the jury, untested against documents that were never examined. The gaps in the investigation, the unanswered questions, the evidence left out – all shaped their understanding of the case and, ultimately, their verdict.

When the jury acquitted the defendant of the charges related to two of the victims, what stood out more was their hesitation over those charges involving the third witness. The case against him had not been dismissed outright. There was doubt, but in the absence of missing evidence, those charges remained undecided – even though key records that might have provided clarity were never examined in the courtroom.

And so, the case remained unresolved. Disturbed by the handling of the case, I wrote to the Chief Constable and the Police Commissioner to raise concerns about procedural failures. Receipt was confirmed, but there was no response – just silence.

Later, word reached me that a retrial had been scheduled. But when the witness failed to attend the hearing, the prosecution presented no evidence, and the case was dismissed. The defendant walked away a free man, while I was left questioning not just the legal process, but the broader system itself.

The trial received coverage in the local newspapers, reflecting the significance of the case, and articles about it remain available online. Yet, beyond the headlines, what stayed with me was not just the verdict, but the way the system itself had failed those it was meant to protect.

Cases didn't collapse because the truth was unknowable, but because the system was never designed to hold itself to account. For witnesses, the choice was hardly a choice at all – why put yourself at the mercy of a system that had already failed you?

During my time working alongside Lancashire Police, Greater Manchester Police, and other forces across England, I had become increasingly aware of systemic failures that mirrored those exposed by Maggie Oliver, the former detective who revealed Greater Manchester Police's mishandling of child sexual exploitation cases in Rochdale.

Like Maggie, I saw vulnerable young people being failed by the very authorities meant to protect them – evidence overlooked, concerns dismissed, and responsibility too often shifted onto the victims rather than the perpetrators. These failures weren't new, and they weren't rare. The same themes kept resurfacing: cases not taken seriously, investigations shut down, and decisions made that prioritised institutional reputation over child protection.

Recent press coverage has scrutinised the handling of child sexual exploitation cases during Keir Starmer's tenure as Director of Public Prosecutions, raising questions about the broader systemic challenges in prosecuting such crimes.

It was the year I left this role that Nazir Afzal, Chief Crown Prosecutor for Greater Manchester, Cumbria, and Lancashire, stepped down. He had been one of the few people willing to challenge the culture of inaction. His most significant decision had been to overturn the earlier refusal to prosecute the Rochdale grooming case. At the time, both Greater Manchester Police and the Crown Prosecution Service (CPS) had refused to proceed, dismissing the victims as unreliable witnesses. When Afzal reviewed the case, he recognised systemic failure and pushed forward. Without his intervention, the 2012 trial – one that exposed years of institutional neglect – would never have happened.

Afzal later acknowledged that fears of being accused of racism had played a role in the delays, but he remained adamant that justice had to be pursued without fear or bias. His leadership forced uncomfortable conversations about why child sexual exploitation cases had been mishandled for so long. But even leaders like Afzal eventually walked away, frustrated by the system's resistance to change.

By then, I had already come to the same conclusion. These weren't isolated failures; they were part of a culture of denial – one that allowed abuse to continue in plain sight. Just as in Rochdale, Rotherham, and countless other towns across the country, those who spoke out were ignored, dismissed, or forced out.

Around the same time, the Jimmy Savile abuse scandal had come to light, revealing how he had evaded prosecution despite allegations spanning decades. The institutions that should have stopped him – the BBC, the NHS, the police – had done nothing. They had looked the other way, allowing him to use his celebrity status to gain access to hospitals, schools, and children's homes under the guise of charity work.

The most disturbing part wasn't just the abuse itself. It was how many people had known, how many chances there had been to stop him, and how many institutions had made the same calculation – that it was easier to ignore the problem than confront it.

In 1986, while allegations against him were already circulating, Savile wrote the forward to '*Benjamin Rabbit and the Stranger Danger*', a children's book warning kids about the risks of talking to strangers. The irony was staggering. Here was a man who represented exactly the danger children were being warned about, yet he was still seen as a trusted public figure. It wasn't just a personal failure – it was a systemic one. The fact that someone like Savile could be held up as a role model while abusing his position spoke volumes about how safeguarding protocols were more about appearances than actual protection.

The scale of institutional failure became even clearer in 2014, when then-Home Secretary Theresa May announced the Independent Inquiry into Child Sexual Abuse (IICSA). That same year, Professor Alexis Jay published her report on child sexual exploitation in Rotherham, exposing the abuse of at least 1,400 children between 1997 and 2013. Jay's findings were damning, but not surprising. The pattern was the same: victims ignored, abusers protected, institutions paralysed by fear and burcaucracy.

Theresa May suggested that concerns about political correctness had played a role in the failures. But others, including Professors Dave Richards and Martin Smith, pointed to something even deeper – bureaucratic barriers, rigid hierarchies, and an unwillingness to confront uncomfortable truths.

These weren't just mistakes; they were decisions. Every missed opportunity to act, every ignored report, every dismissed complaint was a choice made by people who found it easier to do nothing.

Bureaucracy provided the perfect cover. Concerns were shuffled from one department to another, slipping into the systemic black hole, where they vanished without a trace. Decision-making became tangled in protocols and paperwork, delaying action until it was too late. Senior officials, far removed from the reality on the ground, prioritised protecting their organisations over protecting children. Those who did speak up were ignored or punished.

The culture of silence was reinforced at every level. Questioning decisions, even hinting at wrongdoing, was seen as disloyalty. Whistleblowers weren't just dismissed; they were actively silenced. This wasn't about a few bad decisions – it was about an entire system designed to protect itself.

The day after the IICSA inquiry was announced, Baroness Louise Casey was appointed to conduct an independent investigation into Rotherham Council. Her 2015 report pulled no punches: the council was *'not fit for purpose.'* It had ignored warnings, dismissed evidence, and intimidated staff who tried to speak out. A culture of cover-ups and denial had allowed abuse to continue unchecked.

As a result, the entire political leadership of Rotherham Council was removed. South Yorkshire Police Commissioner Shaun Wright, who had overseen children's services during part of the abuse period, resigned in September 2014 in the wake of the Rotherham child sexual exploitation scandal. His resignation came under mounting pressure from the Prime Minister, the Home Secretary, and members of his own party, all calling for him to step down. Although Wright initially resisted, he ultimately cited the public interest in his decision to resign and the need to focus on the victims.

Reading those findings, I recognised much of what Casey described. I had seen it firsthand – the way institutions protected themselves instead of the people they were meant to serve. I had witnessed whistleblowers being shut down, victims being dismissed, and the same patterns repeating over and over.

I was one of those silenced whistleblowers. So was Mark. We had spoken up, believing that telling the truth mattered. Instead, we were shut down, dismissed, and left carrying the weight of the stories no one wanted to hear. But it wasn't just us. Across the country, survivors were finding their voices, only to be met with the same wall of silence. The very systems designed to protect them were the ones letting them down.

While the IICSA examined institutional failings, many survivors felt sidelined – trapped in a bureaucratic process that prioritised legal caution over lived experience. Frustrated by this, some turned to the People's Tribunal, an independent initiative designed to give them a voice on their own terms. Unlike official inquiries, the Tribunal wasn't bound by bureaucratic limitations – it was about truth, not damage control.

The Tribunal wasn't just about collecting stories; it was about amplifying survivors' voices. Testimony wasn't filed away or ignored. It was heard, validated, and made a part of the public record. Its findings were presented directly to Parliament and other government bodies, demanding that survivors' experiences be recognised and that real action be taken.

Alan Collins, legal counsel to the Steering Committee, ensured survivor testimonies were handled with legal precision and integrity. A leading solicitor in child abuse litigation, he had represented victims in high-profile cases like the Jimmy Savile scandal, as well as the Haut de la Garenne case – where allegations of historical child abuse surfaced at a former children's home in Jersey. Collins' experience in these major cases made him a trusted advocate for those seeking justice. His investigative work uncovered paedophile rings, secured justice and compensation for survivors, and brought an international perspective to cases of institutional abuse.

Regina Paulose, chair of the Steering Committee and a respected human rights lawyer, provided the strategic oversight that kept the Tribunal independent, and survivor focused. With her extensive background in human rights and international law, she ensured the Tribunal's work aligned with global legal standards, drawing on her expertise in advocating for justice on behalf of vulnerable communities.

Listening to a member of the Tribunal's steering group speak on the radio was a turning point for me. She didn't just talk about what had happened – she spoke about the long shadow it cast, the way trauma rippled through generations. It was another stark reminder of why this work mattered. These weren't just stories of past abuse; they were stories of ongoing pain, of lives shaped by silence, and of institutions that had yet to reckon with their failures. I knew this place. I'd been there.

The failures of Rotherham, Rochdale, and so many other institutions should have been a reckoning. Yet the culture of silence persists. The lesson is always the same: institutions do not change unless they are forced to. Power protects itself. And unless those who witness wrongdoing speak out – no matter the cost – the cycle will continue, and more lives will be destroyed in its wake.

I'd been in my new role for just a month when I read the Casey Report – I wish I could say I was shocked, but I wasn't. It was just another exposé, another round of excuses, and another stark reminder that children had been failed while those in power looked the other way. The same old patterns of neglect and indifference were there, and it seemed like nothing had really changed. The system was still broken, and the people who were supposed to fix it were still avoiding accountability.

The report described a *toxic workplace culture, poor communication, and serious safeguarding failures'* – it was all too familiar. I had seen it before. And I had no doubt I would see it again.

The same patterns of denial, dysfunction, and deflection had played out in settings where I had worked for decades. Reports ignored, whistleblowers sidelined, and those in power more concerned with protecting reputations than protecting children. As I read through the report, frustration outweighed shock. The warning signs had been there all along. Those who should have acted chose not to. And once again, vulnerable children had been failed – and the system was still broken.

Only Two Residential Homes

I'm lucky, so I'm told.
Only two residential homes.
That makes me better off than others with more moves — how
could I moan?

I'm lucky, so I'm told.
Floors of only two residential homes to scrub.
My knees can't be that sore, or my hands split and bleeding.
After all, it's only two residential homes.

I'm lucky, so I'm told.
My bed not made how I was taught — or beaten to learn to make it.
So, no breakfast for me or the others.
Today we go to school hungry and worn down.
But still, it's only two residential homes.

I'm lucky, so I'm told.
Being cheeky to staff meant standing in the hallway all night long.
Freezing cold, legs so tired you fall down.
Then made to stand in the matron's room the rest of the night,
Because you woke them falling.
Still, I'm lucky — it's only two residential homes.

I'm lucky, so I'm told.
Boot room duties today:
All shoes lined in a row, polished until you see your face —
Or they see theirs.
Otherwise, they're thrown outside.
Just like you.
Still, it's only two residential homes.

I'm lucky, so I'm told.
Laundry duty today.
Beds stripped bare.
Steam so hot, water in the sink burns the skin off your hands
As you wash and soak the sheets all day long.
Still, it's only two residential homes.

I'm lucky, so I'm told.
Held down and beaten black and blue.
Raped by older boys — taking turns.
Against your will, your wishes.
No one hears your screams —
A hand over your mouth.
The other girls can't save you.
They're hiding under the sheets,
Whispering thank God it's not me tonight.
Still, it's only two residential homes. How could I moan?

I'm lucky, so I'm told.
I got fed, clothed, kept warm — so don't kick up a fuss.
Your family wouldn't do that
They don't care — that's why you're here.
Still, it's only two residential homes.

I'm lucky, so I'm told.
I was heard talking in bed.
So I was dragged by my hair,
Down two flights of stairs —
Thrown down the third, into the cellar.
For talking in bed.
Cold. Damp. Wet.
Alone. Scared. Frightened.
Still, it's only two residential homes.

I'm lucky I was only in two residential homes.
But the abuse, neglect, beatings, and sexual assaults
Still left their mark —
On my body,
My mind,
My soul,
And my memory.
A lifelong impact.

Still, I'm lucky, so I'm told.
It was only two residential homes.

Jackie McCartney

12

BEYOND INSPECTION
Leadership, Policy, and the Realities of Care

When I arrived, inspection ratings were slipping, and there had been little preparation for the new regulations. The sector was already under immense strain, and the rapid rollout of new standards only added to the pressure on providers.

The Children's Homes (England) Regulations 2015 were published on 4 March and came into effect just 28 days later, on 1 April. This rushed timeline left providers with little time to adapt, intensifying the strain on an already overburdened system. Despite these challenges, I was determined to face them head-on. I knew the road ahead wouldn't be easy, but I was motivated to take on the task.

The pressure to meet inspection standards, combined with workforce instability and the complex emotional needs of the children, created a perfect storm. Staff were like passengers on a bus, unaware of the direction they were heading, oblivious to the scale of change required, and unprepared for the challenges ahead. The lack of guidance and support left many feeling lost. As the new regulations took effect, the sector grappled with high staff turnover, behavioural challenges among children, and a shifting regulatory landscape. These factors made it even harder to provide the stability and quality of care that was so crucial for the children we served.

Care was happening, but it wasn't the driving force behind decision-making. It ran in the background – managed, not truly led. Registered managers, despite their legal accountability, were not empowered as the professionals they were supposed to be. Their role was critical to reversing the decline, yet the lack of influence within the company structure prevented them from taking the lead. Fixing this required more than compliance – it demanded a fundamental shift in how care was valued and delivered.

The regional structure operated in silos, with responses varying from region to region. Without a unified approach, care delivery lacked consistency. While individual managers worked hard, it became clear that many staff, like passengers with no clear destination, were unaware of the full scope of the challenges and would struggle to meet the new standards. Best practices weren't shared, and responses to regulatory challenges were fragmented and uncoordinated.

To address this, I established a senior management team with registered managers from each region, as well as heads of therapy and education. This collaborative leadership structure helped ensure that homes no longer operated in isolation. It allowed managers to share best practices, standardise approaches, and work closely with education and therapy to develop a more integrated model.

Registered managers were not just babysitters. Legislation required them to be leaders, accountable for delivering high standards of care. Good inspection ratings depended on their ability to lead teams, uphold compliance, and embed quality into service delivery. They carried significant legal responsibility to ensure care wasn't just a box to tick, but a priority.

With inspections fast approaching, the real challenge wasn't just ensuring we met compliance standards; it was about preparing the homes for the transition to a more demanding regulatory framework. This required more than just technical adjustments – it called for a complete rethinking of how care was delivered.

What I saw was a system where therapy was prioritised at the top, education was next, and care was relegated to the bottom. Care needed to be recognised as just as important as therapy and education. From my perspective, that's what needed to change. Care had to be elevated. It was central to the mission. Experience had shown me how critical it was – and how easily those responsible for delivering it could become disconnected from the realities of frontline work.

Care staff carried both emotional and physical demands in creating a 'secure base' a safe, stable environment for young people to heal and grow. Their work extended beyond daily routines – fostering trust, building resilience, and forming connections that would shape a child's future.

For real change, registered managers and care practitioners needed to be recognised as integral parts of the team. Raising their status wasn't just about professional recognition – it was about ensuring better outcomes for the young people who relied on them.

That required a shift in how care was valued and integrated into operations – stronger leadership, clearer career pathways, and meaningful professional development for care teams. It meant fostering a culture where care was seen as equal to therapy and education, where frontline staff had a voice in decision-making and the resources needed to excel.

I was pleased when the board accepted my assessment and approved my request for investment in therapeutic practice, including funding for places on the Therapeutic Childcare degree at Wrexham Glyndŵr University and the introduction of clinical consultation to provide staff with guidance and space for reflection. The goal was to equip managers with specialist training and structured support, enabling them to lead by example, share knowledge with their teams, and integrate therapeutic practices into their daily work to ensure the highest standards of care for the young people.

It was a good job I hadn't dragged my feet, because less than three months after taking up the position, I was required to attend a meeting with one of the regional inspection teams to discuss actions being taken to address the declining ratings of homes in the area. Walking into that meeting room was daunting; I felt like I'd been summoned to the headmaster's office. The large screen displaying past inspection results struck me immediately.

The atmosphere was tense, and it was a stark reminder of the challenges ahead, particularly the regulatory expectations we were facing. Fortunately, with the benefit of my board-approved action plan, I was prepared for the meeting, though less so for what lay ahead.

In my experience, the inconsistencies in inspection interpretations and the ever-shifting standards made it difficult to achieve fair, consistent outcomes. The regulations were applied unevenly across regions, and it was evident on that screen. Some inspectors approached their role with balance and understanding, while others were rigid and fault-focused, often creating tension rather than fostering constructive oversight.

A new manager, just a week into the role, faced an unannounced inspection regardless of the home being closed for refurbishment. Despite informing the inspector, the visit went ahead – apparently, the email hadn't been received. The home was a building site – walls knocked down, carpets ripped up, the kitchen and bathroom stripped bare. With the young person away on holiday, we had seized the opportunity to carry out necessary renovations without disrupting their routine.

Yet, even with these extenuating circumstances, the pressure to meet standards never let up. Real life, even in a children's home, isn't without its disruptions and messes. Renovations, like many things in life, come with their own chaos, but too often, the drive for perfection in inspections ignores the reality that a children's home is not a show home. A home isn't meant to be pristine; it's meant to be lived in, shaped by those who call it home. Yet, the focus on ticking boxes risked turning it into something artificial, a façade, rather than the living, breathing space where children are nurtured and learn about life.

Reflecting on my, before Ofsted, years as a foster parent, Mark and I never saw home improvements or repairs as tasks never to be done with the kids. On the contrary, we often involved them. Whether decorating a room or fixing the car, we saw these moments as opportunities to teach life skills and build connections.

I remember one time when Hannah was helping to strip wallpaper in the lounge. In her mind, she had done a brilliant job – removing both the wallpaper and the plaster! It was one of those moments that makes you laugh and sigh at the same time, but it also reminds me of the importance of being involved in the space you live in and feeling like it's your own. Even in the mess and mishaps, we were building something more than just a home – we were building relationships, trust, and memories. Hannah and I still laugh about this to this day.

It's in those moments – the small, and sometimes bigger, mishaps – that a home truly becomes theirs. It wasn't about making everything perfect, but about being actively involved in the space they lived in. Care that makes a difference isn't just about ticking boxes – it's about letting them make their mark and helping them feel truly part of things.

But when it came to the inspection, none of this context seemed to matter. The house was under renovation, no children were present, and essential areas were out of action. Even the office was packed in boxes, making it near impossible to locate documents or respond to inquiries in real time. In no way could the inspection reflect the home's usual operations – yet, despite this, the inspection went ahead.

The result was a harsh evaluation: over twenty requirements and an *'inadequate'* rating for the public record. The inspector's decision to proceed with the inspection, despite the home being in disarray and unprepared, was not only unfair but also unjustified. It didn't reflect the home's usual standards or the dedication of the staff.

What made this even more frustrating was that it wasn't an isolated incident. Other inspections went ahead under similar conditions – homes with ongoing repairs, staff juggling multiple roles, or key services temporarily unavailable. Despite these challenges, the inspections proceeded, leading to ratings that didn't represent the true quality of care. These decisions damaged reputations impacted the morale of staff who were already working under difficult conditions, and put children's placements at risk.

The only positive from this inspection was the assurance of a re-inspection. While disappointing, it gave us an opportunity to show that, once the renovations were complete and the staff returned, we could meet the required standards. Under the new regulations, homes could now demonstrate progress and correct inaccurate assessments, which helped remove barriers to improvement – especially for the children.

Eight weeks later, the inspector returned unannounced to conduct both the re-inspection and the fit person interview. The manager, having successfully managed homes with strong ratings before, expected a fairly straightforward process.

However, it quickly became clear that this time would be different. During the interview, the manager was unexpectedly confronted with a question about sensitive personal details from their childhood – information that had been recorded but never shared with them. The question specifically referenced the manager's history, information which had never been relevant or disclosed to them before. This felt intrusive and unsettling, especially given its emotional weight.

The abruptness of the revelation, combined with the pressure of the situation, was deeply distressing. Yet, the inspector pressed on, either not noticing or choosing to ignore the distress it caused. It felt like an invasion of privacy – one that had no bearing on the manager's qualifications or ability to fulfil their professional responsibilities. What should have been a straightforward assessment of their suitability turned into an emotional ordeal, casting doubt not only on the integrity of the inspection process but also on the appropriateness of the questioning itself.

Despite this the progress made could not be denied and the home earned a well-deserved 'Good' rating. However, the final report failed to adequately reflect the true extent of the team's commitment and hard work in addressing over twenty requirements in just eight weeks, turning the home around under such challenging circumstances.

But what made this even more difficult to accept was the emotional toll of the fit person interview. The manager, unexpectedly confronted with deeply personal details about their birth – information that had no relevance to the professional context – was left feeling exposed and vulnerable. What should have been a straightforward assessment of the manager's qualifications and integrity became an emotional ordeal. The inspector's approach not only intensified the distress, but it also raised serious concerns about the integrity of the fit person process itself.

We attempted to improve relations, hoping that constructive

dialogue would lead to a more supportive process. But these efforts never gained traction in the region. Initially, I attributed this to an overzealous inspector, new to the role. But over time, I began to wonder if the inspection process itself attracted individuals more interested in exerting control than in ensuring fair, balanced oversight. At times, it felt like we were fighting a battle that had no end.

As the first inspection cycle under the new regulations unfolded, it quickly became clear that the challenges went far beyond this initial experience. The sector was under immense strain, grappling with workforce turnover, increasingly complex needs among children and young people, and heightened regulatory expectations.

Yet, despite these systemic pressures, responsibility for shortcomings was often placed squarely on the shoulders of providers, rather than addressing the broader structural issues within the system. Managers were expected to deliver stability, consistency, and high-quality care – against all odds – and faced consequences for even the smallest deviations from expectations, as interpreted by inspectors, even when those issues were beyond the home's control.

Homes were frequently criticised for children not attending school, even when those children weren't enrolled in any educational institution – circumstances completely beyond the home's control. In other cases, trivial issues, such as not having enough pictures on the walls (even when the children didn't want them), became requirements, overshadowing more important aspects of care. This misattribution of responsibility placed undue pressure on homes and diverted attention from the systemic reforms needed to improve outcomes for children.

While regulatory compliance dominated discussions, a deeper crisis was quietly unfolding. This became undeniably clear when the *2013 Children's Homes Workforce Census* was published in January 2015. It highlighted what we already knew – high staff turnover and serious recruitment challenges. Experienced staff were leaving for other roles or moving between homes, making it harder to build the long-term relationships children in care so desperately need.

High turnover, coupled with growing emotional and behavioural challenges, added immense pressure. Most of the children were dealing with trauma, neglect, and disrupted family relationships – all while staff were trying to keep up with the relentless demands of inspections.

The over-emphasis on compliance, not just in childcare, created an industry of 'tick-box' online training – courses that could be skimmed through quickly, offering the illusion of competency without actually equipping staff with the practical, hands-on skills they needed. What should have been valuable professional development instead became just another another box to tick that failed to build real capacity in the workforce.

Despite the oversight across all regions, the outcomes of inspections varied considerably. A key factor in this variation was the level of experience and expertise among inspectors.

In one region, a relatively new inspector led three of the five inspections. The results were mixed: two homes were rated inadequate, one required improvement, while the other two were rated good. In contrast, another region had all five inspections overseen by an experienced inspector, supported by a long-serving regional inspection manager (RIM) with a master's degree in regulation and compliance.

In that region, there was meaningful engagement. The RIM attended senior management meetings, provided training on the new regulations, and contributed to creating a more collaborative atmosphere during what was, for many, a challenging transition. Here it felt like the inspector was working with the team, not just evaluating them.

But the inconsistency across regions pointed to a broader issue: while many inspectors applied the framework fairly, differences in interpretation sometimes led to outcomes that were unfair or damaging. The lack of consistency created confusion, and in some cases, homes were judged in ways that didn't accurately reflect the care they provided.

Looking back, it's clear that the regulatory landscape had shifted dramatically. The focus had moved away from child-centred care and toward compliance. Balancing regulation, quality of care, and staff wellbeing became increasingly difficult. New requirements, high staff turnover, and inconsistent inspections created a constant state of pressure. Tools meant to support improvement became moving targets, and providers often pushed into survival mode, forced to adjust again and again. Long-term stability for children seemed harder to achieve with each passing day.

In this climate, staff turnover became an even more serious issue – especially in leadership. If a home went more than 26 weeks without a registered manager, it was automatically downgraded, putting even more pressure on recruitment. The registration process itself could take 12 weeks or more, leaving a narrow window to find someone – a near-impossible task in a sector already facing a shortage of experienced candidates.

Tightened regulations and rigid inspectors placed immense pressure on providers. Many shifted focus from the child to the checklist, knowing a single inspection outcome could affect occupancy, funding, even their future. Some staff prioritised paperwork over presence. I once had to pull someone aside during breakfast – they were sitting at the table with a laptop, trying to finish a report. It was a small moment, but it captured something bigger: the pressure to tick boxes was starting to eclipse the reason we were there in the first place.

And still, Ofsted ratings didn't always reflect the true quality of care. Some homes held onto high grades even after serious safeguarding concerns came to light, exposing a system where compliance often mattered more than lived experience. The inspection process became so procedural that toxic cultures were sometimes missed entirely. It wasn't until whistleblowers or police got involved that the full extent of harm was revealed.

Larger organisations had the resources to absorb a poor rating. Smaller ones didn't. Financial pressure, combined with changing expectations, left many struggling. For some, selling to a bigger provider became the only option.

The new regulations were meant to improve care – but in practice, their application often had the opposite effect. What was truly needed was a constructive relationship between inspectors and providers. Oversight should have supported improvement without losing sight of the child at the centre of it all. While some inspectors understood this and worked collaboratively with providers, others approached the task with a 'gotcha' mindset – focused more on fault-finding than fostering real progress.

At times, it felt like a game of *Whack-a-Mole* – fix one requirement, and another inspector with a different point of view would pop up. We were always reacting, never addressing the root causes. Constantly scrambling to meet shifting expectations, but never fully catching up. Never quite achieving the stability children needed most. And while we were stuck on repeat, making little real progress, the wider political landscape began to shift.

In 2015, David Cameron's negotiations over the EU were making headlines. Brexit still felt distant, but the impact wasn't. Budget cuts, shifting policies, and mounting regulatory pressure were already filtering into our work. The support we needed was being stripped away, bit by bit, making it harder to provide stable care for the children who needed it most.

It felt like a mirror – on one side, watching political decisions unfold in Westminster: on the other, managing the fallout on the ground. While politicians debated the future of the EU, we were already living with the consequences. There was little room to breathe, but every now and then, there were moments that felt like a light at the end of the tunnel. Reminders that there was more to life than pressure and politics. And amid it all, life outside work carried on.

Just a month before the referendum, our family had a reason to celebrate – the birth of our second grandchild. His arrival offered respite during a heavy time. He was given the name Mark had once chosen for the son we never had. Seeing that name carried into the next generation was deeply moving. It reminded us that even in the midst of uncertainty, life still offers moments of joy, connection, and quiet hope.

But while we celebrated this new life and wondered about the future our grandchildren would inherit, the political landscape continued to shift, casting long shadows over my work. Promises of austerity and deficit reduction weren't just political slogans – they were becoming painful realities: cuts to essential services, tightened policies, and increasing pressure on the care sector. The gap between political rhetoric and the harsh frontline reality was widening, and it was becoming harder to ignore

On 23 June 2016, the UK held its long-anticipated referendum. I was acutely aware of what my vote would mean for our grandchildren. The world they would grow up in, the opportunities they might have, and the stability of the society they would inherit – all of it rested on this one, weighty decision.

The outcome surprised many: 52 percent voted in favour of leaving the EU. What followed was a period of profound political and economic transition, shaping policy and regulatory debates for years to come.

As the UK moved away from EU frameworks, regulatory oversight became a central concern. The challenge was clear: to ensure governance remained effective, transparent, and accountable – especially in sectors that had long depended on EU regulation.

Children's social care was part of that conversation, though it rarely received the attention given to education. Ofsted's inspections of fostering agencies, residential homes, and local authority services had long revealed familiar problems: chronic funding pressures, high staff turnover, and growing doubts about whether inspection ratings truly reflected the quality of everyday care.

Transparency was another growing concern. Ofsted's frequent use of GDPR to block Freedom of Information requests raised questions about where the line should be drawn between confidentiality and public accountability. These limits only widened the gap between regulators and those working directly with children.

Surprisingly – or maybe not – inspection outcomes remained largely positive. More services were rated Good or Outstanding, results that conveniently reflected well on the regulator, especially as its role came under increasing scrutiny. Yet many were calling for a more nuanced inspection process, one that would provide a clearer picture of both strengths and areas needing improvement. While the ratings suggested progress, the reality on the ground often told a different story. It seemed as if the regulator was more concerned with maintaining a positive image than addressing the real, ongoing challenges.

13

COLLATERAL DAMAGE
When Regulation Fails the Most Vulnerable

The call came in late at night – another young person was being moved to a children's home because there was nowhere else for them to go. When all else failed, that's where they ended up. No long-term plan, no stability – just another crisis placement, after two kinship and seventeen foster placements had already broken down.

Too often, children's homes weren't a choice. They were a last resort – a dumping ground. And when that failed, the next stop, if they were lucky, was supported accommodation.

According to the Department for Education's 2015 report, *'Children Looked After in England (Including Adoption and Care Leavers)'*, only 6 per cent of care leavers aged 19 to 21 were in higher education, compared to 42 per cent of their peers. The message was clear – the system was not setting children in care up for success.

Instead of focusing on how to care for these young people, we were constantly battling a system that prioritised budgets over futures, ratings over relationships, and compliance over compassion. It was exhausting – not just because of what it meant for staff, but because of what it meant for the children.

The way forward, as I saw it was to unify care, education, and therapy. That included the introduction of a clear definition of therapeutic care and education, along with a *'team around the child'* model – designed to provide more collaborative, child-centred support.

Therapeutic care and education understand the developmental and emotional harm caused by adverse childhood experiences.
It is theoretically informed and facilitated by authentic relationships in a richly nurturing environment.
It recognises individual need and relies on therapeutically trained and supported staff working collectively to seek creative strategies to lessen detriment and promote physical, emotional, and spiritual wellbeing.

The CEO embraced the definition and at his request, it was printed on canvas and displayed in offices across the regions. This visible reminder reflected a shared commitment to child-centred care, ensuring that these values were not just spoken but embedded into the very culture of the organisation. It became the foundation for the wider approach – shaping everything from staff training to day-to-day care and ensuring that every decision was rooted in a deep understanding of the complex needs of the children being supported.

As with any organisational change, people responded differently. Fortunately, one of the headteachers was a reliable advocate for the changes and later stepped into the role of head of education, playing a key role in embedding the therapeutic model within the organisation.

With this renewed focus on education and cross-disciplinary support, the regional schools were in a strong position to pursue membership with the Independent Schools Association (ISA), transitioning their inspections from Ofsted to the Independent Schools Inspectorate (ISI). Both Ofsted and ISI inspect schools, but their methods differ. Ofsted, as a government body, applies broad statutory regulations, while ISI, operating under the Department for Education, focuses more on quality improvement within the independent sector.

The move ensured the schools not only met regulatory standards but were also set up for sustainable growth and improvement.

The regional schools soon became a community in their own right, culminating in a combined sports day that celebrated teamwork, achievement, and healthy competition – a perfect reflection of the positive spirit we were cultivating. Under her leadership, communication between the homes and schools improved significantly, ensuring both care staff and students felt supported and fully engaged in the learning process.

But it wasn't just academic progress that brought people together. Festivals and special occasions became cornerstones of school life – moments that built joy, connection, and pride. World Book Day was a highlight. Staff and children threw themselves into it with enthusiasm, dressing as favourite characters, decorating classrooms, and sharing stories in ways that made even the most hesitant readers feel part of something joyful.

The school Bake Off was another much-loved event. Children carefully planned and baked their entries – sometimes with a little help from staff – and proudly presented their creations for judging. Cakes collapsed, biscuits broke, but the laughter, effort, and pride always stole the show. It wasn't about perfection. It was about confidence, participation, and belonging.

Alongside this, we were embedding a stronger therapeutic foundation into everyday school life. Access to speech and language therapy and occupational therapy became core, not optional – key to supporting emotional regulation, communication, and developmental progress. For some children, these supports were life changing.

We also introduced regular clinical consultation, offering staff space to reflect on complex situations, share concerns, and think collaboratively about how best to support each child. It bridged the gap between education, care, and mental health – reinforcing that no one had to carry the emotional weight alone. This culture of shared thinking made our care more consistent, more responsive, and more humane.

Inspirational figures like Bear Grylls and Emma Watson became more than just posters on the wall. Their stories in books they were allowed to keep prompted conversations about resilience, equality, and self-belief – giving children permission to reimagine who they were and who they might become.

Together, these elements shaped a school culture where learning wasn't confined to the classroom, and where every child felt seen, supported, and celebrated – not just for their achievements, but for who they were becoming.

Governance within the schools was also strengthened with the appointment of 'parent' governors from the homes. Their insight into the children's lived experiences helped create a more integrated and responsive approach to school leadership.

Our membership with the Independent Schools Association (ISA) opened new pathways for staff training, professional development, and collaborative learning. The decision to join was an easy one. After meeting the criteria – including a compliance inspection by the Independent Schools Inspectorate (ISI) – the application was approved.

My only regret was that there was no similar alternative for children's homes. Ofsted had been granted that monopoly, leaving little room for alternative approaches or perspectives.

Meanwhile, the summer of 2016 in the UK was as unpredictable as ever– a heatwave in July followed by cooler temperatures and storms in August. What I didn't realise at the time was that a different kind of storm was approaching in my professional life.

When school resumed after the break, the Head of Education informed me that she would be leaving at the end of the term. It was a blow. Her leadership had been instrumental in driving positive change– not just in policy and practice, but in the sense of purpose and unity she helped cultivate.

As the term drew to a close, the school prepared for Christmas with time-honoured traditions: making decorations and cards to take home, baking cakes to share, and rehearsing for the school concert. Taking part in the Candlelit Carol Service at the local church, where the children joined the choir to sing, was the highlight of the season. It was a heartfelt way to end the term – and to say farewell to a much-loved teacher. Her absence was deeply felt. She had been a steady presence, someone people trusted. Losing her left a gap – in the team, and in the work.

Her replacement was also a champion for children, and competent in her own right, but they never quite inspired the same level of collective commitment. The unity we had worked so hard to build began to unravel. Momentum stalled. A legal challenge ahead started to feel heavier– perhaps compounded by the pressure I was increasingly under. By then, it was clear the dispute I was party to wasn't going away.

Even though I was ready to take my day in court, the looming threat of being reported for professional misconduct was difficult to carry. As far as I was concerned, any decision about my professional future was not for a former employer to make. So, I took the step of referring myself to the regulatory body for social workers at the time.

Despite my determination to stand by my principles,

the weight of it all began to take its toll. I had no intention of burdening my current employer with the fallout from a dispute that had nothing to do with them. And so after much reflection, I made the difficult decision to resign. It wasn't an easy choice, but it felt like the only way to protect both my employer and myself. I didn't take that decision lightly, but in the end, I knew it was the right one.

However, stepping away from my role didn't change the bigger picture. The challenges within the sector remained unresolved. Even with the leadership change when Amanda Spielman took over as HMCI in January 2017, the fundamental issues persisted. Services continued to be judged against rigid criteria that too often failed to reflect the complexity of the work.

It was a relief to shift my focus. I had supported Hannah and Robert with independence skills when they lived with us in the early 1980s, moved into Gower House when Sarah was born, and later set up my own service for care leavers in 2003. By 2009, Pete and I had developed a new service together– one that aimed to bridge the gap between care and independence, drawing on everything we'd learned over the years.

Hannah was still in our life as a mature adult. Her journey to adulthood hadn't been without challenge– and neither had Robert's, though we saw far less of him. Hannah had raised her children without social work involvement and was living a good life. She had worked for us during the pub years, before joining us at Brighter Futures as a support mentor– and later, as project leader of the service Pete and I had set up.

Watching her navigate parenthood, work, and everyday life reminded me that the impact of care isn't always immediate. Sometimes, it reveals itself years later – in the way someone builds a home, raises their children with confidence, and breaks the cycle that once threatened to define them. This is the real outcome– a life quietly rebuilt, one step at a time.

I knew the realities of semi-independent living. It wasn't easy, and it wasn't always successful – but I also knew what it could offer when done with the right intention and enough consistency.

Each young person had their own flat, offering privacy, autonomy, and space – often for the first time in their lives. But alongside that independence was a shared communal area, where we encouraged people to come together – to cook, eat, talk, or simply sit in the company of others.

Staff shared a flat on-site and were present 24/7, which made a huge difference. Not just in moments of crisis, but in the quiet, unremarkable parts of the day– the moments where trust actually begins. It meant we could respond in real time, notice the small shifts, and offer support without fanfare. Just as importantly, it meant young people didn't have to explain themselves again and again to new faces. We knew them. That kind of familiarity built something deeper than service delivery – it built relationships, even if it took time.

Taking a more active role again reminded me why I had stayed in this work for so long. It was never about fixing everything. But it gave me the chance to shape support that was real, practical, and grounded in the realities of daily life. Not just about leaving care– but about building the confidence to live beyond it, even if it took years, and even if the path wasn't linear.

Because the truth is, even if you've never been in care, you'd have to be pretty lucky to go through life without facing challenges. The difference is, most people face those challenges with some kind of safety net – a family, a home, a sense that someone's got their back. For young people leaving care, that safety net often doesn't exist. And that's what we were trying to build – not to protect them from life, but to walk beside them through it.

For as long as they wanted us to be there, we stayed. Some

left and were never seen again. Some stayed in regular contact. Others drifted in and out. But none of that really matters. What matters is that they know the kettle is on, and the door is open– whenever they choose to knock.

Towards the end of the year, I was approached by the producers of *Kicked Out: From Care to Chaos*, a documentary following the journey of a young care leaver who had graduated from university against all odds. The researcher wanted to know more about the challenges care leavers were facing, and the barriers that often shape early adulthood.

I suggested the film crew spend a day with us – to see the work we were doing for themselves.

The documentary, fronted by Rebecca Southworth – a care leaver who had graduated from the University of Salford's BA Television and Radio programme with a first-class degree in 2015 – explored the experiences of care leavers and examined why so many face challenges like homelessness, instability, addiction, and mental health struggles. Rebecca traced her own story throughout, offering a deeply personal look at how the system can set young people up to fail. Her work was rightly recognised, winning the Royal Television Society NW Award for Best Current Affairs Programme in 2017.

Rebecca's story highlighted not only the adversity faced by care leavers, but also the crucial role that stable relationships play in shaping better futures.

At the time, supported accommodation was under heavy fire in the media. Hannah and I had hoped the documentary might offer some balance – to show another side of the story. But our contribution never made the final cut.

Just two months later, in October 2017, Tamsin attended the first *Your Life, Your Story* (YLYS) event, where themes of resilience and systemic change took centre stage. During the event, she read *I AM* – a powerful poem she had written while working with a group of care leavers. Raw and unflinching, the poem captured the complexity of their experiences, giving voice to the pain, resilience, and hope so often overlooked by policy makers and society.

Tamsin's words resonated deeply. In that moment, personal testimony and public urgency came together – and the call for change felt louder, more human, and impossible to ignore.

In 2009, the same year Pete and I set up our semi-independent accommodation for care leavers, the Cave Review addressed systemic issues in children's social care. The review echoed my own concerns, highlighting how the system's overemphasis on compliance was overshadowing the need for relational care. It called for a more flexible, child-focused approach to better support the independence and well-being of both children and care leavers.

These findings validated my belief that the system was too focused on risk and ticking boxes, rather than prioritising meaningful, relational care. At the time, semi-independent accommodation wasn't Ofsted-regulated, and I hoped it never would be. I always said, if that day ever came, I would find it difficult to stay.

From the start, Pete and I built our service around age-appropriate support – offering not just accommodation, but a living, learning experience with emotional support in a caring environment. Our focus was on helping young people build independence, equipping them with the skills and confidence to thrive beyond the sheltered world of children's social care.

In another poem, *Forgotten*, Tamsin brings to light the harsh realities of a system that fails to meet the true needs of vulnerable young people – those denied the consistent, nurturing environment essential for their growth. Rather than providing the emotional support and guidance necessary for these young people to thrive, the system perpetuates patterns of neglect, trapping them in a cycle with far-reaching, long-term consequences.

Through her poignant words, Tamsin paints a vivid picture of a system more fixated on ticking boxes and meeting regulatory targets than on safeguarding the well-being of the very individuals it was meant to protect. The failure to provide universal support to families has been at the heart of many of the challenges within the care system. For decades, policy has shifted away from broad, accessible services and toward a more reactive, means-tested approach. Families are left without support until they reach crisis point – and by then, the damage is done. This reactive approach only highlights the inadequacies in how we treat care and protection for vulnerable children.

It shouldn't be about stepping in when things go wrong – it should always be there. Support should be available before families reach breaking point. By the time a family is on the radar of the care system, it is often too late to prevent long-term damage to a child's development and well-being. True, preventative care would focus on strengthening families and providing support long before children are at risk. If we are serious about protecting children and supporting families, this fundamental shift is what is needed most.

The system has failed to recognise that universal support, accessible to all, is far more effective than the current means-tested model. This approach, which has increasingly dominated policy, traps families who don't meet strict criteria into neglecting care until it's too late. For many, being just above the threshold for support leaves them without the help they need. And it's not just about income.

The stigma associated with means-tested support is deeply harmful, and it's not just about the financial aid – or lack thereof. It's the labels, the branding that comes with it. I think of the kids on free school meals, singled out and forced to stand in a separate queue at lunchtime, visibly marked as different from their peers.

Children, feel these divisions acutely. These labels stick with them, creating shame and alienation. No wonder the pull of a new pair of designer trainers, the promise of a new phone and a night in a hotel room with a mini bar sounds appealing. These bribes offer a brief escape from a life stacked against them, creating an illusion of belonging and worth – something the state refuses to provide. It chips away at self-esteem and sense of identity, and those emotional scars last much longer than any policy or system can hope to address. The system isn't just failing them; it's turning them into easy prey. It's trapping them in a world they never had a chance to escape.

In *Forgotten*, Tamsin powerfully captures the tragic consequences of a system that fails to provide consistent, accessible support to families. Too many young people are left to navigate the world without the skills, stability, or emotional grounding they need, simply because the system doesn't offer them the help they deserve at the right time. The system should be about preparing children for life– equipping them with the tools they need for independence, not just stepping in when it's too late to help them thrive.

The same applies when they cross the threshold of the care system. The failure to provide a meaningful foundation during their time in care doesn't simply disappear when they turn 18 or 21. It stays with them, shaping their future in ways that cannot be ignored. If we continue to focus on ticking boxes and applying compliance-driven regulations, we risk robbing these young people of the chance at a fulfilling, self-sufficient life.

This isn't just about extending care or prolonging dependence – it's about providing the right kind of support from the start. Tamsin's words in *Forgotten* show us the stark reality of what happens when we don't give young people what they need in time.

The solution is not stepping in when it's too late or more regulation; it's about creating a system that ensures young people, and their families, have the support they need long before things fall apart. And when things do go wrong, a system equipped to repair and rebuild – not just patch things up for the moment.

I AM

I am.
I am the fabric on which you left your stain.
I am the mind that's tortured and torn.
I am the shredded file that you threw in the bin.
I am the child prostitute—
but there is no such thing.

I am the music that is always playing within.
I am beautifully broken;
gold fills the cracks that you chiselled in my skin.

I am the crown that you wore
when you wanted new contracts—
money, money, money... k'ching.

I am the sociopath,
too damaged by age five to feel—
apart from rage and fear, that is.

I am the empath,
a sponge absorbing all shame, pain, and grief.

I am the mother too scared to ask for help
in case it happens again.
I am the mother not even knowing where to begin.

I am the college lecturer,
hiding his demons mostly in a bottle of gin.

I am the graduate.
I am the dropout.
I am the highflyer and the low rider.
I am all of these things.

I am the one who lays awake at night.
I am the one who sleeps with pills or drink.
I am the one with autoimmune diseases—
the body keeps the score, you see,
no matter how many smiles are worn.

I am the child locked in the cupboard.
I am the Black boy in the cell—
ssh… we won't tell if you don't.

I am Daddy's girl,
with multiple fractures long since healed.
I am the one who regresses to a toddler
when life throws shit beneath my wheels.

I am the boy they call the fantasist.
Wouldn't a child raised by wolves seem more real?
Irony.

I am pissed off with your bureaucracy
and a system that has failed.
I am done with being wheeled out at your fancy events
for a voucher or three,
while your CEO creams a six-figure salary
from the children you steal.

I am not going to be silenced.
I am a warrior with a voice—please, let me be heard.
Whether I'm riding on a wave crest
or homeless in the dirt:
I matter. Can you see?

I am the overachiever you clap and give awards to—
but I'm also the one carving scars in prison walls.

I am cosy in my penthouse.
I'm crawling in the gutter.

I am living to a ripe old age.
I am hanging from a rope—
ten days dead in my flat, no one even knows.

I am a statistic in the papers.
I am a number on your books.

I am everything you said.
I am everything you said I'm not.

I am a conundrum, easily read.
I am a human.
I am precious.
I am living.
I'm not dead.

I am lost.
I am found.
I am all and none of the above.

I AM A CHILD THAT'S BEEN IN CARE.
AND WHAT I NEED IS... LOVE.

—Tamsin Trevorrow

FORGOTTEN

Like a refugee in his own land—
a land that has forgotten him.

The care child wanders,
with no hand to hold when it is cold,
no hand to stop the blows
from an unseen foe that strikes—
strikes in the night
when curled, he lays on a cardboard box.

A box wet and stained with rain and tears
in a lonely town,
on an un-named street.
Forgotten.

No longer remembered by the State—
his corporate parent,
who arrived too late to save him.
Too late to save him from the monsters in his head,
the monsters who used to join him
in his soiled single bed
when he was young… oh, so young.

Too old now, they celebrate.
They can sign him off their books with an almost clean slate.
Hurray!
A big fat tick in the corporate box.
Ofsted regulated—what a load of…
Who regulates Ofsted, anyway? he says
Irony.

He's now twenty-one.
The 'job' is done.

He slips into anonymity—
a nameless face in a human sea.
Not so many friends.
Definitely no family.

The monster's return.
No longer under his quilt,
but still embedded
in his train-wrecked head.

They would not give therapy when he was three.
"Too young" they said.
Would not give it when he was five... eight... ten.

"Onto the tablets," they said.
"That's best for him then."

The tablets that numbed the pain
and gave them the excuse
to release a sigh and say:
Cured?

Cured?
No—repressed.
Repressed by chains of numb and dead.
But numb and dead he stayed...
until the bells of age twenty-one
sang their toll and sealed his fate.

Out you go, *they say.*
"There's your flat, and a ton or two,
to see you on your merry way"

The way to homelessness.
Because he was not equipped
to make the perilous journey into adulthood.

He forgot his pills—
and the walls caved in.
As the monsters were not gone;
They were caged within.
The chaos unleashed on him
like bike chain whips on baby skin.

Where can he go?
*Where can he **begin**?*

So instead, he curls—
holding a syringe as his hot water bottle,
on his cardboard box.
A box wet with rain and tears
in a lonely town,
on an un-named street.

Forgotten

—Tamsin Trevorrow

14

YOUR LIFE YOUR STORY
Lived Experience and the Battle for Change

The week before I stepped away from regulated children's homes, the world changed in an instant. At Manchester Arena, a night of music ended in horror. An explosion ripped through the foyer, leaving twenty-two dead, hundreds injured, and a nation in mourning. Among the victims were children and teenagers – the very people I'd spent a lifetime trying to protect.

It was a harsh reminder of how quickly safety can be shattered – and how urgently we needed real, meaningful safeguards. The attack exposed just how vulnerable young people can be, drawn into dangerous situations by those who prey on their isolation and insecurity. Just as gangs and traffickers exploit vulnerable children, extremist networks target those who feel disconnected, unheard, and desperate for a sense of belonging.

The story of the Bethnal Green Girls – Shamima Begum, Kadiza Sultana, and Amira Abase, all aged 15 at the time – lured to Syria by ISIS in 2015, is a stark reminder of how easily vulnerable young people can be manipulated into extremism. These girls, reportedly seeking a sense of belonging and meaning, highlight the importance of staying alert to the risks of radicalisation.

Shamima Begum's citizenship was revoked by the UK government in 2019, a decision framed as both a punishment and a deterrent. However, it did little to address the root causes of radicalisation. The decision came after she was discovered in a refugee camp in Syria, but it did nothing to tackle the vulnerability that led her to join ISIS in the first place. Kadiza Sultana, tragically, was killed in a bombing in 2016, meaning her citizenship was never revoked. As for Amira Abase, her fate remains uncertain – she is believed to still be in Syria, and there has been little public information regarding whether her citizenship was ever revoked.

While the exact influence remains unsaid, it's possible that the decision was influenced, at least in part, by the 2017 Manchester Arena bombing. What is clear, however, is that the UK government's approach – focusing more on punishment than prevention – failed to address the underlying issues of vulnerability and radicalisation. Subsequent attacks have shown that this approach did not prevent future threats, highlighting the need for a more proactive, preventative strategy.

After the Bethnal Green Girls went missing, we raised concerns about a young woman in our supported accommodation. Her older boyfriend had introduced her to *Queens of Islam*, a documentary that romanticised extremist views. Despite the seriousness of our concerns, they were dismissed, and worse, we were accused of racism. Once again, the systems meant to protect young people failed to act. Much like the Bethnal Green Girls, this young woman may have been vulnerable, seeking a sense of belonging – a crucial red flag in recognising and intervening against radicalisation. But we will never know, because the full consequences of systemic failure in people's lives are rarely revealed.

The Prevent strategy, introduced as part of the Counterterrorism and Security Act 2015, was meant to intervene early and prevent individuals from being drawn into radicalisation. Yet, the tragedy at Manchester Arena demonstrated just how difficult it is to act before harm is done. The attacker, once a promising student, withdrew from his peers, showing signs of troubling change. But these warning signs were missed, and the response came too late.

Similarly, the failure to address the signs of radicalisation we noticed in the young woman in our supported accommodation highlighted just how ineffective the system can be at genuinely protecting vulnerable individuals. Prevent, the government's strategy to stop people from being drawn into terrorism, is meant to act as a safety net. However, when authorities dismiss concerns raised by care providers closest to the young people, those individuals remain exposed to serious risks. In our case, the signs of radicalisation were clear but ignored, and worse still, we were chastised for raising them.

This wasn't just a missed opportunity; it was a stark reminder that when those directly involved in a young person's care are disregarded, the system fails to protect not only those most at risk but also those who find themselves in the wrong place at the wrong time – like 25 people tragically killed in Manchester Arena, three little girls in Southport, and the many more who were injured and whose lives were forever changed. All of these victims, along with their loved ones, were let down by the very system meant to protect them.

The suggestion that the young man found guilty of the Southport tragedy was not radicalised highlights a key issue: the system's narrow definition of radicalisation. This young autistic man, 17 years old, may not fit the typical profile, but the failure to intervene points to a broader problem. A rigid definition often overlooks early signs of vulnerability, such as mental health struggles, social isolation, or neurodevelopmental conditions – factors that can make young people susceptible to extreme content on social media. Whether or not this young man was radicalised, this case reinforces the need for a more flexible approach to intervention – one that allows us to better support vulnerable individuals, including those with autism, and ultimately prevent such tragedies.

Similarly, the rigid definition that separates care from support also limits intervention in complex cases. The focus on pushing young people toward independence – without considering the emotional or practical support they need – fails to take into account the realities of their individual circumstances. Just as early signs of radicalisation were missed, the system fails to provide the preparation needed for adult life. This lack of support can have equally tragic consequences, both for the individual and society. The growing number of vulnerable young people coming of age and ending up in prison cells is testament to this failure – a direct result of a system that prioritises protocol over real, flexible care and support.

An important oversight in this failure is the science of brain development. Neuroscience shows that the human brain, especially the areas responsible for decision-making, impulse control, and emotional regulation, continues to develop well into a person's twenties. Young people's brains are still maturing, which affects their ability to handle complex emotional and social situations, and makes them more vulnerable to manipulation or influence. The system's failure to recognise this crucial aspect of development means that vulnerable young people are expected to transition to full independence far too soon – without the necessary support structures in place.

The rigid definitions of care, support, and radicalisation ignore the fact that young people, especially those from disadvantaged backgrounds, need time and guidance to build the skills, resilience, and understanding required to navigate adult life. Failing to account for these developmental realities can result in tragic outcomes, as the system pushes young people to take on responsibilities they are not equipped to handle, whether that's managing their own finances, coping with mental health challenges, or resisting radicalisation.

The justice system's failure to account for brain development and the nuanced needs of young people has far-reaching consequences. At the core of this failure is the rigid, narrow definitions that shape how we understand and address vulnerability, whether in the context of radicalisation, care, or support. These definitions, which fail to consider the realities of individual circumstances and development, leave young people exposed to risks they are not fully equipped to handle.

This failure isn't just a problem with the Prevent strategy; it's part of a broader issue with how young people's care and support are handled. In both the justice system and in youth care, young people are often treated as if they have the same cognitive and emotional maturity as adults, yet science tells us otherwise. The human brain, particularly the prefrontal cortex, responsible for decision-making, impulse control, and emotional regulation, is not fully developed until the mid-20s. Neuroscience has shown that young people's brains are still in a critical stage of development, which means they are more vulnerable to emotional and social pressures, and more likely to make impulsive decisions without fully understanding the consequences.

Yet the justice system continues to treat young people with the same expectations as adults. The system's rigid definitions of accountability, responsibility, and radicalisation fail to consider the fact that adolescents and young adults are still developing the cognitive abilities needed to make sound decisions. A narrow approach, whether in defining radicalisation or care, doesn't recognise that young people may not be ready for full independence or may need more emotional and psychological support than they are given. Instead, they are expected to take on adult responsibilities before their brains are fully equipped to handle them.

This over-reliance on compliance with rigid protocols also prevents professionals from doing the job they are trained to do. Instead of using their expertise to assess and address the unique needs of vulnerable young people, they are forced to follow strict guidelines that may not fit the situation at hand. This stifles their ability to intervene in ways that could prevent harm, whether that's recognising the early signs of radicalisation or offering the right kind of emotional support. The system's insistence on protocol over professional judgment creates a barrier to the real, flexible care and intervention young people need.

For example, the system often pushes young people towards independence without providing the emotional and practical support they need to succeed. They may be expected to manage their own finances, medications, or living arrangements, even when they have not developed the necessary skills or emotional maturity to do so.

This focus on pushing for independence – without the proper preparation or support – can have tragic consequences. It leads to vulnerable young people being pushed too far, too fast, and they end up failing to meet expectations. Whether it's a case of radicalisation, mental health struggles, or general independence, these failures lead to tragic outcomes, both for the individuals involved and society as a whole.

In fact, this lack of support too often ends with young people finding themselves caught in a cycle of failure, to often ending up in prison cells – a direct result of the system that prioritises protocol over flexible care. Instead of providing rehabilitation and tailored interventions, young people are pushed into environments that are ill-equipped to meet their emotional and developmental needs, leaving them ill-prepared for adulthood and far more vulnerable to negative influences, including radicalisation.

One of the greatest failures of the current system is the inability to see young people as they are: developing, vulnerable individuals who need support, not just a narrowly defined, rigidly applied approach. The science of brain development has shown that young people's brains are still developing, which means their capacity for understanding consequences and regulating emotions is limited. The system's refusal to account for this developmental reality leads to unfair punishment and a lack of rehabilitation.

If we are to truly protect vulnerable young people and help them transition into healthy, responsible adults, the system must embrace a more flexible and nuanced understanding of care, support, and radicalisation. It's not enough to apply rigid definitions that ignore the developmental realities young people face. We must be willing to adapt, to recognise early signs of vulnerability – whether they manifest in radicalisation, emotional distress, or social isolation – and intervene before it's too late.

In light of this when I first heard the term 'careless' used to describe supported accommodation it felt particularly unfair. It's a broad, sweeping accusation that lumps all providers together. It wasn't that nobody cared – it was the definition set by Ofsted that separated care from support, making it impossible to offer the nuanced help young people truly needed. Worse still, those of us genuinely trying to empower young people were at risk of being penalised or even prosecuted for running an 'unregistered children's home.' As it turned out, this was an empty threat. Ofsted did not act against providers blatantly breaking the law. Instead, the lack of adequate enforcement allowed the problem to grow.

When I stepped into my new role, I focused on strengthening the service building on its foundations to create something meaningful amid the uncertainty of change. The service had always been about providing opportunities for young people who struggled to find stability in other settings. It was a living, learning experience – one where they could develop the skills, confidence, and resilience needed for adulthood. What set it apart, in my view, was the absence of Ofsted-style regulation, which allowed true innovation to flourish.

We focused on personal responsibility and self-regulation. By giving young people more control over their lives and fostering a sense of community, we helped them develop essential life skills – empathy, emotional intelligence, and problem-solving. In a timely way, they gained practical skills, such as budgeting, meal preparation, and maintaining their living spaces. They were trusted to manage their time and decisions, fostering both confidence and accountability.

This shift from overprotection to autonomy, from suspicion to trust, allowed young people to embrace responsibility for themselves and their future. For many, it was the first time they had been empowered to make decisions that shaped their own lives. The emotional support from staff, combined with the freedom to learn from mistakes, helped them grow – not just as individuals, but as part of a community. We aimed to equip them with the tools to navigate life beyond the sheltered world of children's social care and establish themselves in the wider community.

Though not deliberately modelled on places like *Peper Harow* and the *Cotswold Community*, our approach shared many of their core principles: personal responsibility, self-regulation, and community. Founded in the 1960s and 1970s, these pioneering communities were among the first to challenge conventional care models by focusing on therapeutic, relational support for young people, rather than just institutional or rigidly regulated care. While they were shaped by a different era and environment, the core principle remained the same: by giving young people greater control over their lives and fostering a sense of belonging, they helped build the skills needed for adulthood.

Peper Harow and the *Cotswold Community* demonstrated the effectiveness of structured, relationship-based care. Their success – evidenced by reduced reoffending rates among young offenders – highlighted the importance of stability, therapeutic intervention, and a sense of community in promoting long-term change. These principles evolved after the closure of approved schools, shaping a care model that prioritised rehabilitation over punishment, though they remained far from universal.

We offered young people their own self-contained flats and opportunities to participate in support sessions, residents' meetings, and a weekly communal meal. Life skills workshops covered essential tasks, from laundry and cooking to budgeting, managing relationships, and emotional regulation. Placements weren't imposed; they were based on a clear agreement outlining expectations for the service, the young person, and the local authority. To be eligible, residents were expected to be in education, training, or employment – or actively seeking it.

Yet, funding restrictions created a significant barrier. Support was tied to chronological age rather than actual readiness, meaning some young people had to leave before they were ready, risking failure just as they were beginning to find their feet. It made no sense to invest millions in raising a child in care, only to withdraw support at a critical time when a little more guidance could have made all the difference.

For some, however, the journey was far from straightforward. Many had grown up in children's homes and foster care, while others had come from failed adoptions or entered care as teenagers. Some had already been exposed to exploitation, radicalisation, or mental health challenges. Others struggled with substance misuse and disengagement from education, training, or employment. Many also suffered from undiagnosed anxiety and depression, making it difficult to participate in group activities or seek help when needed. This often led to cycles of isolation, hindering their development.

Despite our best efforts, some struggled to adjust, revealing the limitations of the support we could provide. It became clear that some young people had been so profoundly harmed by their past experiences that they required more specialised care – structured environments with higher staff ratios, clinical intervention, and support that would come at a significantly higher cost.

Over a decade had passed since investigative journalist Harriett Sergeant's influential 2006 report, 'Handle with Care: An Investigation into the Care System,' which offered a critical analysis of the UK's childcare system and its failures. I remember hearing Harriett present her findings at the Children's Commissioners Conference in 2006, marking my thirtieth year as a caregiver. Yet, some in the audience were unwilling to accept the truth, ignoring early warnings.

Ten years later, as I organised the national care leavers' conference in London, I could think of no better title than 'Handle with Therapeutic Care.' This conference raised awareness about the experiences and challenges of care leavers transitioning into adulthood.

Harriett's report captured the fundamental shortcomings of the care system, highlighting the gap between what children need and what the state provides. Her words underscore the moral responsibility of the care system – not just to provide safety, but to create a stable foundation for a better future. Yet, for many young people, even the most basic expectations –

safety, consistency, and opportunities – remain unmet, leaving them vulnerable at a critical time in their lives.

"The state cannot replace the unconditional love of a parent, but it can provide an alternative to a violent and chaotic home life. At the very least, it should keep young people in its care safe and give them what they ask for: stability, continuity, and education."

Supported by The Care Leavers Foundation and TCTC, the 'Handle with Therapeutic Care' conference explored why care leavers still face challenges and how the system could improve. Data shows that many children in care experience multiple placements, with some having had numerous moves before even reaching a children's home. This instability erodes trust, disrupts education, and affects emotional development, making it harder for young people to form relationships, develop coping skills, and feel a sense of belonging.

Yet, despite this knowledge, little has changed. Those of us living with young people every day are rarely consulted about how instability affects their behaviour, the challenges we face, or the support needed to create meaningful stability. It seems easier to assign blame than to listen to caregivers.

The reality is that it's the system – not the caregivers – that sets these young people up for failure. Pushing them toward independence before they are ready leaves them ill-equipped for adulthood. Rather than preparing them for success, the system casts them into the world unprepared for the challenges ahead.

This is not merely a failure of bureaucracy but a reflection of deeper, generational flaws – the legacy of past failures. These systemic issues, including poverty, mental health struggles, and a lack of community support, have been passed down through generations, condemning vulnerable children to face the same struggles without the resources to overcome them. By neglecting to address these root causes, we perpetuate a cycle of disadvantage, making it harder for young people in care to break free.

In 2007, Tony Blair's government transferred responsibility for children's social care from the Commission for Social Care Inspection to Ofsted. At the time, the Commission had raised valid concerns about the imbalance between focusing on protection and addressing deeper systemic issues affecting families, such as parental struggles with mental health, poverty, and substance abuse. While these concerns were acknowledged, Blair's government pressed ahead with the reforms.

This shift in oversight marked the beginning of a new era for children's social care, with Ofsted assuming greater control. Over the next decade, the number of teenagers entering care rose sharply, often due to exploitation, criminal activity, neglect, and homelessness. This surge placed mounting pressure on an already overburdened system, further exacerbated by increasing regulation and budget cuts.

As a result, local authorities turned to supported accommodation for young people aged 16 and over who were ready for semi-independent living. It provided a stepping stone to independence, helping young people transition out of care and into adulthood. Supported accommodation was never suitable for those who needed more comprehensive care. It was simply not resourced to provide the consistent emotional, educational, and social support that young people still in need of a structured environment required.

With budgets under pressure and the cost of semi-independent accommodation significantly lower than children's homes, local authorities moved young people out of care at 16 into projects like ours. We provided 24-hour staff support at a fraction of the price of a children's home placement. However, over time this decision became driven increasingly by finance, turning what should have been a stable transition into adulthood into a cost-cutting measure.

As the number of young people in care continued to rise, it became clear that this model was being stretched far beyond its original purpose to stretch insufficient funds. Seeing an opportunity for higher rents and greater profits, landlords in low-cost rental markets began offering accommodation with minimal floating support. This was even cheaper for councils and more profitable for landlords, but it came at the expense of young people who needed more than just occasional check-ins to successfully navigate independent living.

Floating support – a low-cost alternative to staffed accommodation – relied on pre-arranged check-ins, often just a few hours a week, instead of providing on-site, 24-hour support. While it was supposed to bridge the gap between full-time care and independence, in practice, it often left young people isolated, with limited immediate help when they needed it most.

At 18, many young people were expected to navigate adult life alone, often with no more than a phone number for a support worker. This marked the point when the safety net disappeared.

The consequences of these decisions reach far beyond the care system. Many young people could have taken a different path if early intervention had been prioritised. Instead, multiple placements and instability left them ill-prepared for adulthood. Without the right support, breaking free from negative cycles becomes increasingly difficult.

It's easy to be critical, but hindsight offers valuable lessons. Lived experience, from both sides of the care journey, holds the insights needed for real change. Progress begins with listening to those who have walked the path – and change doesn't start with statistics; it starts with stories.

15

THE COLLECTIVE VOICE
Speaking Truth, Driving Change

Stories have the power to drive change. They illuminate injustice, amplify unheard voices, and challenge broken systems. When used effectively, storytelling can transform policy, reframe public perceptions, and give those who have been silenced a voice.

'Your Life Your Story' (YLYS) was born out of this belief. It was built on the understanding that the most powerful tool care-experienced adults and caregivers have is their own truth – and the acceptance that two truths can exist in the same space. A child can be grateful for the support they received in care and still carry deep pain from the experiences that brought them there. A worker can do their absolute best and still be part of a system that lets children down. Holding space for both truths is where real connection and change begins.

When used effectively, supported accommodation plays a vital role in the transition to adult life. It provides a structured but flexible environment where young people can learn responsibility, take manageable risks, and develop resilience. But with rising demand and stretched budgets, cost-cutting often takes priority over quality, leaving too many young people without the support they need to thrive.

The consequences of these funding decisions extend beyond the care system. Overstretched public services – including the police – end up under even greater pressure when young people don't get the help they need. Media narratives tend to focus on negative stories, reinforcing public misconceptions and making things even harder for care leavers and those trying to support them.

The scale of these challenges becomes even clearer when looking at the long-term impact of missed opportunities. Many young people could have taken a different path if early intervention had been a priority. Instead, they often experience multiple placements that fail to meet their needs, leaving them without the stability required to build confidence and independence and easy prey for those willing to take advantage of this.

Expecting rapid change from young people who have faced years of instability is unrealistic. By adolescence, many have already endured significant difficulties that shape their sense of self, trust in others, and ability to cope with challenges. Without the right support, breaking free from negative patterns can feel impossible.

It can be disheartening to reflect on these issues. The pressures on the system often make real change feel out of reach. But hindsight offers valuable lessons. The voices of those who have experienced the system first-hand hold the insights needed to create better policies and support structures. Listening to different perspectives is key to finding real solutions. When discussions are limited to politically preferred viewpoints, opportunities for meaningful change are lost. True progress comes from acknowledging a range of experiences and using them to shape something better.

But it's not just children in care who are let down. As a parent, I saw this firsthand with Sarah. Throughout her education, her struggles with dyslexia went unnoticed. Like many others, she was labelled a behaviour problem instead of receiving the support she needed. It wasn't until after she had completed her statutory education – or perhaps more accurately, after being failed by it – that she was formally diagnosed. Her story is a stark reminder that far too many young people, not just those in care, are let down by systems that should be equipping them for success.

Looking back, I remember Sir Al Aynsley-Green, the first Children's Commissioner, who took on the role in 2005. Sarah was ten, and I was working with Pete at the time. His time in the role highlighted many deep systemic issues in children's services. He worked hard to bring attention to the failings in child protection and the lack of support for vulnerable children, though it wasn't without challenges.

The role of the Children's Commissioner was created by the *Children Act 2004*, following the tragic death of Victoria Climbié in 2000. Despite contact from social services, police, and the NHS, no one acted on the clear signs of abuse. Her death exposed the serious flaws in the system and the need for change.

Sir Al was a strong advocate for children, especially those in care and those with disabilities, as well as those facing other significant challenges. But the role wasn't without its controversies. Even though he worked tirelessly to highlight these issues and push for reforms, he often found himself in disagreement with government officials. His criticisms of the government's handling of children's welfare sometimes created tension, as some felt he was highlighting uncomfortable truths. It sounds familiar.

Years later, in his book '*The British Betrayal of Childhood*', Sir Al reflected on how, despite decades of work, children's services continued to fall short. His words rang true then, and they still do now. There is no shortage of evidence to validate this – after all this time, we are still failing the very children we set out to protect.

Amid this challenging landscape, the idea for Your Life Your Story (YLYS) emerged– an initiative inspired by the literary aspirations shared by many care leavers over the years with Janet Rich, the founder of The Care Leavers Foundation and a pioneer of Care Leavers' Week. Pete and I were long-time supporters of the charity, and I was highly motivated to take on the responsibility of organising the event. It became a much needed and welcome distraction from the dispute that was weighing heavily on me.

Thankfully, the matter was resolved just four weeks before YLYS 2017, though I was still awaiting the outcome of my self-referral to both the Health and Care Professions Council (HCPC) and the Information Commissioner's Office (ICO). I was worried about making the referral, but the person I spoke to reassured me, saying that many other whistleblowers had spoken out about high-profile cases of institutional abuse and kept the proof – most notably, the Jimmy Savile case.

Years before one such individual was the social worker Alison Taylor, whose courageous stand against institutional abuse in children's homes in Wales ultimately contributed to the Waterhouse Inquiry. Despite her unwavering integrity and dedication, Taylor faced severe professional retaliation, losing her career in social work – a deeply unjust consequence of standing up for vulnerable children and young people. Though disillusioned, she remained undeterred, channelling her sense of injustice and grief into writing.

Her debut novel, '*Simeon's Bride*' (1995), garnered critical acclaim for its powerful portrayal of corruption and abuse within institutions, drawing heavily from her real-life experiences. She followed this with '*In Guilty Night*' (1996), a poignant and haunting exploration of child abuse and its lasting emotional and psychological scars. Although she never intended to become a crime writer, her pivot to fiction allowed her to continue her advocacy, giving voice to those silenced by systemic failures. Through her work, Alison illuminated stories that might otherwise have remained hidden, proving that the pen can indeed be mightier than the sword.

Reading some of Alison's work, I recognised echoes of my own experiences. '*In Guilty Night*' was more than just fiction; it reflected the institutional failures I had witnessed firsthand. Its unflinching exploration of betrayal, guilt, and the lasting impact of childhood trauma felt achingly familiar.

Alison's work did more than tell a story – it captured the haunting legacy of abuse and neglect, offering a window into the emotional and psychological scars carried by those failed by the very systems meant to protect them. Like Alison, I'd come to see how power and bureaucracy often overshadowed morality, leaving the most vulnerable to bear the brunt of institutional failure.

The novel's raw authenticity reminded me of Alison's own disillusionment when we later connected. She spoke plainly about the cost of standing up for what was right and the deep injustice of a system that punished whistleblowers while letting abusers get away. Yet, even in her disillusionment, she held firm in her belief that stories – her own and others' – could shine a light on the truth and make a difference.

Her words stayed with me as I awaited the outcome of my self-referral to the HCPC and ICO. Meanwhile, I kept busy with the final preparations for the first YLYS event, set to take place during Care Leavers' Week.

Three years earlier, by chance, Mark and I had reconnected with David during a stay at a hotel in the Lake District. He was the boy who had spoken out about Mrs. Marsden before being moved to the teenage boys' hostel where Mark worked. That chance meeting reignited our connection, and we've stayed in touch ever since. When I told him about the event, he immediately offered to come and show his support.

The event brought together sixteen care-experienced adults, ranging in age from eighteen to sixty, along with published care-experienced authors Rosie Canning, Lisa Cherry, and Paolo Hewitt. In an emotionally supportive space, participants learned the techniques of storytelling, sharing their experiences through writing. David played a key role, helping me welcome attendees who had travelled from all corners of the UK.

One young woman, clutching her guitar and trembling with anxiety, chose to go straight to her room when she arrived. Others were less intimidated, and during dinner, the room buzzed with nervous chatter as we tucked into our meals. As the initial tension began to fade, our shared care experience facilitated an immediate bond among everyone.

That evening, when I finally retired to my room, an email from the regulator, the Health and Care Professions Council (HCPC), was waiting for me. It had been an intense day, and this was my first chance to check my emails. It read:

"We have now reviewed all the information we have received about your concern. This included the information you provided, along with information from the ICO. We have taken the view that this case involves contractual and/or employment matters, not issues that would reflect upon your fitness to practise. We are also mindful that the data protection element of this matter has been considered by the ICO, which is taking no further action."

As I read those words, relief nearly overwhelmed me. It had been a stressful and uncertain time, but this message brought closure. Finally, the matter was settled. I had reported child protection failures, and the evidence of this was contained within legally privileged communications, ensuring the issue couldn't be hidden if those affected chose to pursue complaints in the future.

Now, I could focus on the event and support the participants without distraction. I closed my laptop and prepared for bed, feeling a renewed sense of purpose and determination to face whatever challenges lay ahead.

The next day, we assembled to learn the techniques of storytelling. But what followed was far richer than that. Memories were shared, poems were written, songs were performed, and bonds formed as tears were shed, both in sadness and in jest.

I was reminded of the conversations I'd shared with my parents, the custodians of my childhood memories, and with my own children, as well as Hannah and Robert, who are still in our life. Each of us carries the weight of our histories, but we also hold the potential for change – not just in our lives but in the lives of others.

As autumn gave way to winter, a few of us, inspired by YLYS, kept in touch. David began writing his first book. Yusuf, who'd also attended the event, was busy exhibiting his art and developing his unique style of spoken verse.

Then, out of nowhere, I received a message on Facebook. By some uncanny twist of fate, the message was from one of the children who'd lived at the home with David. Memories flooded back of a little girl with fair hair and piercing blue eyes – sent to live with relatives when the local authority closed the home due to cost-cutting. Thirty-seven years had passed, but some things you never forget. I replied, telling her that I thought I'd looked after her when she was eleven – she replied:

"OMG... I've finally tracked you down at last!"

Her message inspired me to write '*Not Forgotten*' – a true

story about a cruel manager, six vulnerable children, and the boy who tried to save them.

Writing this poem allowed me to reconnect with my personal story. It didn't matter that some might have preferred it remained untold – this was my story, and I had found a way to share it. More than that, I had discovered a way for others to find their own voices and tell their own stories. In that moment, I knew I had to find a way to keep YLYS alive.

But storytelling alone wasn't enough. The weight of my experiences – everything I had witnessed, the failures of the system, the harm done to vulnerable young people and those who care for them – still weighed heavily on me.

After YLYS 2017, I wrote to the Independent Inquiry into Child Sexual Exploitation, raising concerns about systemic failings within institutions. I was disheartened when a civil servant responded, telling me that my concerns fell outside the scope of the inquiry. Undeterred, I wrote again but received more replies that failed to address my concerns:

"As you will appreciate, given the wide remit of the Inquiry, it is not possible to investigate every allegation of institutional failure. A member of the Inquiry team will be in touch at a later date if we have further queries."

No further contact was made, and I was not surprised. The insincerity of the system never failed to disappoint.

In my professional world, the year ended with the launch of Amanda Spielman's first annual Ofsted report on 13 December 2017, as HMCI. When presenting it, she stated, "The life chances of the vast majority of young people in 2017 are the best they have ever been. That is the story our inspection reports are telling."

According to Ofsted data, 83 percent of children's homes were rated as Good or Outstanding. As I read those words and absorbed the glowing statistics, I couldn't help but think of the children whose stories were absent from the report. The children I had worked with, the ones whose voices went unheard, and the ones still suffering in homes that were far from the shining example Ofsted was painting.

The report seemed more focused on protecting Ofsted's reputation and securing its future, rather than addressing the harsh realities many children were still facing in care. The stark contrast between this data and the ongoing struggles of vulnerable young people made it clear to me: the system may have been patting itself on the back, but it wasn't really listening.

Not Forgotten

'OMG… I've finally tracked you down.'
Your timely words seemed meant to be,
but you could not have known how much they'd mean to me.
It's forty years since we last met in that awful place,
where cruelty went unpunished, and justice was disgraced.

There were fireworks in the attic and confiscated toys.
Colouring books were all you had, designed to mute your noise.
A cold bath if you wet the bed, stood barefoot in the snow.
Deliveries hijacked; food packed to go.

When visitors came, the scene was set for deceptive illusion,
bay-windowed lounge unlocked, children on parade,
reciting party pieces in humiliating charade,
with tea and cake to celebrate this perilous delusion.

Years later, it was no surprise to discover
the boy who spoke out was stripped and beaten by police,
'moved' and branded liar.

For time served leaves me without doubt,
abusers will be reprieved.
As long as truth is worthless
and vested interest valued higher,
children and young people will be dispersed,
scattered – like it doesn't matter.

Ruptured relationships cannot survive uncertainty,
and self-belief withers
when trust is shattered by impunity,
by those willing to collude in crimes against humanity.

—Amanda Knowles MBE

16

A LIFE IN REFLECTION
Unleashing the Power of Connection

Despite these professional frustrations, life outside work brought joy and reflection. In our family, the new year always marked the beginning of birthday season. This year was special as I celebrated my sixtieth. Emma and Sarah surprised me with afternoon tea at The Ritz in London. Joining us were my sisters and my mum, who, being twenty-five years my senior, effortlessly stole the show.

Upon arrival, the staff assumed it was her birthday and escorted her to the table – much to our amusement she lapped up the fuss and said nothing. Even after realising their mistake, the waiters continued treating her like the guest of honour, adding a playful touch to the occasion. It was a truly memorable day, with *'Great Nan,'* as she's affectionately known, basking in compliments on how remarkable she looked for eighty-five.

As I reflect on moments like these, I can't help but think of my own journey, perhaps because, with age, memories have a way of becoming clearer. It's funny how certain recollections, no matter how small, can resurface with time. Until I was thirteen, I had been blissfully unaware of my father's passion for other women – a truth that would later shape my understanding of love and loyalty.

When he met my mum at a town hall dance in the early 1950s, it wasn't long before he swept her off her feet. Within weeks, they were married – she was expecting her first child – my brother, the only boy. I was the third child in the family, but before I came along, the dynamics between them were already shifting in ways I would come to understand only much later. My father, full of charm, had a way of making everything feel effortless – even love. But I would eventually learn that not all of his affections were so easily contained.

Early childhood was simple, but good. Every week, Dad brought home his wages in a small brown envelope, and Mum, who stayed at home, made sure we had everything we needed. We lived on a post-war council estate, our clothes were often second-hand from jumble sales, and holidays were rarely anything more than a day trip to the seaside– while holidays abroad were becoming more common for other people.

Tourists, wearing unmistakable red, white, and green sombreros, carrying Spanish dolls in brightly coloured dresses and woven straw donkeys – trophies from far-off lands that felt a world away from our own. On the rare occasions we saw my dad's older brother and his wife, who had no children of their own, they were always eager to boast about their travels. As kids, we listened, wide-eyed and perhaps a little envious, as they spoke of places we could only dream about. It all seemed so distant – a life we only read about in books.

While I wasn't a bookworm like my older sister, I did enjoy the book I received for good attendance at Sunday school. It was about an air hostess named Mandy, and for a while, I couldn't help but daydream about becoming one myself. The story captured my imagination, offering a glimpse into a world that seemed so distant from my own.

Despite the modesty of it all, we were loved. Our beds were clean, we were never cold, and our tummies were full. Looking back, those simple comforts meant everything to us. It was in these early years that I learned the difference between wants and needs.

It was my maternal grandmother who made the trip to Rhyl possible. A stalwart of the local community, Nan had long been involved in fundraising and had served on the committee that ran Rhyl Holmes, a convalescent home for children from Stoke-on-Trent. Her efforts ensured that children like us, from working-class families, could get away for a much-needed rest and recovery. Thanks to her, my older brother, sister, and I were able to spend two weeks at Rhyl Convalescent Home in North Wales for children. I was just seven and had recently had my tonsils out.

At first, the idea of a two-week holiday by the seaside seemed exciting, but when the day arrived, I did feel a knot of anxiety about leaving my parents behind. As the bus pulled away, I felt a strange sense of separation, almost as if I would never see them again.

When we arrived at the home, it was a large, red brick building close to the sea. The nurses were kind, making sure we were checked in and settled. As we unpacked, the building felt imposing yet comfortable – not quite a hospital, though the nurses wore uniforms. It all felt strange, but we were together, and that made it easier to adjust.

Our days followed a simple routine, even though we were only there for two weeks. Mornings started with porridge, toast, and jam. After breakfast, we were allowed outside into the garden where there were a couple of swings. Dinner was always stew or meat with boiled vegetables, and at teatime, we had bread and butter with jam. Before bed, we lined up for a cup of milk, then made our way back to the dormitory, tucked in, and ready for another day. We went for a boat ride on a nearby lake and to the pictures to watch the Saturday morning film. Sundays were reserved for board games, reading, and church.

The highlight of each day was the trip to the beach. We'd walk in a line, feeling the cool sea breeze on our faces. The water was freezing, but we didn't mind. We ran barefoot on the sand, our feet sinking into the dampness, built sandcastles, and laughed as the waves splashed against our legs. Having my brother and sister there made it feel less like being away from home, and for those two weeks, ordinary became extraordinary.

But my most vivid memory wasn't of the beach. It was the day we went to the theatre. The theatre felt enormous to me, its red seats stretching high above us as the lights dimmed and we settled into our 'scratchy' seats. I don't remember much about the show, but I will never forget the moment the compère called me up to the stage. Standing there, in front of the audience, with my big brother and sister watching from their seats, felt incredibly special. I still hold onto the one photograph from that holiday – a snapshot of a simpler time.

By the time my younger sister was born three years later, we had moved to a new house, and I had to start over at a different junior school. Adjusting was hard – my childhood friends were far away, I struggled to fit in, and at home, I was no longer the baby of the family. Though I didn't realise it at the time, I was vulnerable.

I believed the lady who lived a few doors further up the street liked me, and I craved her attention. Before long, I became a regular visitor to her home, where she lived with her bedridden husband. She bought me a hairbrush, comb, and mirror dressing-table set – a gift I had longed for, one that made me feel special. When I abruptly stopped visiting, no one seemed to notice. Years later, when the memory resurfaced, I threw the set away. It had become tarnished by the reawakening of reality.

During my early years working in children's social care

and social work, I sat through countless training sessions on child abuse – hearing the stories of others, learning the signs, and understanding intervention frameworks. But I never recognised myself in any of it. I had buried the abuse so deep, compartmentalising it to the point where it was not my story.

The lessons, the statistics, the warnings about vulnerability – none of it was about me. To this day, I don't know what triggered the memory, but even now, it still evokes shame. Even though I know it's not mine to carry, emotionally, it still feels as though it is – and somehow, because I went willingly to that house, I feel as though I am to blame.

After primary school, I moved to the local comprehensive and reunited with my best friend. Though we weren't in the same class, we rekindled our friendship and spent time gossiping about school dramas, the latest friendships, fights and fallouts. Around this time, my mum began working part-time, and with more money coming in, little luxuries like a telephone and a second-hand car began to appear in our home.

For a while, it seemed as though my parents were falling in love again. They started going out together on Saturday evenings with Dad's work friend and his wife. I'd babysit their three kids, and for a time, life felt content. It was nice seeing Mum looking pretty and dressed up in a way I wasn't used to.

But things soon changed when Dad's affair with his friend's wife came to light. He came in person to our house to tell Dad that he had kicked her out. We had just returned from a shopping trip when we saw him approaching. As soon as Dad saw him, my sister and I were sent upstairs; even so, we heard every word. She was pregnant. Dad didn't leave us to set up home with her, as she had expected. Instead, the mother of his unborn child slept in our living room while arrangements were made for her to have the pregnancy terminated – a procedure that was only allowed under strict conditions back then.

At thirteen, after it was all over, I was enlisted to help her move into her new home. I still feel the weight of that day, especially walking into a shabby bedsit that felt cold and empty. We just stood there, unsure of what to say. Her dream of building a life with Dad was shattered, and my feelings toward him in tatters. As I stood there, surrounded by the emptiness of her new home, I realised the extent to which my father's actions had shattered lives. It wasn't just her broken dreams that I carried with me, but a profound sense of helplessness and disappointment that would resonate deeply in my work with vulnerable young people.

I had been mortified when I was made to watch him cut my sister's hair to keep the boys at bay. The cruelty was never in doubt, but now the hypocrisy was undeniable. This woman had paid a high price for falling for my dad's charm and so had her very young family. It was a travesty. As I said goodbye, the sound of the door locking behind me stayed with me. I remember the long bus ride home, lost in thought. Even now, I can't shake the memory of leaving her there, alone, with nothing but a few belongings, broken promises, and a broken heart. At home, it was never mentioned again – as if we were all pretending it hadn't happened. The chapter was closed.

At school, I became disinterested and misbehaved as a way to escape class. I could usually be found in the girls' toilets, having a fag, or in the sick bay, feigning illness – if I hadn't already left for the day. By the time I finished my GCEs, I was ready to leave and start working. Higher education wasn't something most working-class kids considered in the 1970s, and my dream of becoming an air hostess had long been forgotten.

Though higher education wasn't an option for most working-class kids in the 1970s, it became clear to me later in life that opportunities – whether in education or care – are the key to breaking cycles of depravation. This realisation drove me to support young people in care, helping them see that their futures were worth fighting for. As I entered the field of children's care, I knew all too well the consequences of emotional instability and the urgent need for safety, consistency, and nurturing environments.

These formative years, full of love followed by confusion, shaped my view of care and protection. Looking back, I realise these early lessons were not just about love, but also about stability and safety – concepts that would later become my guiding principles in children's social care. It was in these early moments of emotional complexity – of love, loss, and vulnerability – that I began to understand the importance of stability in a child's life. This understanding would later become the core of my work in children's social care: knowing how quickly stability can be lost, and how desperately it needs to be rebuilt.

Years later, after multiple moves and witnessing my dad's struggles with his mental health, I learned that he and his brother had been taken into care as children. That revelation helped explain much about his past, but it did little to lessen the emotional toll on us. After a serious suicide attempt, Dad was hospitalised, and Mum – finally worn down – returned to her roots. By then, her own mental health was in decline, worn out by years of instability and disappointment.

The breakdown of my parents' marriage was a painful experience that left lasting scars. Through it, I began to understand the complexities of love and loyalty – and how, sometimes, we must rebuild ourselves from the wreckage of broken relationships. That journey of emotional resilience would later resonate with the young people I worked with – many of whom were forced to rebuild their lives after trauma and betrayal. These early lessons shaped how I saw the young people in my care, who often found themselves navigating the same painful dynamics I had experienced.

My siblings and I were scattered across the country – you

could say we were dropped off in various locations. It was in these places that we met our partners and where the story of the next generation began. Over the years, the distance between us grew: my brother living in the suburbs of Glasgow, my sisters on the outskirts of London, and me in Lancashire.

When Dad was finally ready for discharge, none of us felt able to take him in. Instead, it was his brother, Alan – the one he'd been in care with – who stepped up, offering him a home in Oxford. Dad rebuilt his life, remarried, and found a new sense of purpose. I went to the wedding, but it was traumatic. I cried, though my tears were not tears of joy. I realised there was no longer a place for him in my life. He had reinvented himself, leaving behind the man I once knew – a talented man who, though full of charm, lacked empathy. I could not pretend he was the person he wanted the world to see. And he didn't need me to blow his cover.

His reinvented self didn't need me to remind him of his past. And in turn, I had to let go of mine in order to move forward.

The month after my milestone birthday, marking the start of my seventh decade on this planet, also marked forty-two years in the children's workforce. It was a reminder of the long journey I had travelled. I was back in London for the launch of Christine Bradley's latest book at the Foundling Museum, an institution dedicated to commemorating Britain's first children's charity, founded in 1739 by philanthropist Thomas Coram.

Christine's book, "*Revealing the Inner World of Traumatised Children*", demystifies the complexities of working with young people who have experienced trauma, serving as a guide for future caregivers and emphasising the importance of empathy, patience, and understanding. In her words, it is her legacy.

Reflecting on my own forty-two years in the children's workforce, I was reminded not only of how far we've come but also of the enduring importance of the knowledge and compassion preserved by people like Christine – individuals who have shaped both the field and the lives of children. If only the system could embrace this same empathy and understanding, the impact could be transformative. And what a year it turned out to be.

On 19 March, Mark and I celebrated forty-one years of marriage. As I reflected on all that had changed since we began our life journey together – two young kids full of hope and big dreams, unaware of the twists and turns ahead – something unexpected arrived: a letter that left me speechless. The formality of it was unmistakable, and as I read the opening lines, I had to stop and read them again, convinced I must have misunderstood.

"Dear Madam, The Prime Minister has asked me to inform you, in strict confidence, that, accepting the advice of the Main Honours Committee, she proposes to submit your name to The Queen..."

I stared at the page, trying to absorb what it meant. My name. Submitted to The Queen. The gravity of those words sank in, and for a moment, I couldn't quite grasp what they meant. Of all the letters I might have expected to receive, this was not one of them. An MBE... me!

In that moment, I hoped it would add credibility to my voice – legitimacy to the stories I was trying to amplify, and the truths I had spent a lifetime standing up for. Not for status, but so that when I spoke – especially in rooms where difficult things needed saying – people might just listen. It wasn't about honour. It was about permission. A way to go where others feared to tread, and to be heard when silence had too often been the safest option.

At first, I was stunned. It had come as a complete surprise – but soon after, I learned that my family, professional friends, and colleagues had known about the nomination for over two years. The vetting process, I was told, was both lengthy and thorough.

What humbled me most was learning that the nomination had come from colleagues – past and present – whose respect and recognition meant so much. It was a testament not just to me, but to the collective journey we had all been on together. This honour wasn't just about me; it reflected the shared effort of everyone who had been part of the work.

The hardest part, though, was keeping it to myself. I'd been informed I was to receive an MBE for services to residential care – but until the official announcement, I wasn't allowed to share the news with anyone. So, like always, it was a case of keeping my head down, my mouth shut, and getting on with the job.

While I was secretly bursting with pride, I was also already thinking about how I could use the honour to shine a light on the voices that mattered most – the care-experienced people who had lived it, and those in the work who had cared for them. The ones who were there at 3am when no one else was. The ones who sat in the stillness, through the chaos, the heartbreak, the silence. The ones who stayed, even when it would've been easier to walk away. The ones who showed up – again and again – because they knew that sometimes, that's what care really means.

But while those on the ground were showing up for children in the ways that mattered, the system continued to struggle with clarity and accountability.

In 2016, Ofsted had introduced a clearer legal definition to distinguish between regulated children's homes and supported accommodation for young people aged sixteen and over. The definition sought to outline the legal distinctions between these services and the consequences of operating illegal children's homes, but its impact was minimal. While it was unequivocally unlawful to place a thirteen-year-old in accommodation designed for those preparing to leave care at sixteen and above, the reality was that this practice still occurred.

Some providers understood the regulations and would never have considered such placements, while others were either unaware of the legal requirements or chose to ignore them altogether. As a result, thirteen-year-olds were placed in unregistered children's homes – an illegal and alarming practice that often went unchecked.

In theory, the guidance should have drawn a firm line between what was legal and what wasn't. But in practice, the line was blurred almost immediately. I saw placements that made no sense – young teenagers, placed in settings meant for care leavers preparing for adulthood. These weren't children ready to navigate independence – they were scared, traumatised, and in desperate need of care, not just a bed and a front door key.

The definition may have changed on paper, but the culture hadn't caught up. There was still too much room for interpretation, too little accountability, and too many children falling through the cracks. You only had to look at the referrals to prove it – like so many other things, it was happening in plain sight.

Three years later, Ofsted had identified 292 illegal homes that should have been registered – an alarming rise from just 136 the previous year. It was believed that hundreds of children and young people, many under the age of sixteen, were living in these homes in direct violation of the law. These children should have been placed in regulated homes, yet weak enforcement allowed these illegal placements to persist.

For these children, insufficiently trained staff and poor supervision often led to an overreliance on control measures like physical restraint – a poor substitute for the safe and secure care they so desperately needed. Local authorities making referrals and some providers exploiting the demand for financial gain routinely disregarded the guidance. While not all providers operated illegally, Ofsted's lack of effective enforcement meant that these dangerous practices often went unaddressed, making it easier for purchasers and providers to bypass the rules.

Looking back, the care system has always been shaped by economic decisions made by those in power. Since the new millennium, successive governments have relied on market forces, assuming that competition would drive quality up and costs down. While this might have seemed logical in theory, in practice, it introduced risks that were not fully recognised. Independent regulation was intended to protect children and young people and uphold standards, but it fell short. It failed to ensure that the right people were in place to deliver essential services and did not do enough to keep the wrong ones out. This was where things began to unravel, creating gaps that left children and young people vulnerable.

And when it all began to go wrong, the blame game took over. Fingers were pointed at the private sector, but that narrative oversimplified the issue. The growth of private providers wasn't an unintended consequence – it was a direct result of political decisions to reduce state involvement and rely on market mechanisms. The problem wasn't the existence of the private sector; it was that the safeguards weren't strong enough to ensure all providers prioritised the needs of children and young people over financial interests. Without proper oversight, the balance had tipped too far in the wrong direction.

While watching this situation develop, I spent the summer balancing my day job, raising funds, and planning '*YLYS 2018*'. Thankfully, I had received much-appreciated support from well-known care-experienced adults who had stayed in touch, along with a generous donation from a well-known care-experienced author and trainer.

Soon after schools resumed for the autumn term, Pete was approached by the director of a small children's home company, someone he had known since setting up his first business at the beginning of the millennium. The company was in financial difficulty and in need of rescue.

Our initial response was no, but on reflection it felt like something we couldn't ignore. The government was promoting the Staying Close approach, designed to help young people transition out of the care system by maintaining close relationships with their former foster carers or children's homes. With our supported accommodation services located near these children's homes, we saw the potential to develop a *'throughcare'* service. This would smooth the transition from care to independent living – an opportunity too good to pass up.

Three weeks later, I took YLYS to the Lancaster campus of Cumbria University. Joining me was an inspiring lineup: poet and playwright Louise Wallwein MBE; writer, editor, and educator Dr Josie Pearse; Clare Fisher, Lecturer in Creative Writing and author of *'All the Good Things'*, and Una, author of *'Becoming Unbecoming'*, a memoir in comic form. To capture the essence of the event, I commissioned my neighbour's son, Ben – then a recent university graduate and aspiring filmmaker – to create a video of the event.

After the event, care-experienced participant and registered social worker Saira Jayne Jones – now a director of YLYS – shared the following reflection:

"Throughout a full and thought-provoking programme, voices were shared, the power of our truths unleashed, and relationships developed as if we had somehow been there for much longer. The space we held for each other felt safe, honest, unquestioning, and non-judgemental, like you were never more than an arm's length away from people who just 'got it.' The facts were unimportant; the connection came through feeling, knowing, and the shared threads of

existence. We all became more than we were before we arrived, taking away not only the practical writing skills, we had been developing but also a sense of being in it together."

In November, David's book, *Oi*, was published. Although I was familiar with his story of life in care, the version held in social services' archives was sanitised. Hearing the story from the perspective of a child left to die with life-changing injuries at the hands of his mother was an entirely different experience. The rawness in his voice and the pain etched into every word were, at times, almost too much to bear. I had to put the book down and let the moment pass – and reviews from others echoed this sentiment:

"I don't have many words; this book has stunned me. This is a MUST read. I've only read the first three chapters so far and made the mistake of reading chapter three while at work (had to stop due to tears). An insightful, raw, unbelievably true story."

2018 was shaping up to be an eventful year, marked by meaningful collaborations, powerful storytelling, and significant milestones. With YLYS 2018 already on the calendar, we were brimming with excitement, eager to expand our reach and amplify the voices and stories that had too long been silenced.

The stories we told were no longer just reflections of the past – they were shaping the future. With every word spoken and every line written, we were reclaiming our narratives, proving that lived experience was not just something to be acknowledged but something that demanded attention. The momentum was building, and for the first time in a long while, it felt like real change was within reach.

When Pete and I shared our plans to create a throughcare service – linking children's homes with our supported accommodation to ease the transition from care to independent living with Mark – he asked if we were mad. From his point of view, the thought of dealing with the scrutiny, the inspections, and the stress was enough to make anyone hesitate. But we understood the challenges – or at least, we thought we did.

17

NAVIGATING THE STORM
Fighting for Integrity in Care

The deal was sealed just a day before Mark and I were set to fly to Walt Disney World, Florida, with our family for Christmas. We were buzzing with excitement, eager for the adventure ahead. But as we queued to check in, we sensed tension in the air – it wasn't just pre-flight nerves. Drones had grounded all flights over Gatwick Airport, throwing the festive travel plans of thousands, including ours, into chaos.

Once we had cleared check-in and security, we took our time with the customary rip-off airport breakfast and after that, we sat there for hours. Eyes fixed on the flight information screens that refused to budge from *'flight delayed.'* Hope waned with each passing moment, making me wonder if our flight would ever be called. We took turns keeping the kids happy and entertained, doing our best to appear more jolly than we actually felt. And then the announcement came: the 10.40am flight to Orlando was cancelled. My heart sank. We'd been saving for this trip for such a long time. The disappointment hit me like a ton weight, but I just couldn't bring myself to give up hope of getting there.

I spent the next couple of hours on the phone, listening

to what felt like endless hold music, explaining our situation over and over. My tenacity was tested, but I refused to give up. Finally, after what felt like forever, I managed to secure flights from Heathrow for the next day, rerouting us through Dallas... and onto Florida the day after that. It seemed like the perfect solution to a stressful situation. It was the only solution, and finally, I could breathe a sigh of relief, knowing we'd soon be on our way.

After a long day at the airport, we left via the arrivals lounge, even though we'd never actually departed. We were greeted by a swarm of journalists and photographers eager to report the latest tale of an airport in disarray. By then, it was breakfast time in Texas, and a quick call to Gareth and Julia, who had been living in the U.S. for over thirty years, turned our unexpected detour into a mini reunion.

I thought I'd already lived through my worst travel nightmare after the curse of the Ash Cloud, but fortunately, this disruption came with a silver lining. Although we saw Gareth and Julia now and then for holidays and special occasions, the stop in Dallas turned out to be an unexpected delight. There was something especially heartwarming about seeing our children together again as adults, reminiscing about their childhood adventures, while watching their own children begin to create memories of their own.

We even managed a day trip to Fort Worth, or 'Cow Town,' as it's affectionately known. It felt surreal walking back into the place after all those years. We sat on the same bar stools made from saddles, had a drink at the Victorian bar, and felt the old fans above spinning with pulleys to keep the place cool in the Texan heat. It was like stepping back in time. Emma and Sarah were about the same age as our grandchildren the last time we sat in this spot, all those years ago. And in that moment, it felt like nothing had changed at all. The years, the distance, the changes in life – gone in the blink of an eye. It was just as it had always been, and for a few minutes, it was as if time hadn't moved on at all.

That's the thing about true friends – time and distance may separate you, but when you come back together, you just pick up where you left off.

Except that over the years since our earlier visits, the whole experience had become more 'Disney-fied.' The curated atmosphere and choreographed performances for the tourists had replaced much of the raw authenticity we remembered. Watching a cattle drive and taking photos of our grandchildren riding a longhorn bull before the mock gunfight was fun. Even though it wasn't quite how Mark and I remembered it, the experience still held a certain charm – captured forever in a group photo taken against a backdrop of Stars and Stripes.

After our time in Fort Worth, we flew onto Florida late the next day and made our way to the hotel. The kids were tired, and we were exhausted, but we felt a sense of relief that the worst of the travel chaos seemed to be behind us. However, that relief was short-lived. When we finally arrived, we hit another snag – our reservation had been resold due to the delay. The email I'd sent, letting them know we'd be arriving late, had likely been ignored.

At the reception desk, I tried to explain the situation to a staff member who seemed indifferent to our plight. It felt like a scene straight out of the Nativity – weary travellers, no room at the inn – except it was far from holy and way more distressing. Instead of being treated as delayed guests, we were made to feel like an inconvenience.

Hotel policy states that if you don't check in by the designated time, you're a 'no-show,' and your room can be re-let. Only in our case, we weren't absent – we were delayed, and I had informed them we were still on our way. A fact both the policy and the staff chose to ignore, and I wasn't about to let that go.

After what felt like twelve more rounds with Tyson Fury and a great deal of persistence, we were eventually offered alternative accommodation, though it was at a distance from the facilities and a far cry from the poolside rooms we had originally paid for.

To my thinking, that's the arrogance of supply and demand – the belief, perhaps even the certainty, that someone else will book the room, take the seat, and pay the rate, leaving the customer to be grateful for whatever they're given. It's an unfair and frustrating practice, and sadly, it's catching on. We've been conditioned to accept it, often without even realising. It's now standard policy in many city centre restaurants to cancel your table if you're more than ten minutes late, no matter the reason.

The implication is clear: you are replaceable. There's always someone else waiting. And we play along, quietly, even when the service is poor, or the experience falls short. Who hasn't choked down a disappointing meal and still smiled politely at the server, insisting everything was fine? We've learned that to complain is to cause a scene, to be '*difficult*', even when we're the ones being shortchanged. Somewhere along the line, we stopped being guests or customers and became statistics in a booking system – and the unspoken rule is simple: shut up and put up.

This willingness to put profits before people has become absolute. But I wasn't about to let them get away with it. It wasn't just about the disappointment or the inconvenience – it was about the principle. I wasn't going to walk away from a situation not of my making without standing up for what was right. In that moment, though, I was just thankful to have a roof over our head and I resolved to deal with the rest when I got home.

After what turned out to be another exhausting game of '*planned ignore*' and '*fob-off emails*,' persistence finally paid off when I called the CEO, who agreed to compensate us for their mistake. Getting to that point took every ounce of determination, but the acknowledgment and redress felt like a small victory against a system designed to wear you down and make you settle for less than what's right. I sometimes wonder how many battles we're expected to fight before we finally throw in the towel.

In the end though the real consolation came when the Disney experience turned out to be truly magical. Just being there, reliving the joyful memories from when Sarah and Emma were little girls, swept up in the same wonder that had brought us there all those years ago. In her excitement, Sarah ran straight into Pluto, sending him toppling onto his bottom – much to everyone's amusement. Emma, wide-eyed in disbelief, stood frozen, unsure whether to laugh or be worried – the way only a big sister can when her little sister causes chaos.

Before we left, I sent postcards – one from Mickey, one from Minnie – thanking them for being such good girls. They arrived a few weeks after we got home, and it wasn't until years later that they realised it had been me all along.

And yet again, Walt Disney World didn't disappoint. With its twinkling lights, towering Christmas trees, and the magical snowfall on Main Street, USA, it delivered everything we'd wished for. The Christingle service on Christmas Eve and the Christmas Day dinner with Disney princesses made the experience unforgettable. I have to give credit where it's due to the Americans for that – they really do this stuff very well.

The magic stayed with us long after. Emma, now grown, sent postcards to her own children – one from Mickey, one from Minnie – a tradition born from a moment of childhood wonder that stayed with her.

We made it back to the UK just in time to ring in the New Year, holding on to the magic a little longer, grateful for the memories that would stay with us – and the stories that will be shared with my grandchildren and beyond, reminding them of the moments that shaped us and the joy we found in each other.

There's an old saying I've always held dear: *'One day, you'll be a memory – make sure it's a good one.'* It's a reminder to live in a way that leaves a lasting, positive impact. Hopefully, our adventures in Disney – and the ones still to come – will be the stories carried forward long after I am gone.

It wasn't the first time Pete, and I had returned to work in the new year, taking responsibility for children's homes that were new to us. Of the three homes, only one was owned by the company; the other two were rented from landlords. Unlike the high standards we maintained in our properties, these homes fell well below what we would have accepted. The landlords showed little interest in making improvements, leaving the financial and logistical burden of necessary maintenance and repairs to the previous owners. This neglect was a significant factor in the company's demise, and one that contributed to the sale. It was hardly a win-win; the only winners in that deal were the landlords.

We had always preferred to own the homes we operated. Ownership provided long-term stability, allowed for meaningful investment over quick fixes, and gave us greater control over the quality of care we could provide. With this in mind, we decided to give notice on one of the rented homes. Despite its Good Ofsted rating, it was hard to see how it had earned that status. The home was extremely small, in desperate need of modernisation, and its location – right next to a motorway junction – made it unsuitable in our eyes.

Before finalising the acquisition, we had engaged with Ofsted to discuss our plans, including a request to increase the registration capacity of two of the homes from two to three children. This change was crucial – not only for financial viability but also to maintain its affordability for placing authorities. What we didn't know though was that a new Regulatory Inspection Manager (RIM) had taken over responsibility for our homes.

So, it was a shock when our variation request and the manager's application for registration were both refused.

After 20 years in the children's workforce, the manager was disqualified – a reality I still can't get my head around. Nor can I quite grasp why it took another 12 months before the variation request was finally approved – just two weeks before the tribunal appeal hearing we'd been compelled to spend so much time preparing for. The whole episode felt unnecessary and unjustified, and I couldn't help but wonder why. It crossed my mind that the sudden change in RIM might explain it – an information gap, or some other reason, perhaps – but I knew there was no way we'd ever really find out. All I do know is that it was a complete waste of time, effort, and money – resources that could have been used far more productively.

While larger providers often have the resources to absorb such setbacks, for a smaller organisation like ours, the financial strain was immediate and deeply felt. The emotional toll was just as significant. The constant pressure of managing cash flow, navigating endless paperwork, and keeping operations running amid unexpected hurdles was exhausting. But it wasn't just the financial stress – it was the relentless sense that no matter how hard we worked, there was always another Ofsted inspector waiting just around the corner.

What made the situation particularly frustrating was the inconsistency I had witnessed firsthand. I knew of other homes that had been approved for three or more children in spaces no larger – and in some cases, smaller – than ours. These disparities raised serious concerns about whether decisions were being made based on consistent criteria and whether the policy was being applied unevenly.

Across different regions, I encountered regulatory decisions that often seemed contradictory. Some homes were approved to accommodate additional children despite having very limited space, while others were denied – even when they provided more appropriate and spacious environments.

In one instance, a three-bedroom semi with a small dining kitchen was registered for three children, even though there wasn't enough room for them to sit together at mealtimes. I even came across one home where staff slept on a crudely made bed in the office, and another where a staff member slept on a bed built into a cupboard under the stairs. It was like something out of *Harry Potter* – all to make space for one more child.

In my experience, staff comfort has almost never been a priority. I've slept in rooms that, as Sarah once put it were, "no better than a dog basket." That line stayed with me - and it's why I've made staff comfort something I pay close attention to. In the homes I became responsible for, it was not ignored. A decent bed with a good mattress, a TV, a bedside lamp, and somewhere to hang your clothes are the very least we can offer to show staff that their comfort and wellbeing matter too. It cannot be right by any standard to expect a member of staff on duty for several days to sleep on bare floorboards with nothing but a sheet. And if you think I'm exaggerating, think again – that kind of thing really does go on.

For some, it was all about occupancy and pipelines – the more heads on beds, the bigger the margins, and the lower the costs, the bigger the dividends. There were times when I wanted to place a photograph of a young person on the boardroom table – a reminder of the futures in our hands. For some it seems this is the sole focus.

These issues extended to fostering, where some homes were overcrowded – housing six or more children. In some cases, there were more children than you'd typically find in a small children's home. While fostering is a vital service, some placements blurred the lines between foster care and residential care. I even heard of foster homes where every room, including the basement, had two sets of bunk beds.

The core issue lies in the gap between expectation and reality. Children are told they will be placed in a loving, stable family, yet for many, the reality falls short. Instead of stability, they experience overcrowding, multiple moves, temporary placements, and environments that feel more like institutions than homes. This not only erodes trust but also reinforces feelings of rejection.

Respite care complicates this further, as it sends the message that children aren't truly part of the family. While it's meant to support foster carers, it can make children feel disposable – especially when they're moved to another placement while their carers take breaks or holidays.

Unlike biological children, who typically stay with relatives or travel with their families, foster children often feel like outsiders, deepening their sense of not belonging. If the service cannot consistently provide the family experience it promises, it should either align its practices with that commitment – prioritising permanence, emotional security, and belonging – or change the name and be honest about the reality. Children deserve truth as much as they deserve stability.

Calling something a family doesn't make it one. Real change requires delivering on that promise – or rethinking the service to reflect what it truly offers. Research by the Department for Education in 2019 showed that children who experience multiple placement moves are at greater risk of mental health issues and school exclusion.

Over time, this not only deepens the emotional and psychological toll on the child, but it also increases reliance on specialist services, creating long-term costs that far exceed any initial savings. Yet rather than addressing these root causes, regulatory efforts continue to focus primarily on oversight.

As media scrutiny of the sector intensified, *Newsnight* launched its campaign on *Britain's Hidden Children's Homes*.

When the programme's producer approached me for comment, I questioned the angle – children's homes were registered and regulated, so I didn't understand why they were being portrayed as '*hidden*.' As the conversation progressed, it became clear that the focus was actually on supported accommodation, where young people aged 16 and over lived with less structured supervision.

Mark and I had set up Brighter Futures in 2002 to provide accommodation and support for young people who had been pushed out of the care system, often long before they reached the age of eighteen. For many, the alternative was cheap, unreliable bed and breakfast accommodation. We took every step to ensure we were operating within the law, securing the appropriate permissions at the time. A year or so later, after objections were raised about an application to register a children's home nearby, we found ourselves accused of running an unregistered children's home.

But after a visit from the regulator, they confirmed once again that our operations were fully legal. We were operating within the legal framework, but the scrutiny we faced highlighted the challenges of working in such a complex and often misunderstood sector. The difficulties of navigating the system had only just begun. What had changed was the increasing media scrutiny on the sector, as the conversation around supported accommodation and the broader challenges within the care system gained momentum. As public concern was rising in response to media coverage, it became clear that merely operating within the law wasn't enough.

While I agreed that there were valid concerns about poor-quality services run by landlords with no experience in social care, it had to be said that equally valid concerns existed within regulated children's homes. Regulated or not, these services continued to operate because local authorities were willing to place young people with them. The issue wasn't just about tightening regulation; it was about addressing the root causes – reassessing regulation, scrutinising placement decisions, and rethinking the overall approach to social care. In my opinion, without confronting these overarching factors, simply adding more regulation would only make the problem worse.

Ofsted ratings had become the kite mark – the Red Tractor – of children's social care. They satisfied placing authorities, insurance companies, and the government. Nobody, it seemed, was looking beyond the end of their nose. But none of this was of interest to the programme makers.

Instead, when the programme aired, it opened with a senior police officer describing a case in which a young person had been missing for several days, triggering a county-wide search. The officer used this as an example of the risks posed by unregulated settings. But the issue of missing children is not exclusive to these settings. Young people go missing from registered children's homes as well – often due to external influences, peer pressure, or personal struggles, rather than a lack of care.

The police are equally outspoken about children missing from registered children's homes, but that clearly didn't fit with the programme's aims. By focusing solely on settings not regulated by Ofsted, the narrative reinforced a misleading distinction – implying that regulation equates to safety, and that risk exists only where oversight is weaker. The reality, however, is far more complex.

Media coverage can be a powerful tool for raising awareness, but it often oversimplifies complex issues. Public and political reactions to children's residential care have long been driven by outrage, fear, and media pressure – resulting in knee-jerk policy changes rather than real, meaningful reform.

The selective decisions made by programme makers about whose voices are heard – and, more importantly, whose are not – can create a false impression of expertise. Visibility is often mistaken for authority, and individuals with limited relevant experience are elevated to positions of influence on deeply complex issues. We've seen similar patterns across other matters of public interest – climate change, for example – where media coverage often favours those who fit a particular narrative, real or engineered, rather than those with genuine expertise or frontline experience. This practice not only distorts the conversation but can also disregard the contributions of those who have firsthand, substantial experience, and a deeper understanding of the challenges at hand.

This selective framing has been explored by various academics, including Richard Webster, whose book *The Great Children's Home Panic* (1997) examined how moral panics surrounding children's homes have shaped public perception and policy. Webster argued that waves of hysteria and media-driven fear led to over-regulation and sweeping reforms – some of which, he believed, caused more harm than good. He questioned whether the vilification of children's homes was always justified and cautioned against the unquestioning acceptance of abuse allegations without proper due process. His work reminds us that while the need for oversight and accountability is paramount, the pendulum of regulation can sometimes swing too far, creating an environment where the welfare of children may not always be the primary focus.

Webster does not deny that abuse occurred in children's homes – nor do I. However, he highlights how sensational stories, particularly those involving abuse, led to widespread fear and the vilification of children's homes. His work questions whether the moral panic surrounding these settings was justified, suggesting that the intense focus on regulation often obscured the deeper question of what was truly needed to support children effectively.

Webster's conclusions have been the subject of considerable debate. Critics argue that he underestimated the prevalence and severity of abuse, and that his scepticism toward large-scale investigations risked minimising or dismissing the experiences of genuine victims. Beatrix Campbell, a journalist, writer, and activist known for her work on child protection and social care issues, for example, challenged his views, accusing him of being overly sympathetic to those convicted of running abusive regimes. Others have questioned his methodology, suggesting that his analysis lacked the depth needed to fully understand the systemic nature of abuse in some institutions.

All of that said, his work raises important questions about the consequences of moral panic. The stigma surrounding children's homes – reinforced by high-profile scandals and hidden agendas – has often led to policy decisions that focus more on manipulating public perception than addressing the actual needs of children. In many cases, this has resulted in instability, risk-averse decision-making, and a reluctance to acknowledge when residential care might be the best option.

The moral panic around children's homes is not just damaging – it's dangerous. Scandals and media reports frequently distort the truth, shaping public opinion and, in turn, influencing government policies that may ultimately do more harm than good. We need to challenge the assumptions that fuel this panic and focus instead on building a system that genuinely serves vulnerable children. That means moving away from penalising care providers for the failures of a broken system. It means calling for a balanced approach – one that holds institutions accountable without sacrificing the welfare of the very children they're meant to support.

I bear witness to how reactionary reforms – often driven more by media pressure than the realities of care – can create new challenges rather than resolve existing ones. The constant stress of navigating ever-changing regulatory hurdles, combined with the frustration of achieving little systemic change despite significant effort, took its toll.

When our only registered manager resigned due to stress, it was a stark reminder of just how taxing social care roles can be on mental and physical health. In her resignation, she wrote that the job had become unmanageable, that the constant pressure was affecting her well-being – and that she simply couldn't go on.

The demands had always been high, but Ofsted inspections were the final straw. A job at McDonald's wasn't just a better option – it was a relief. She loved it. And she wasn't alone.

Research from the Social Care Workforce Research Unit has shown that stress and burnout are among the most common reasons registered managers leave their roles, with regulation cited as a key source of pressure. (Skills for Care has also reported that registered managers are leaving faster than they can be replaced, with more than forty percent citing stress or lack of support as the reason for leaving.)

I understood that exhaustion all too well. Fifteen months after a testing return to the world of regulated children's social care, a break wasn't just something I wanted – it was something I desperately needed. The pressure had been relentless, and I was exhausted in every sense: mentally, physically, emotionally. Even Mark had begun to voice concern about the toll it was taking on me. I needed space to breathe, to step back from the day-to-day responsibility, and to remember what life felt like outside the constant demands of care. I needed a holiday.

In all the years I had worked in children's social care, I'd known stress. I'd worked long hours, carried emotional weight, and made decisions that kept me awake at night. But this was different. There were times it felt like I was running uphill just to stand still. I didn't realise how much I was carrying – how heavy it had become – until Mark pointed it out. I wasn't just tired. I was worn down.

Something had to give. And for the first time in a long time, I was ready to give myself permission to stop.

We went to Goa with Mark's brother and his wife, escaping to the laid-back vibe of India's west coast. The place had everything – beautiful beaches, a bit of culture, and enough energy to make you feel alive. The days were warm, the nights were lively, and we made the most of it.

We wandered through busy markets, ate amazing food, and let ourselves unwind. It was exactly what we needed – time to reconnect, take a breath, and recharge.

As I felt the sun on my skin and settled into lazy days, I found a small but real sense of peace – something I hadn't felt in months. The constant setbacks, the emotional toll, the endless regulatory hurdles – had worn me down. But here, under the warmth of the sun and away from the noise, I could finally breathe. It wasn't just the time off I needed; it was the space to think. And with that space came perspective – a clearer view of everything we'd been through, and why it mattered.

But even with all Goa had to offer, the reminders of struggle were never far away. Children played barefoot in the dust, families sold handmade crafts by the roadside, and beggars moved quietly through the crowds. Small children, guided by unseen hands, worked the tourist areas, hoping for a few coins. It was impossible to ignore. In a place so full of beauty and colour, the gap between those with so much and those with so little was striking.

It reminded me how fragile life can be for vulnerable young people, no matter where in the world they are. As I stood nearby, I noticed a group of caregivers raising funds for a local home. One of them handed me a flyer for a Bollywood-style gala they were hosting. When I asked if we could go, Mark and his brother bought tickets without hesitation – they were taking us out for the evening. But this wasn't just about a night out. It was about supporting something that might actually make a difference.

The event did not disappoint. It was a spectacular display of colour, music, and dance that captivated us from start to finish. My sister-in-law stole the show when she accepted the invitation to join the dancers on stage – thrilling the audience with her spontaneous moves and vibrant energy. Her joy, set against the meaningful cause behind the event, made it unforgettable.

The evening was filled with colour and happiness, but it didn't erase the bitter truth. Goa's vibrant markets and beautiful beaches also highlighted the stark disparities that persist around the world. Children played in the streets, their laughter often interrupted by calls for charity – a reminder that many, like the young people I'd worked with back home, were caught in cycles of poverty that shaped their futures. Their lives seemed defined not just by what they had, but by what they lacked.

18

AGAINST THE ODDS
Navigating Family, Crisis, and Safeguarding Failures

As I lay in the warmth of the sun, finally enjoying some much-needed peace, my thoughts turned to Mark's first reaction to our plans. His initial scepticism hadn't shaken us at the time, but now, with the quiet surrounding me, I began to wonder if he had a point.

During the fundraiser, I learned about Anita Edgar and Matthew Kurian's inspiring journey to create El Shaddai, a charity that started in Goa. In 1997, Anita, on a two-week holiday, saw children searching for food in hotel rubbish and felt compelled to act. By chance, she met Matthew, a minister who shared her desire to create safe homes for street children. It was one of those serendipitous connections, the kind that feel meant to be, much like my own connection with Pete. Within a year, El Shaddai was officially registered. Their story stayed with me – a powerful reminder of how vision, courage, and persistence can create real change.

Later that evening, a conversation with one of the charity's sponsors led me to pick up 'Blink' by Malcolm Gladwell. She spoke about the book with such conviction, saying it had changed her life. Intrigued, I decided to read it myself.

The book explores the ability to make quick, instinctive judgments based on experience. One of Gladwell's most striking examples is the story of a controversial kouros statue, scientifically verified as authentic, yet immediately doubted by art experts. Their instincts, honed over years, ultimately proved more reliable than the tests.

It reminded me of Shaun Greenhalgh, the infamous Bolton forger Mark knew from school. When the story hit the headlines, Mark told me Shaun had always been a talented artist but felt snubbed by the art world – a rejection that he thought may have driven him to prove a point in the most spectacular way.

One of his most notorious forgeries was the *Amarna Princess*, a statue Bolton Museum proudly purchased in 2003 for £440,000, believing it to be a rare piece of ancient Egyptian history. For three years, it was displayed as a prized artefact until experts uncovered the truth. It hadn't come from Egypt at all. Shaun had crafted it in his garden shed using clay from the local DIY store and stained it with tea to give it an aged appearance.

His parents had helped forge the paperwork, claiming the piece had been passed down through a family collection. The deception finally unravelled in 2005, when a police investigation into the family's dealings uncovered a hoard of fakes, moulds, and forged documents. And yet, even after its true origins were revealed, the statue still draws the crowds – only now, as a masterpiece of deception.

Reflecting on this, I saw clear parallels. Just as art experts, police officers, and doctors develop instincts that go beyond data, so too do caregivers. '*Blink*' reinforced the importance of experience – reminding me that good judgment isn't only about what can be measured, but also about recognising when something doesn't feel right.

It was the same instinct I had about the deputy I inherited while managing the children's centre – and the same unease that niggled me the day I met Ralph Morris at Castle Hill School, when I went to see Robert. Both were fakes, hiding behind a veneer of title and trust. Experience had already told me something was wrong, long before I had the words – or the evidence – to explain it.

Our return to the UK was, fortunately, well timed. Just a day earlier, Boris Johnson had announced new guidance to halt nonessential travel and social contact. We had been blissfully unaware that this marked the beginning of a global upheaval. As we boarded our flight home, we were still in holiday mode – relaxed, sun-tanned, and reluctant to leave this beautiful place. There was talk of a virus on the news, of course, but we barely heard it – we had taken respite from what was happening elsewhere in the world.

We couldn't have known that in a matter of days, airports would close, cities would sleep, and life as we knew it would grind to a halt.

The day after we arrived home, Mark and I celebrated forty-three years of marriage. Four days later, the UK was in lockdown. The country fell quiet, routines collapsed, and uncertainty settled in. Like everyone else, we were trying to make sense of it all. But not everyone had the option of retreating to the kitchen table with a laptop. Some of us had to carry on – because not all jobs could be done from behind a screen.

The hospitals didn't close. The supermarkets stayed open. Delivery drivers kept going, as did the bin men, the carers, the cleaners, and the countless others who kept the country running while most of it came to a halt. Vulnerable children were still in care and staff were still showing up to look after them.

And for those of us responsible for services, the pressure didn't ease. If anything, it grew. We were juggling pandemic risk assessments on paper with the realities of daily life: safeguarding, infection control, staff shortages, and the emotional toll of trying to protect others in a world that suddenly felt unsafe.

So, I stepped in. There had been enough upheaval. The young people needed consistency, and the team needed support. That was my responsibility – it came with the territory. Leadership isn't about collecting accolades; it's about showing up for the people who rely on you, even when there's no immediate gratification or reward.

"Leadership is not about being in charge. Leadership is about taking care of those in your charge." – Simon Sinek

The work can be thankless and overwhelming at times, but that's what we sign up for. What mattered most was keeping the young people safe, ensuring they had the stability they needed, and guiding the team safely through the uncertainty.

The truth is the cracks were already there. The pandemic just forced them wide open. What held us together – what kept us going – wasn't policy or process. It was people. People who showed up. People who stayed. People who carried what needed to be carried – together.

Some of the structures we were relying on weren't built to support us. Not really. And nowhere was that more obvious than in the registration process.

In theory, it was about safeguarding – about making sure the right people were in place to run children's homes. In practice, it often felt anything but fair or reliable.

The process was inconsistent. One person might be interviewed in the home, another in a regional office. Sometimes there was a notetaker. Sometimes not. Requests for notes were routinely refused, with GDPR given as the reason. And all too often, applicants – despite what was at stake – weren't given a proper chance to respond before decisions were made.

On paper, 28 days to appeal a Notice of Proposal to refuse registration may sound reasonable. But when you're trying to make sense of complex allegations, gather evidence, and find legal support, 28 days disappears fast – especially when a Freedom of Information (FOI) request could swallow that and then some. The consequence of a failed appeal isn't just a refusal – it's disqualification from the children's workforce. But not all of it, as I would learn in years to come.

Previously, applicants could withdraw voluntarily if concerns were raised – stepping back without destroying their careers. But that option was quietly removed. Even if someone was willing to walk away, they could still be disqualified. Ofsted had decided that in some cases, there were people who simply shouldn't be in the sector – and they wanted the power to make that judgment final.

When I queried the lack of feedback after the fit person interview, Ofsted told me it was a new approach that was within current guidance. Inspectors had previously given applicants a heads-up if refusal was likely, allowing them the option to withdraw – a right Ofsted had to accept.

But in cases where they believed someone shouldn't be working in social care; they didn't want that person to quietly step away. They wanted the ability to formally refuse them – which meant automatic disqualification from the children's workforce. To make it 'fair', they stopped giving immediate feedback to anyone – removing that opportunity from applicants as they saw fit.

Although the right to withdraw has since been partially reinstated, the damage was already done. People lost their reputations – and in some cases, their careers – without ever having a fair chance to defend themselves. For many, it became punishment without process. For all, it was life changing.

And all of this sits within the fit person process, part of the Care Standards Act 2000 – legislation that, as written, failed to reliably account for what a privatised future might look like. Its application is largely left to Ofsted's discretion – and that's where things get messy. Unlike employment law, which gives individuals the right to respond before decisions are made, this process offers few safeguards. People were blindsided – no warning, no opportunity to challenge – until it was already too late.

Of course, we need to make sure children's homes are managed by the right people. But disqualifying time-served, qualified, and experienced professionals without due process doesn't keep children safe – it leaves them more exposed. It strips the sector of hard-won knowledge and stability at a time when both are desperately needed. And when Ofsted refuses to publish disqualification data, it only fuels concern.

If the process is fair and consistent, why not be transparent? This wasn't a request for personal information – it was a request for data. The kind of data that would help build trust. The kind of data that, should already be in the public domain.

Meanwhile, recruitment was becoming harder by the day. Skilled managers were becoming an endangered species, and vacancies often went unfilled for months. High demand and short supply pushed up salaries – and that cost was passed on to purchasers. Realising the opportunity, who could blame a qualified manager for accepting the most lucrative offer? High turnover became inevitable, and continuity suffered as a result.

When registration is refused, legal barriers make it worse. The only option is a tribunal appeal – with legal fees ranging from £10,000 to £15,000. Completely out of reach for most, and even more so if you're unemployed. So, they walk away. And the sector potentially loses another good person unnecessarily.

The fit-person process is supposed to assess whether someone has the skills, integrity, and experience to lead. But more and more people were starting to ask whether it actually did that. Did it measure leadership? Contribution? Integrity? Or had it become a tool to shut people out – not because they posed a risk, but because the process itself was not fit for purpose?

The short appeal window, the cost of legal advice, and the fact that you can only challenge once a decision has already been made – none of it inspires confidence. None of it feels just.

And silence was not an option. This wasn't just about policy – it was about justice. I spoke with people who had been directly affected, with sector leaders and legal professionals, to understand the scale of the harm. I launched a petition to challenge the disqualification process and push for a judicial review. It didn't gain enough support to reach Parliament – but that doesn't mean the issue has gone away. The need for reform is urgent. Like so many injustices, it's easy to ignore until it lands on your doorstep. That's exactly why I spoke up – and why I'll keep going.

Because the cost of injustice in this system is personal. When someone is disqualified after years of service, it's not just the end of a career. It's financial strain. Emotional strain. Reputational harm. Good people – who have given everything to the care and protection of children – get shut out by a system that shut them down without a fair hearing. And it doesn't just hurt them. It hurts the whole system.

When those professionals walk away, children lose the adults they trust. Relationships break. Teams weaken. The workforce thins. Progress is interrupted, and it becomes harder to offer the stability and care those children deserve.

Disqualifying people without proper safeguards or a meaningful right of reply doesn't protect children. It protects a broken system.

Registered managers knew what was at stake. Disqualification meant being out of work, with no employment rights and serious financial consequences – and they had seen it happen to others. Years after the introduction of the fit-person process, a warning was finally added to the start of the interview. Some inspectors delivered it bluntly: *"Do you realise that if you fail this interview, you will never work with children again?"*

From that moment, the tone was set. It didn't feel like a conversation about skills or experience – it felt like an interrogation. The message was clear: the stakes were high, the scrutiny intense, and there was very little room for error. That single question put fear front and centre, making it impossible to forget what was at risk.

For many, that anxiety never left. The pressure, the unpredictability of inspections, and the constant risk of 'getting it wrong' pushed people over the edge. Some moved into roles as Regulation 44 visitors or Responsible Individuals – still involved, but at a safer distance from Ofsted. Some left altogether.

Under Ofsted's critical eye, the shelf life of those on the front line – caregivers, teachers, social workers – was getting shorter. The emotional toll, the pressure, and the fear that even a small misstep could have serious consequences left fewer people willing or able to stay the course.

The impact was undeniable. Services lost experienced, dedicated professionals. Teams became stretched, overworked, and increasingly reliant on less experienced staff still finding their feet. And most worrying of all, children – already vulnerable and in need of stability – were left with fewer trusted adults to support them.

But this wasn't just a workforce crisis – it was a systemic failure. Safeguarding and regulation are meant to protect children. But they must also ensure fair, transparent, and effective processes for those working in the sector. When oversight feels more like punishment than support – when good professionals are driven out rather than developed, trusted, and retained – safeguarding itself is weakened.

There is no escaping the truth: flawed oversight damages lives. In high-profile cases like the Rotherham child exploitation scandal, professionals failed to act, allowing harm to continue unchecked. At the same time, others have had their careers and reputations destroyed by investigations built on flawed or incomplete information.

Regulation is supposed to be a safety net. But when it fails to distinguish between genuine safeguarding risks and procedural errors, it becomes a blunt instrument – harming both the people it was meant to protect, and those trying to protect them.

The Bichard Inquiry, launched after the Soham murders, led to reforms aimed at improving accountability – including the introduction of the Local Authority Designated Officer (LADO) role to ensure allegations were handled fairly. But despite these changes, the same fundamental issues remained. Some professionals still found themselves unaware of accusations made against them, judged on decisions made without full context, and left with no real opportunity to defend themselves. Meanwhile, others slipped through the net, continuing to work in the sector despite serious concerns about their conduct.

These weren't just bureaucratic failures. They had real consequences – for careers, for safeguarding, and for trust in the system itself.

For those who remained in the sector, the Fit Person interview became yet another ordeal. In theory, it was designed to assess competence and suitability. In practice, many professionals said it was more like an interrogation than an interview. Some walked out unsure of what had just happened – only that their future now rested in the hands of people who held all the power, but not necessarily all the facts.

The weight of these experiences didn't fall only on those

being assessed. It rippled across entire teams, creating anxiety and uncertainty for staff – and for the young people they were there to support. Delays, inconsistent decision-making, and the sheer unpredictability of the process undermined trust in a system that should have inspired confidence.

It wasn't just the policies that were doing harm – it was how people were being treated in practice. A notetaker described a hostile atmosphere: relentless questioning, minimal breaks, and only a single small bottle of water during an interview that went on for hours. Social workers, staff, and even young people raised concerns. Over time, the pressure began to wear people down. Long hours, constant exposure to trauma, and the emotional demands of the work all took their toll. Some burned out. Others kept going, but with less to give.

And the pressure never let up. Ofsted's prove-it game was relentless. Every decision, every conversation, every instinct had to be written down, justified, and ready to withstand scrutiny – not just in the moment, but weeks, months, or even years later. Their mantra was clear: *"If it's not written down, it didn't happen."* It wasn't enough to do the right thing – you had to evidence it, exactly, repeatedly, and in a format that ticked all the right boxes. But even then, documentation was flawed by interpretation. I learned very early in my career that what is transmitted is not always what's received. Anyone who has ever played a game of Chinese Whispers will tell you the same.

Over time, it stopped being about care and became a compliance exercise. Less about children. More about covering your back. It chipped away at trust – not just between professionals and inspectors, but sometimes within teams. People second-guessed themselves. Some doubted their own judgment and became reluctant to make decisions at all – afraid of getting it wrong, or of not being able to defend their actions later. The work became procedural. It became risk averse. It became something else entirely.

Researchers call it *'compassion fatigue'* – a form of secondary trauma that builds up when you're exposed to pain for too long without the space or support to process it. Even the most committed staff can begin to feel numb, drained, and worn out.

But this isn't just about coping better. It's about creating the right conditions to do the work well – and still have something left to give at the end of the day. Because the quality of care children receive depends on the wellbeing of the adults around them. And yet, even as I tried to hold space for others, life had its own way of testing my own strength.

The news was grim: COVID-19 deaths in the UK had surpassed 40,000. Just a month later, Patrick – Mum's second husband and the love of her life – passed away. As soon as we got the call, Mark and I set off, though it took over an hour to reach her.

My sisters were four hours away, in Hampshire and Ipswich. My brother, living with cancer and unable to risk travelling, was in Scotland. Patrick's COPD had worsened during lockdown, and by the time we arrived, the ambulance crew had already confirmed he was gone.

His funeral, limited to close family, was streamed for those who couldn't attend – including my brother. Like so many families during the pandemic, we felt the cruel weight of separation. Grief made heavier by distance and circumstance. Meanwhile, the nation celebrated resilience.

In July, Captain Tom was knighted by the Queen at Windsor Castle. Bailouts were announced for theatres, museums, and cultural venues, as well as the food, hospitality, film, and TV industries. Public sector workers – including doctors and teachers – received an above-inflation pay rise. And while the Institute for Fiscal Studies warned that taxes might need to increase to fund these measures, spirits were briefly lifted by news of promising vaccine developments.

As I continued to navigate the challenges within the system, I found myself reflecting more often on the importance of resilience – not just in institutions, but in our personal lives. The weight of responsibility, the fight for fairness, and the frustration of a system that too often failed those it was meant to protect had taken its toll.

And yet, even in the midst of it all, there were still moments of joy. Glimpses of life beyond the struggle.

19

UBUNTU
I Am Because We Are

When seven Greek islands were removed from the quarantine exemption list for travellers arriving in England, we were relieved to learn that mainland Greece remained quarantine-free. This meant Sarah and Josh's wedding could still go ahead – a rare piece of good news in a year of uncertainty. Then, when Prime Minister Boris Johnson reassured the public that the government was doing *'everything in its power'* to avoid another lockdown, it finally felt like things were falling into place.

Two weeks later, on a beautiful sunny day, Mark and I boarded the plane with my mum. It was bittersweet, knowing that Patrick's passing had made this trip possible for her. Still, as we touched down, the warm Mediterranean breeze greeted us, lifting our spirits as we eagerly awaited the flight from London carrying Emma, our son-in-law Jacob, and our precious grandchildren.

The drive from the airport took just under an hour, winding through the Taygetos Mountains. We passed tiny villages, endless olive groves, and the occasional goat standing stubbornly in the road. As we descended toward the coast, the sea came into view – brilliant blue, shimmering in the afternoon sun. And then, there it was: Stoupa. This was where Sarah and Josh had chosen to get married, and it wasn't just because of the stunning beaches or warm evening air. Josh's father had lived here before he passed away, and holding the wedding in Stoupa was their way of honouring him, of making sure he was part of their day. It felt right. After such a difficult year, this was something joyful, something to hold onto.

But Stoupa is more than just a beautiful place – it has a story of its own. This was where Nikos Kazantzakis found the inspiration for Zorba the Greek. He spent time here with George Zorbas, a miner whose larger-than-life personality shaped the novel. If you haven't read it (or seen the film), Zorba the Greek is about a bookish intellectual who steps away from his studies to start a lignite mine in Crete. He meets Zorba, a wild, passionate, unpredictable man who teaches him that life isn't meant to be analysed – it's meant to be lived.

The story has its share of heartbreak, but at its core, it's about resilience. No matter what happens, Zorba dances. In the final scene, after everything has collapsed, he doesn't dwell on failure – he just throws his arms out, kicks up the dust, and dances on the beach, laughing in the face of it all. That scene became iconic, and Zorba became a symbol of embracing life, no matter what it throws at you.

Standing there in Stoupa, where the real Zorba once lived, I couldn't help but think about how much his story connects to my own professional life. The unpredictability, the highs and lows, the heartbreak, the absurdity of it all – it seems to sum it up perfectly. There have been moments when I felt like the narrator, trying to make sense of a system that doesn't always make sense. And there have been times when, despite everything, the only thing left to do was to keep going, keep moving forward, and maybe even dance a little.

Three days later, on the jetty overlooking the harbour, Sarah and Josh tied the knot. Although the absence of friends who couldn't travel from America and New Zealand was deeply felt, the celebration that followed was perfect in every way. The taverna's patio was draped in twinkling fairy lights, casting a warm, romantic glow over the gathering. As guests mingled and applauded the arrival of the newlyweds, all eyes were drawn to Sarah, her hair in loose waves adorned with a delicate floral crown, wearing a stunning boho dress that perfectly matched the rustic charm of the setting.

Our beautiful granddaughter and handsome grandson played a special part in the day as the sweetest little bridesmaid and pageboy. With a tiny wreath of flowers on her head and an infectious smile, our granddaughter walked down the jetty with such grace, stepping carefully, fully focused on getting it just right. Beside her, our grandson, determined to keep pace, stayed close. Watching over them with pride was Emma, their loving mum. As they followed Sarah to the end of the jetty, her husband-to-be looked on, his eyes filled with love and anticipation. That moment reflected everything this day was about.

As the day unfolded, the air was rich with the aromas of Greek cuisine – grilled lamb, chicken, and seafood, served alongside ripe tomatoes, cucumbers, baskets of warm, crusty bread, and bowls of tzatziki. Plates of sweet baklava followed, all washed down with champagne and local wine. After the speeches, the celebrations continued with traditional Greek dancing and plate smashing, much to the shock and delight of our grandchildren. Later, as night fell, guests gathered on rugs around a campfire, listening to the haunting sound of a lone saxophone playing on the lantern-lit beach.

It was a perfect evening – one that reluctantly gave way to reality. The celebration was over all too soon, and we returned to the sobering news of a four-week lockdown beginning on

Bonfire Night. Just before that, new travel rules were announced, requiring most travellers from Greece to quarantine for two weeks.

Fortunately, we escaped that, and despite the looming restrictions, Sarah's wedding felt like a miracle – a moment that somehow happened, against all the odds. In a year shaped by so much uncertainty, it was a reminder of what truly matters.

It wasn't just about Sarah and Josh getting married. It was about family, and the strength of the bonds that hold us together when everything else feels like it's falling apart. As we danced, the music seemed to defy the pandemic – a celebration of life that refused to be dimmed. The laughter, the clinking of glasses, the joy of being together – it all felt like an act of quiet resistance in the middle of a difficult year.

To this day, I think of it as a miracle wedding – not just for Sarah and Josh, but for all of us. In a year overshadowed by restrictions, grief, and constant change, it was a gift. A reminder that even in the hardest times, life still finds ways to surprise us with beauty and connection.

It wasn't just the vows or the setting. It was the resilience behind it all – our ability to adapt, to show up for each other, and to celebrate what we have, even when the world around us is standing still. That night, under the stars, it didn't feel like just a wedding. It felt like a turning point. A moment of light, reminding us that no matter what life throws our way, our shared humanity – if we allow it – will always bring us back to what matters most.

But elsewhere trust was unravelling. On the eve of England's second lockdown in 2020, the government came under fire for its handling of COVID data. During a Downing Street press conference on 31 October, questions were raised about the lack of transparency behind the Office for National Statistics' death projections. The government admitted there had been mistakes in its briefing but stood by the broader message: COVID was putting the NHS under immense strain.

I didn't doubt the NHS was struggling – how could it not be? But I also knew COVID-19 wasn't the whole story. After years working in health and social care, I'd seen the cracks in the system long before the pandemic. The virus didn't create these problems – it just made them impossible to ignore.

One moment, from back in 2002, when I was working as a hospital social worker has stayed with me. I was on a hospital ward and saw an elderly woman calling out for help. She was clearly in pain. Staff were nearby, but no one responded. I waited, assuming someone would step in. No one did. Eventually, I raised it – and was brushed off. It wasn't an isolated incident. I'd seen it before, and I saw it again many times after. Staff were present, but often disengaged, stretched too thin, or caught in a system that didn't prioritise patient care the way it should.

The problem wasn't that people didn't care. They did – and it showed. But over time, the system changed. Hospitals became less about care and more about targets, budgets, and box-ticking. Even before COVID, the balance between efficiency and empathy had started to shift. The pandemic didn't cause that shift – it just exposed it.

Nearly two decades later, those same cracks were no longer hidden – they were in plain sight. COVID didn't just strain the NHS; it overwhelmed it. But what stood out wasn't only the pressure or the flaws – it was the relentless effort of frontline staff, doing their best under impossible conditions, even as the government was quietly outsourcing key responsibilities behind the scenes.

At the same time, the public narrative told through daily briefings often felt disconnected. Charts and statistics dominated – hospital capacity, case numbers, infection rates – yet the data was frequently framed to defend policy, not to tell the whole story. The crisis was real, the numbers were real – but the human cost behind them was harder to see. And that was something no graph could ever capture.

It made me think more about how data is used – not just to inform, but to influence. It's not only about the numbers themselves, but how they're framed, what's emphasised, and what's left out. The same dataset can tell very different stories, depending on who's telling them – and what they want people to believe.

This wasn't a new phenomenon, but COVID put it under the spotlight. I'd long been interested in how messaging influences behaviour – how statistics, when carefully packaged, can push a particular agenda. That curiosity goes back to when I first learned about the Behavioural Insights Team (BIT), introduced under David Cameron. The 'Nudge Unit', as it was known, used psychology and behavioural economics to subtly shape public behaviour.

It reminded me of a conversation I had with my dad as a child, about subliminal advertising – how hidden messages could slip beneath our conscious awareness and influence us without us even realising. He told me those techniques were banned the year I was born.

Both approaches struck me as sneaky. Subliminal advertising, with its covert messaging, and behavioural insights, with their structured, carefully designed nudges – both were about steering people, just by different means. It felt like a new version of an old trick. This wasn't just about manipulating perception – it was about how data was presented, framed, and sometimes distorted to influence decisions.

The problem with relying too heavily on data is that it can be incomplete, outdated, or built on flawed assumptions. And when decisions are driven purely by numbers, the system often fails to address the underlying issues – confirmation bias, inequality, and chronic underfunding – that are already there. Rather than solving these problems, data-driven approaches can reinforce them. Children's lives were reduced to data points and performance metrics, while their real struggles, emotions, and needs were overlooked.

And it wasn't just happening in social care. Algorithms were playing a growing role in shaping decisions across every part of life – what news people saw, which adverts followed them around, even which voices were amplified online. These tools were meant to make things more efficient, but they also had an invisible influence, quietly nudging people in particular directions – often without them realising.

It took time for people to understand just how powerful those algorithms had become – especially on social media. The role they played in the 2016 US election and the Brexit referendum should have been a clear warning. Tailored content could manipulate beliefs, fuel division, and spread misinformation at an alarming scale. But not everyone paid attention. It was only when the impact began to show up in the lives of young people that the consequences became harder to ignore.

The more I thought about how algorithms were shaping decisions, the more I started to see the same pattern elsewhere – particularly in how success was measured and accountability operated in public services. In children's social care, data had taken centre stage. The focus had shifted from understanding lived experiences to producing the right numbers. Regulation, too, had become less about children and families, and more about what could be shown on a spreadsheet.

I saw this firsthand with Ofsted. Inspections were supposed to uphold standards, but increasingly, they felt procedural. Success was being defined through quantifiable outcomes – placement moves, school attendance, adoption figures. But those numbers never captured what mattered most: the emotional toll of instability, the reasons behind a child's school refusal, the slow, quiet work of rebuilding trust. They couldn't reflect the strength of relationships or the day-to-day reality of supporting children and families through incredibly complex situations.

Too often, data shaped the narrative. A drop in care entries was presented as a win, even when higher thresholds meant families in crisis weren't getting early help. An increase in adoptions was labelled a success, without asking whether children had been moved on too quickly, or whether enough had been done to keep families together. In chasing targets, long-term impacts – like the trauma of unnecessary separation – were overlooked.

This was never clearer than during inspections. I remember another late night, reviewing a draft report – determined to correct inaccuracies and make sense of what had been written. That's when I came across the *Regulators' Code*, outlining principles like fairness, transparency, and proportionality. But what I was witnessing didn't reflect any of that.

Regulation hadn't always felt this way. Before Ofsted took over, inspections allowed more room for dialogue. Under the Commission for Social Care Inspection (CSCI), inspectors understood the complexity of care. Success wasn't reduced to metrics. There were honest conversations. Scrutiny was still part of it, but it felt purposeful. The goal was improvement, not just compliance.

After Ofsted took over in 2007, the tone changed. Inspections became more rigid, with judgments pinned to performance data. The intention may have been consistency, but the nuance of the work was often lost. The numbers told one part of the story – but not the whole one.

What stood out to me over time – something I never saw reflected in inspection reports – was the number of children returning to care from failed adoptions. I hadn't tracked adoption statistics closely, but I'd seen what happened when placements broke down. Children came back carrying more pain, more mistrust, more instability. These experiences didn't fit neatly into frameworks or key indicators, but they shaped the system profoundly.

Inspections no longer felt like a space for reflection or growth. They brought the weight of judgement. We found ourselves preparing defensively – gathering documents, cross-checking evidence – not because it made the service better, but because we knew how easily the narrative could be shaped without context. The focus had shifted – from improving practice to protecting performance.

Of course, accountability matters – especially in services that work with vulnerable children. But when regulation shifts to biased compliance, it raises difficult questions. Does a standardised, data-driven approach truly improve care, or does it reduce services to tick-box exercises? Does it raise standards, or does it create a culture where professionals are more focused on inspection outcomes than meaningful change?

These were the questions I kept coming back to in the early hours, trying to make sense of a system that seemed to be losing sight of what mattered most: the children themselves.

The more I sat with those questions, the clearer it became that this wasn't just a matter of inconvenience – rigid, data-focused regulation was having real consequences. When services spend more time proving their worth than delivering care, something is deeply wrong. The shift had created a climate of anxiety, where providers became more concerned with compliance than with what children actually need.

At times, challenging inspection findings felt necessary. But pushing back carried risks. Ofsted held the power to shape public perception, and questioning its judgments could be seen not as a commitment to fairness, but as defiance. Still, with so much at stake, silence wasn't always an option.

Regulation is meant to uphold standards and provide oversight – but when the process becomes a power struggle rather than a shared pursuit of fairness, the entire system suffers. When authority goes unchecked, it diverts care and erodes trust in the very systems meant to protect children.

And I wasn't alone in these concerns. Many colleagues felt the same. Reports, forums, and conversations increasingly pointed to a pattern: regulators more focused on protecting their authority than listening, learning, or correcting course. Mistakes weren't acknowledged – they were defended. And when that happens, it becomes even harder to do the work that really makes a difference.

This wasn't just a recent shift – it had deeper roots. When Ofsted took over the inspection of children's social care in 2007, it brought with it a framework designed for education. The model emphasised standardisation, measurable outcomes, and performance data. On paper, that may have seemed logical. But children's social care is not a school – and applying an education-based model to such a complex, relational, and human field was always going to fall short.

In this new system, success became something that could be tracked numerically – placement stability, school attendance, safeguarding alerts. These were the data points inspectors could log, monitor, and compare.

But the realities of children's lives don't fit neatly into performance metrics. Trust, emotional safety, meaningful relationships – these are central to care, yet they became secondary to whatever could be counted. Take safeguarding alerts, as one example. These were often treated as signs of failure rather than as evidence of vigilance or early intervention. And the language used matters.

What one person considers a serious safeguarding concern, another may not. Ofsted resisted defining it for a long time, and when guidance was finally introduced, it did little to resolve the inconsistency. This kind of subjectivity has real consequences: homes that reported more concerns were often scrutinised more heavily, regardless of context. It created a culture where openness could be punished, and silence mistaken for success.

This shift didn't just change the way services were judged. It changed how they operated. The pressure to produce good outcomes turned inspections into high-stakes events – events that could affect funding, leadership, and long-term viability. A single failure to notify Ofsted of a 'serious incident' could result in an inadequate rating for leadership and management – even though the term 'serious' was not clearly defined. It was left to professional judgment, but when there was disagreement, it was the inspector's view that carried weight.

Regulation, though, was only part of the story. The cracks in the system had been visible for years – ignored, downplayed, or lost in endless debates about structure and funding. Then the pandemic hit, and those cracks became impossible to ignore. The pressure revealed just how fragile, fragmented, and overstretched the system really was.

And yet, rather than tackling the deeper injustices, much of the public debate – often shaped by media headlines – remained focused on the role of independent providers. It became a convenient distraction from the real failures that left vulnerable children at risk.

Independent providers – once viewed as part of the solution – were increasingly cast as villains in the ongoing public-versus-private debate. Small providers were unfairly lumped together with large corporate providers increasingly backed by private equity. The nuance was lost, and with it, the recognition of the vital role many of these smaller services played. As a result, their futures were put at risk. Meanwhile, the noise of ideological conflict drowned out the real, urgent issues: chronic underfunding, rising thresholds, workforce burnout, and a slow erosion of trust across the sector.

As the challenges in the care system continued to grow, so did the calls for reform. The failures were undeniable, yet tangible action remained just out of reach. Many of us – especially those who had spent years working for change – were looking for something to hope for, a sign that improvement was possible.

On 15 January 2021, the government finally announced the long-awaited Independent Review of Children's Social Care. That very same day, Yusuf passed away – just ten days before his fifty-eighth birthday. For those of us who had known him and benefitted from his wisdom, the timing was bittersweet – a painful reminder of what had been lost.

His death was a deeply personal loss. But it also brought into sharper focus the long-term consequences of childhood adversity, especially for adults raised in state care. For many, the impact doesn't end when they leave care. The effects echo across a lifetime. Research into Adverse Childhood Experiences (ACEs) shows that exposure to high levels of trauma in childhood significantly increases the risk of poor physical and mental health outcomes. Some studies suggest that having six or more ACEs can reduce life expectancy by as much as 20 years.

In his 2018 TED Talk, Benjamin Perks, himself a care leaver and UNICEF diplomat reminded us that childhood adversity doesn't have to become a life sentence. That message is more than a statistic – it reflects the lived experience of so many care-experienced individuals. ACEs are linked to a wide range of long-term challenges, including autoimmune disorders, heart disease, and chronic mental health conditions.

Three years later, the pandemic only widened those inequalities. Yusuf, who had an underlying health condition, was particularly vulnerable to COVID. Sadly, he was one of those who didn't survive.

After watching Ben's TED Talk, I reached out and invited him to present to the TCTC Children's Interest Group I was chairing at the time. Much to my surprise, not only did he agree – but during the session, he revealed that he, too, was care-experienced. Here was a UNICEF diplomat, openly sharing his personal history with a room full of professionals. His honesty reinforced something I've long believed: that real change begins with authenticity and human connection. But more than that, the lived experience of both those receiving care and those providing it must be at the heart of any reform.

Yusuf's passing wasn't just a loss for his family – it was a devastating loss for the children he was fostering. These children had formed strong attachments to him, and his sudden absence left a deep emotional impact – one that's too often overlooked in moments like this. It was a stark reminder of just how essential caregivers are to the children they support. Because without caregivers, there simply is no care.

They are the foundation of any system built to protect and nurture children. Without them, no amount of regulation, policy, or funding can fill the gap. Yet too often, the system treats them as secondary – as if the needs of children and those who care for them are separate, when in fact they are profoundly connected.

We need to confront the fundamental flaws in the care system. This means moving away from fear-driven regulation and toward reform that centres care, connection, and well-being. A functioning care system must support both children and those who look after them. If we continue to overlook caregivers, we will keep failing the very children the system is meant to serve – and the adults they become will continue to carry the weight of that failure.

Yusuf believed in being the difference – in showing up, staying present, and doing the work that mattered, even when the system made it hard. If we want real reform, we must start

there: with people like Yusuf, who are willing to be the difference
– in deeds, not words.

A COLOUR FULL LIFE
(A TRIBUTE TO YUSUF PAUL)

From this window, like the moon, we close the distance.
*The distance between you
and our collective sorrow.*

*With thoughts and verse,
a kaleidoscope of painted hues,
we somehow hope to capture
the very essence of you.*

Man of Purple:
*The serene stability of blue,
transcending all inflicted wounds,
bleeding calm instead of hate—
combined with the fierce energy of red:
resolute, committed, fixed, certain, uncompromising.*

*Purple, representing wisdom and dignity—
both of which you treasured.
Power and ambition—
both of which you grasped.
Devotion and creativity—
both of which you lived.*

Man of Black:
*Without black, all colours have no depth—
no depth, no variation.
Black, representing strength and authority—
both of which you embodied.
Elegance and sophistication—
both of which you carried so well.*

Although we now grieve your loss,
you will always dwell in that sacred place:
our collective love,
where no shadow of loss can ever hold you captive again.

May you continue to inspire us,
until we again see your beautiful face—
in that place where no tear falls,
and there are no more goodbyes.

Until then we salute you
and celebrate your life full of colour:

YOUR COLOURFUL LIFE.

—Tamsin Trevorrow

Little Girl in a Red Coat

I never thought a having a daughter—
but when you came to my world,
I knew you were her.

Your curly hair bounced in the wind,
and your eyes were round and brown,
like conkers glinting in the sun.

"You make me laugh," you said to me.

We bought you a red coat,
red with black collar.
I see you now:
white socks, black shiny shoes,
red coat, stepping out the door...

Without me.
Into your new life.
Small hand in your new daddy's hand,
your other hand still wrapped around my heart.

—Sarah McCormack

20

WHEN REFORM FAILS THE MOST VULNERABLE
Innovation or Illusion

On 16 March 2021, World Social Work Day embraced the theme of Ubuntu – an African philosophy that highlights the interconnectedness of individuals within a community, promoting values like compassion, mutual respect, and collective responsibility. In alignment with this theme, *Your Life Your Story (YLYS)* honoured Yusuf with a heartfelt tribute titled *'Ubuntu: I Am Because We Are'*, celebrating his unwavering commitment to fostering unity and community well-being. Central to Ubuntu is the belief that individuals cannot thrive in isolation; their well-being is tied to the welfare of the wider community. This perspective promotes communal harmony and reminds us that true success is measured not by individual achievements but by how we help others to thrive.

Just a few weeks later, on 17 April, the world watched as Queen Elizabeth II sat alone at her husband's funeral. The image was striking – a moment of resilience, but also one of profound isolation. Her solitude spoke volumes – a quiet, public reminder of the truth at the heart of Ubuntu: that even in grief, even in silence, we remain connected.

This philosophy – rooted in care, dignity, and the intrinsic value of every individual – should have been at the heart of children's social care in England. Instead, the system was drowning in politics, bureaucracy, and media-driven policymaking. Rather than centring care and compassion, reform after reform moved in the opposite direction – prioritising votes and financial incentives over the needs of children.

One clear example of this short-term thinking can be seen in adoption policy.

The six-month time limit on adoption decisions, introduced to reduce delay, reflects a broader tendency toward reactive policymaking. While the goal of securing early permanence may have been well-intentioned, it often prioritised speed over substance. Social workers, under intense pressure to meet deadlines, were left making life-changing decisions without the space for relational judgement or ethical nuance. In trying to prevent drift, the system risked making rushed, irreversible choices that favoured compliance over care.

I have known many adopted children who re-entered the care system. This is not a rare occurrence – and yet, it remains largely unexamined. There is currently no official record of adoption breakdowns, a silence that reflects a troubling lack of interest in long-term outcomes. Without this data, we cannot claim to be learning from the past, nor can we make informed decisions about the future.

These systemic pressures extend beyond frontline delivery or regulatory shortcomings – they are rooted in the economics of care itself. Whether services are delivered by the public sector, private companies, or charities, financial frameworks increasingly determine what kind of care is available – and to whom.

Not-for-profit organisations, often seen as the ethical alternative, are not without contradiction. While their stated mission is to serve vulnerable communities, some have come under scrutiny for the growing gap between leadership pay and frontline provision. In 2022, Barnardo's highest-paid employee earned between £250,000 and £260,000, while the median CEO salary for large charities rose to £175,000 in 2023 – figures that stand in stark contrast to the financial rewards available to those delivering direct care. Similar concerns have been raised about Oxfam, Cancer Research UK, and the NSPCC, highlighting an increasingly uncomfortable divide between mission and money.

Beyond salaries, the financial models of many not-for-profits often mirror those of private companies. Many rely on repayable finance – loans, investment capital, and other credit-based instruments – to sustain operations. Banks and financial institutions do not lend without expecting returns. As a result, organisations must prioritise financial viability, often at the expense of their core mission.

This growing reliance on debt financing creates pressure to generate predictable income streams. Instead of focusing solely on children's needs, organisations are forced to make decisions shaped by financial obligations. While financial responsibility is necessary, the risk is that funding and repayment requirements begin to drive strategy – pushing care to the margins. It raises a difficult ethical question: when choices must be made, whose interests are being served?

The rise of private equity-backed providers in social care has only intensified this debate. Critics argue that financial motives too often override children's wellbeing – and in some cases, those concerns are well-founded. But the debate is frequently too narrow, fixated on profit alone, rather than acknowledging that inefficiencies and misaligned incentives exist across all sectors – public, private, and voluntary.

Rising demand, workforce shortages, and complex regulatory frameworks have driven up costs across the board. Focusing solely on removing for-profit providers risks ignoring the deeper, structural failures: inconsistent commissioning, fragmented oversight, the increasing reliance on agency staff, and inefficiencies within the public sector all contribute to a system struggling to meet need.

Some argue that financial viability is non-negotiable – without it, care providers simply wouldn't exist. There is truth in that. The sector lacks adequate funding, and without financial support – whether public or private – homes cannot be built, staff cannot be hired, and essential services would collapse. Others point out that not all private providers are driven purely by profit. Some reinvest in their services and raise standards in ways that overstretched public and voluntary providers cannot always match.

However, when financial sustainability becomes the dominant priority, the quality of care inevitably suffers. Even in not-for-profit settings, the pressure to secure contracts and maintain income streams can shift decisions away from those who need the most support.

In large organisations, success is often measured by occupancy rates, budget savings, and expansion – rather than by emotional stability, trusted relationships, or long-term wellbeing. Yet these are the very things that matter most to children in care, and too often, they are the first to be compromised.

These financial pressures don't just shape how care is delivered – they also influence who is entrusted to lead it.

The inconsistencies in Ofsted's *fit person* process are not merely bureaucratic failings; they carry real and lasting consequences. The process lacks transparency, fairness, and, too frequently, basic humanity. In February 2021, grappling with the fallout of these decisions I wrote '*Why it is necessary to end the unfair disqualification of caregivers'*. It was my attempt to give voice to what so many were feeling, but few felt able to say out loud.

At the same time, a lack of transparency in decision-making has allowed individuals with troubling histories to re-register under new organisations – continuing to run services despite past failings. Even Ofsted's own reports acknowledge these inconsistencies, yet they persist.

Surely, given the level of responsibility placed on registered managers – and the impact their role has on the lives of some of the most vulnerable children in society – it would make far more sense to elevate their professional status. Registered managers should be recognised and registered in the same way as social workers, supported by a clear and independent framework for accountability. Most importantly, the fit person process must be disentangled from all commercial interests, ethical or otherwise. This is a matter of safeguarding, not business.

More broadly, inspections have become more of a bureaucratic formality than a tool for genuine improvement. A well-written policy can carry more weight than the actual quality of day-to-day care. Inconsistent enforcement, regulatory loopholes, and the quiet re-registration of managers from failing services contribute to a cycle of failure. The disconnect between oversight and lived experience means serious issues often go unnoticed – until a crisis forces a response.

Caregivers are the foundation of any system designed to protect and nurture children. Without them, no regulation, policy, or funding can fill the gap. Yet too often, the system treats caregivers as secondary – failing to recognise that the wellbeing of children is inseparable from the wellbeing of those who support them. No amount of policy, funding, or compliance can repair a system that has lost its heart.

Ofsted's high-stakes inspection regime has only deepened these pressures. While standards matter, the rigid framework has fostered a culture of caution – discouraging providers from accepting children with complex needs for fear of jeopardising their ratings. Smaller providers, unable to absorb this scrutiny, have been forced to close or sell to larger corporations. The resulting consolidation has disrupted placements, severed critical relationships, and left local authorities with fewer options – further destabilising the lives of children in care.

Blair's reforms serve as a cautionary tale of the risks when market-driven solutions are introduced without proper safeguards. Self-interest exists in every sector – whether in inflated executive salaries, nepotism in public administration, or profit-seeking in private companies. But the focus must go beyond ideological debates. Regulation needs to do more than tick boxes; it must ensure transparency, accountability, and genuine child-centred care. When oversight fails to challenge systemic issues, it doesn't just weaken protections – it enables the very problems it was meant to prevent.

Every child placed in a home that values ratings over relationships, every professional burned out by bureaucracy, and every whistleblower silenced by fear reflects a system that's lost sight of its purpose.

Safeguarding can't thrive in a culture of fear, and care won't improve in systems driven by compliance. And reform won't work if those doing the work are treated as disposable.

It's time to return to the values that matter most – compassion, integrity, accountability, and care. This isn't just about policy change; it's a cultural shift. Until we refocus on child-centred care, and support those who deliver it, no reform will lead to lasting change.

When the internal market was introduced to me in the 1990s, training on the purchaser-provider split focused on identifying who the customer was. In theory, the customer is central to the system, but in practice, there are multiple customers to consider:

the child, the family, local authorities, and the taxpayer who ultimately foots the bill. Each of these groups has different needs and expectations, which complicates the challenge of delivering a service that effectively meets all of them.

Reflecting on my years of experience across different sectors, I've observed a growing trend of bringing in so-called *'innovators'* to lead reform. This movement gained momentum in children's social care in the late 1990s under Tony Blair's leadership. While his famous mantra was *'Education, education, education,'* his real focus seemed to be *'Privatise, privatise, privatise.'* In his drive for change, he overlooked the risks of handing public services over to the market without proper safeguards.

I've worked across the public, voluntary, and private sectors, and I've seen how investment can play a positive role. Private funding has led to the creation of specialist therapeutic homes, advanced training programs, and improved facilities – all of which have benefited children. Many services continue to be run by people who genuinely care and want to create spaces where children can heal and thrive.

But something changed. What began as an opportunity to improve services slowly turned into a business model where financial returns often took precedence over child welfare. Independent providers were no longer just complementing public services; big business began to take over, shifting the focus from people to profit.

Care became a commodity – no longer a duty, but a service to be bought and sold. With the rise of private equity in children's care, decisions shifted from being made by those with expertise in residential childcare to those focused on occupancy, Ofsted ratings and financial performance. The law of supply and demand took over. There were more children needing care than homes available, and instead of investing in quality placements, prices were driven up.

At the same time, corporate investors and opportunists with no background in social care saw returns that were unavailable elsewhere in the market. They didn't enter the sector to improve outcomes – they came to extract profit. What began as an opportunity to raise standards became a lucrative industry, where financial gain eclipsed ethical responsibility. Regulation, intended to safeguard against such risks, has too often lacked transparency and consistency – and ignoring this has allowed the misuse of power to go unchecked. Rather than challenging poor practice, it has fostered fear-led compliance and a culture of blame, undermining the very trust on which good care depends.

Yet, many of us who joined the independent sector in those early days weren't driven by profit. We were motivated by disillusionment – the sense that change wasn't possible within the under-resourced, heavily bureaucratic public sector. We were experienced professionals who wanted to build something better. And for a time, we did.

The independent sector brought fresh thinking, challenged outdated practice, and created homes that felt aspirational rather than institutional. But gradually, the focus shifted. What began as a values-led approach gave way to market forces, and care became increasingly shaped by commercial priorities rather than children's needs.

The same competition that once raised standards began to drive up costs. Profit margins of up to 40 percent appeared in some company accounts – but the gains didn't go into care. They were channelled into executive pay and shareholder dividends, while many caregivers – the people actually looking after children – were left to survive on less than the living Wage.

By 2016, the effects of an increasingly market-driven care system were impossible to ignore. Private providers were accused of profiteering – some, undoubtedly, were. Others were barely staying afloat. But regardless of their balance sheets, the pressure fell hardest on the homes themselves. Empty beds didn't stay empty for long. Children were placed rapidly, often without proper consideration of fit or need. Same-day placement requests became increasingly common, reflecting a system more focused on availability than suitability. Fostering agencies, meanwhile, were largely spared the same scrutiny.

On paper, matching decisions lie with the registered manager – a responsibility set out clearly in the Children's Homes (England) Regulations 2015, particularly under the standards on care planning and leadership. But in practice, those decisions are often made higher up the chain. Managers may be overruled by those prioritising commercial or operational demands – yet they remain legally and professionally accountable for what follows.

It's a well-established contradiction in the sector: the power to decide is often taken away, but the weight of responsibility remains. Managers are left with an impossible choice – comply and carry the risk, or step away.

In reality, it turns the manager into a scapegoat. They're the ones left holding the risk – legally, professionally, and emotionally – when a placement breaks down or a child is harmed. Their name is on the registration. Their judgment is questioned in inspections. And it's their name on the report, even when the decision wasn't truly theirs. It creates a system where accountability is blurred, but blame is sharply focused. And in the long run, it demoralises staff and drives good managers out – people who might have stayed, had they been trusted to do the job they're held responsible for.

As one residential worker put it simply: *'The responsibility is immense, but the rewards don't reflect that.'* A team leader had just quit to become a dog walker – because it was less stressful, paid more, and offered a better work-life balance. For many, it wasn't just about being away from home for 24 hours, two or three times a week, or about the money – it was about feeling valued.

That sense of being undervalued ran deeper than pay. Regulation became increasingly rigid, slowly choking the innovation that once defined the sector. Ofsted inspections fostered a culture of fear, where compliance began to matter more than care. Bureaucracy ballooned, and risk aversion took over. Proving good practice on paper became more important than actually delivering it on the ground.

The system has become so fixated on process and compliance that it's lost sight of what it truly means to care. Until we address that disconnect, no amount of regulations, frameworks, or reforms will bring the change that children and caregivers so urgently need.

For a while, I think the mixed economy worked well – the eggs weren't all in one basket. But in their haste to privatise, the Blair government failed to anticipate the long-term impact of big business. In the end, it simply replaced one monopoly with another, leaving the sector dominated by a handful of powerful players. What was intended to introduce competition and choice has, in practice, been widely criticised for consolidating power and diminishing service quality, and holding the public purse to ransom.

It became less about how to care – and more about how to compete. Despite political promises that greater privatisation would increase competition, improve quality, and drive down prices, the opposite happened. Costs kept rising – driven not only by profit margins, but also by growing layers of regulation and oversight that added complexity without necessarily improving care.

As the culture shifted, so did people's choices. Not everyone left for better pay or status – but some did. While most caregivers remain deeply committed, there are always those who put self-interest above the needs of children. Some really do walk out on Christmas Eve to avoid working the Christmas rota.

Policy has helped shape a system built on financial success – one that too often rewards the wrong things. Climbing the ladder is faster, better paid, and more appealing. But with the title and salary comes greater responsibility and accountability. In a world where one mistake can end a career, that weight is heavy – and too often unrecognised. Fast-track leadership schemes were introduced to attract talent and drive change, but alongside regulatory pressure and a culture of blame, they've contributed to a workforce stretched thin – where the emotional and ethical demands of care are frequently sidelined.

But even so, the landscape wasn't entirely lost. Despite the dominance of corporate providers, some held onto their values and resisted the pressure to cut corners. It reminded me of the high street – how supermarkets and big chains reshaped it, pushing out many independents and leaving something unrecognisable behind. But not all disappeared. butcher, the baker, the hardware shop and the cafe – so-called lifestyle businesses – survived not by competing on scale, but by offering trust, reliability, and human connection. Their livelihoods depended on their reputation, and that meant showing up, doing things properly, and being known for it.

The same can be said of children's social care. While the big players took over, a handful of smaller, values-led providers kept going. Some continued to strive for high standards, even while hanging on by a thread. Their survival is a quiet reminder of what independent provision once stood for – and why I still believe it brought something vital to children's social care: a refusal to accept that care homes had to be bleak, underfunded places where children merely survived rather than thrived.

But I also saw how quickly those ideals eroded without the right safeguards. The balance tipped. Independent care, once a force for positive change, became an industry. And the children – who should have remained at the heart of it all – were no longer seen as individuals to be cared for, but as commodities to be traded in the referral auction, where the lowest bid sealed their fate.

21

BEYOND SLOGANS
Missed Opportunities

The problem was never the existence of private providers. It was the unchecked rise of profit-driven motives, paired with a regulatory system that prioritised compliance over professional judgement and people. Instead of supporting caregivers to help children heal from trauma, we built a system where they are overworked and underpaid – while investors and executives make millions.

What was lost wasn't just the balance between sectors. The system lost sight of what care is truly about. Parenting is at the heart of what care should aim to replicate or restore for children who can't live with their birth families. It's not simply about providing shelter or meeting basic needs – it's about protection, emotional security, consistency, and trust. These are the foundations that support healthy development into adulthood – shaping not only a child's sense of self, but their physical and mental health for years to come.

And the responsibility is enormous. Because the kind of care children receive shapes the kind of adults they become. It influences how they see the world, how they build relationships, how they respond to adversity – and ultimately, how they go on to shape future generations. It's the kind of responsibility that stops you in your tracks – the quiet recognition that your actions will shape someone else's life, and perhaps the lives of those who follow.

Unless we build a system that values and supports caregiving as the core of what care is – with the investment, respect, and stability it deserves – no policy, funding stream, or structural reform will ever create the lasting change children need, or the future they deserve.

This shift away from parenting hasn't only affected children – it's reshaped caregiving itself. Those in direct care roles have been steadily devalued. Residential care workers remain among the lowest-paid and least recognised in the system. Despite the emotional intensity and complexity of their work, sustained investment in training, support, and retention has been minimal.

The structure of social care is designed in a way that pulls skilled professionals away from caregiving. Career progression typically leads to roles in management, regulation, or consultancy – positions that distance people from the very children they trained to support. This leaves those who are often the least experienced, least qualified, and least supported facing the highest emotional demands with the fewest resources. It's a system that struggles to keep expertise where it's needed most.

I think of the manager as the head of the family – someone who sets the tone, provides stability, and supports those in their care. But in some cases, new managers don't stay long enough to complete the fit person process. Others fail and are disqualified from working in the children's workforce, and some who are registered are simply not up to the job. This constant turnover creates instability at the top, leaving staff without consistent leadership and children without a reliable source of support. Those left behind are expected to shoulder complex emotional responsibilities without the training or backup they need.

To begin addressing this, we need to invest in stable, long-term leadership. That means improving recruitment processes, offering meaningful support and training for new managers, and ensuring they feel valued and equipped to stay. Just as a family relies on a steady, capable head, so too do care teams and the children they look after. Stability at the top creates the foundation for a safe, consistent environment – something every child in care deserves.

The issue becomes even clearer when you look at how leadership roles have evolved under pressure. A children's home can't legally be registered without a manager in place – but once the home is open, it doesn't automatically close if the manager leaves. The provider can keep it running while they search for someone new. In theory, that makes sense – you don't want to disrupt children unnecessarily. But in practice, it creates a grey area. Some homes end up operating in limbo for months. And that's where things start to go wrong.

As the pool of experienced managers with a proven track record shrank, and demand for placements grew, salaries for registered managers soared. In some cases, they now earn more than double what a resident doctor makes – despite doctors undergoing years of education, training, and supervision. But this isn't about skill or complexity – it's about necessity. No manager, no registration. So, providers pay whatever it takes to open the doors – or choose to run without registration, knowing the risk of prosecution is low.

In response, multi-home registrations were introduced. Under this model, a single manager can oversee multiple homes – up to four buildings and six children – if they can demonstrate effective oversight. On paper, it appears efficient. In practice, it raises concerns about consistency, quality, and the ability to build meaningful relationships with both staff and children.

In a system that emphasises relational care, it's difficult to see how one person can lead multiple teams and provide support across different sites. The very relationships meant to anchor healing and stability risk becoming diluted. This sits uneasily alongside the standards set out in *The Children's Homes (England) Regulations 2015*, which emphasise stability, consistency, and individualised care.

Ofsted's own thematic reviews have highlighted the pressures placed on managers working across multiple homes, including signs of overstretch and quiet corner cutting. Its original position was clear: one home, one manager – exceptions allowed only with strong rationale and proven capacity. The policy allowing one manager to oversee two homes was broadened and formalised, despite concerns from across the sector.

This shift was driven largely by large providers, the Department for Education, and Ofsted. Smaller organisations and those delivering day-to-day care were not meaningfully involved in shaping the policy. Concerns about limited consultation were raised by care-experienced advocates, small providers, and professional bodies – many of whom reported being excluded entirely or invited in only after decisions had already been made.

This matters not just in principle, but in regulation. Under the Regulators' Code, oversight bodies are required to minimise unnecessary burdens and consider how they can support compliance and growth – particularly for small businesses. Yet the expansion of multi-home registrations, and the increasing administrative complexity of running a children's home, often favours large-scale operators with centralised infrastructure and legal support. For smaller, values-driven providers, the system is becoming harder to navigate – and harder to survive in. What was meant to streamline oversight instead risks reinforcing the dominance of the few, at the expense of the many.

While this was unfolding, some providers re-registered homes that had been rated inadequate – effectively erasing their inspection histories from public view. Ofsted does not openly permit this as a way to avoid accountability, but the regulatory framework allows new registrations to be treated as fresh starts, even when little has changed. Whether technically within the rules or not, the fact that this occurs highlights how much energy is directed toward managing appearances rather than addressing the underlying issues.

Transferring existing homes into a new multi-home registration involves a fresh application and the cancellation of existing registrations. On paper, that's just part of the process. But in practice, it wipes the slate clean—removing past inspection reports from public view and eliminating scrutiny, rather than fixing problems.

This might be allowed, technically – but that doesn't make it right. Without proper safeguards, it becomes another way to manage appearances instead of improving care. And in a system built on trust, that's a risk other people's children should never be exposed to.

In doing so, the system may have inadvertently built a mechanism for sidestepping scrutiny. And that raises urgent questions: do our safeguards ensure accountability – or do they simply collude with failure?

It's yet another example of the system adapting around its flaws instead of fixing them. Temporary fixes are dressed up as innovation, while the real issues – workforce shortages, weak leadership, and deeply flawed oversight – remain unresolved.

The system rewards paperwork over presence, compliance over compassion, and efficiency over empathy. That's where it's gone wrong. If we want to build something better, we need to start by valuing the people who show up and stay – the ones who sit through the silences, stay through the chaos, and hold the space when everything else falls apart. That's what care really is: consistency, kindness, and trust. When we start measuring that – not just what gets recorded – we might finally build a system that works for children.

Even if privatisation had never happened, one issue remained –not enough people wanted to do the hands-on work of caring for these children.

And so, the workforce crisis deepened. Fewer people were willing to foster. Residential homes couldn't recruit or retain enough staff. Caring for children who had already been let down became just another problem no one wanted to face. And that was the real failure.

You can change policies, restructure services, re-register providers, and increase funding – but none of it matters if there aren't enough people willing and supported to do the hard, human work of care. The system was already at breaking point: buckling under workforce shortages, patchwork fixes, and a widening gap between those making the decisions and those living with the consequences.

In 2021, the government launched its Independent Review of Children's Social Care, presenting it as a bold reimagining of the system. But to many of us, it felt more like a public relations exercise. The urgency to act had existed for years – so why now, in the middle of a pandemic? And more importantly, would this review lead to meaningful reform, or simply deepen the structural failures that had persisted for decades?

From the outset, there were signs this would not be a radical critique. The appointment of Josh MacAlister – founder of the government-backed Frontline programme – raised immediate concerns. His fast-track model, long embedded in policy, had already been criticised for focusing on recruitment over readiness.

How could a review led by someone so closely aligned with the Department for Education ever claim true independence?

It quickly became clear the government wasn't seeking a fresh perspective. They wanted someone who would work within existing parameters and deliver a controllable narrative.

Shortly after the review was announced, a meeting was arranged with the chair by close colleagues, Saira Jayne and I were invited to represent Yusuf's interest through Your Life Your Story. It should have been a chance to ensure his advocacy and the issues he fought to highlight were heard. But none of it made it into a review that claimed to centre lived experience. If this process had genuinely intended to learn from those who had spent their lives pushing for change, Yusuf's voice would have been integral. Instead, its absence stood as a stark reminder of what many believed, the review really was: a stage-managed process designed to preserve the status quo.

As the process unfolded, those concerns were confirmed. The Experts by Experience panel was intended to harness care-experienced voices, yet over 900 applicants were not selected – fuelling widespread frustration and a sense of exclusion. Critics questioned the lack of transparency in selection criteria and the missed opportunity to include voices with both lived and worked insight. The panel looked like window dressing to me – the appearance of participation without a willingness to hear uncomfortable truths.

Perhaps most telling was the review's treatment of residential care. It was sidelined, while the report leaned heavily in favour of family-based placements. That wasn't an oversight – it reflected a long-standing policy direction. Since the mid-1970s, when paid fostering was introduced, successive governments have positioned it as a more cost-effective alternative to residential care, even as concerns about marketisation, oversight, and placement stability have continued to grow.

Over the past 25 years, policy has increasingly reshaped foster care into a model where caregivers operate from their own homes, supported by tax breaks, allowances, and financial incentives. These measures were originally designed to encourage more people to open their homes to children in care. But over time, concerns have emerged – not about fostering itself, but about how the model has evolved to prioritise financial motivation over the child's best interests.

Foster care has long been the more affordable option for governments, and this financial reality has significantly influenced its expansion. While often promoted as a family-based, ethical alternative to residential care, both systems ultimately aim to provide safe, stable homes for vulnerable children. Fostering can offer great benefits, but it isn't always the right fit – particularly for older children or those with complex emotional, psychological, or behavioural needs. In such cases, placements frequently break down and fail to provide the consistency required for long-term recovery.

In 2019, the Children's Commissioner for England's *Stability Index* reported that many children experience multiple failed placements before residential care is even considered. That year alone, more than 8,000 children moved between three or more different homes within twelve months. This cycle deepens trauma, undermines stability, and disrupts both emotional and educational development – ultimately increasing the need for intensive, long-term support and placing greater pressure on an already strained system.

Further concerns have been raised about safeguarding and oversight within foster care. Investigations by the Independent Inquiry into Child Sexual Abuse (IICSA), which published its final report in October 2022, revealed disturbing cases of abuse and neglect in foster placements – incidents that had gone unnoticed or unreported due to systemic gaps in regulation and accountability.

More recently, data from 2022–2023 shows that there were 3,085 allegations of abuse against foster carers in England, with 1,895 of those made by children themselves. Together, these findings raise urgent questions about how well the current model protects the children it's meant to serve.

Despite these issues, public perception of foster care continues to be shaped by government messaging. Campaigns such as *Stable Homes, Built on Love* have framed fostering as a compassionate, family-based solution – one that offers both moral and economic appeal. But this narrative often sits uneasily alongside the longstanding challenges of placement instability, inconsistent outcomes, and limited oversight..

The closer you looked, the clearer it became: the Independent Review of Children's Social Care was never designed to expose uncomfortable truths. It felt carefully managed – constructed to preserve an existing narrative rather than interrogate it. And the connections between those shaping the review and senior figures in government, regulatory bodies, and the private sector were hard to ignore.

Take Isabelle Trowler, for example. Appointed Chief Social Worker for Children and Families in 2013, she had previously led Hackney's children's services, where she co-developed the Reclaiming Social Work model with Steve Goodman. The two went on to establish Morning Lane Associates, a consultancy that received significant government funding to deliver training and embed the model nationally – deepening their influence within the Department for Education.

Amanda Spielman's appointment as Chief Inspector of Ofsted in 2016 raised similar concerns. With no teaching background and strong ties to Ark Schools – a powerful multi-academy trust – her selection went ahead despite objections from the Education Select Committee, who questioned her lack of safeguarding experience.

The appointment of Dame Rachel de Souza as Children's Commissioner in 2021 followed the same pattern. As Chief Executive of the Inspiration Trust, another politically aligned multi-academy trust, she was confirmed in post despite a split vote by the Education Select Committee – this time over concerns about her independence and depth of experience.

Then came the appointment of Josh MacAlister to lead the Independent Review. As founder of the government-backed Frontline programme, his selection was made without any open recruitment – extraordinary for what was billed as a once-in-a-generation opportunity to reform a failing system. In a sector that claims to value transparency and equal opportunity, it felt like a closed shop. The destination had already been decided.

It wasn't just about who got the job – but who never had the chance. Those with lived and worked experience, and bold alternatives to the status quo, were excluded from the outset. It was yet another reminder of that old truth: it's not what you know – it's who you know.

And those relationships mattered. They shaped decisions, directed funding, and determined whose voices were heard – and whose were not. The result was a review that avoided the hard questions. The root causes of failure – unchecked marketisation, excessive bureaucracy, and the financialisation of care – went largely unexamined. Rather than challenge the system, the review entrenched it, handing influence back to those who had helped create it.

This wasn't accidental. It was political. Beginning with the Private Finance Initiative (PFI) in the 1990s, successive governments invited private capital into public systems like health and social care. Marketed as innovation, it embedded private interests into the foundations of public service. Social care soon followed.

This shift wasn't about efficiency – or even outcomes. It was about offloading responsibility, hiding debt, and opening up new markets. What began with buildings expanded into essential services – residential care, fostering, supported accommodation – all reframed as investment opportunities. But once profit becomes the goal, priorities shift.

22

RED TAPE AND REALITY
When Regulations Replace Relationships

This was a moment to tell the truth: that children's social care had become a marketplace, shaped not by the needs of children, but by the interests of those benefiting from its commercialisation. But the review didn't go there. Instead, it leaned on familiar slogans – now with a single word added for comfort: *'a safe, stable, and loving home for every child'* – offered for sentiment, not substance. The language shifted, but the blueprint stayed the same.

The result? More of the same. More policies dressed up as progress. More consolidation of power in the hands of those already steering the agenda. The government could claim decisive action while ensuring the recommendations aligned neatly with existing goals: cutting costs, expanding fostering, and minimal investment in residential care. What really mattered – continuity, quality, and the ability to identify and meet complex needs – was lost beneath layers of bureaucracy and well-defended budgets.

If this was meant to be a landmark review, why did it read like a rehashed policy paper – recycled, without substance or renewal? Why didn't it interrogate the impact of past reforms? Why avoid delivering something that might actually make the difference children need?

The absence of real answers only deepened the sense that this wasn't about meaningful reform. Once again, the same tired narrative was trotted out – residential care is too expensive, fostering is the fix, and the only way forward is to cut costs.

From where I stand after half a century in this work, I can say with certainty that the core issue isn't just underfunding or bureaucracy – it's the refusal to admit when policy has failed. For years, political decisions have shaped a system not around what children need, but around what governments have been willing to pay for.

Generations of children – and the adults they become – have lived with the consequences. The drive to provide care on the cheap, to reduce children to spreadsheets and contracts, has created a culture where short-term fixes are passed off as progress. The Independent Review had the platform to name this for what it is. It didn't. And until there's the courage to speak that truth, nothing will truly change.

It became clear this review wasn't about fixing a broken system. It was about protecting the status quo. A missed opportunity, yes – but more than that, a deliberate decision to avoid disruption. The arrogance of power lies in the assumption that no one will question the deep interconnections between those shaping the future of care.

Academics like Joe Hanley from the Open University have mapped how tightly these connections are woven into the machinery of policymaking – and how effectively they serve to preserve the status quo. Authors like Owen Jones, in *The Establishment*, have gone further, exposing how networks of power and influence work not only to shape policy but to shut down dissent and maintain control – often under the guise of reform.

In the end, the review was anything but independent. It was part of a bigger picture – one where decision-making remains concentrated in the hands of a few, lived experience is sidelined, and recycled narratives are repackaged as innovation to justify more empty promises.

Over nearly half a century in children's services, I've watched politicised appointments steadily erode the independence we so desperately need in roles designed to hold the system to account. These positions aren't ceremonial – they're meant to challenge, to advocate, to protect. But too often, political will overrides public interest.

I've been around long enough to recognise when independence is being compromised. These roles should belong to the children they claim to represent – not to the political agendas of the day. They should be accountable to Parliament, not obedient to ministers.

Children's social care has never been anything less than a political football – passed between parties more focused on looking decisive than on doing what truly matters. Time and again, it's been used to sell simple solutions to complex social issues – from youth crime and antisocial behaviour to school exclusions and mental health. Politicians promise to 'fix' children, rather than confront the conditions that fail them: poverty, trauma, instability, and the chronic underfunding of the universal systems meant to support them.

Care and health have long been staples of political manifestos – but too often, they don't translate into policies that deliver. When even select committees are ignored and scrutiny becomes a formality, we're left with a system that suppresses challenge and rewards compliance.

If those charged with speaking truth to power are chosen for their willingness to toe the line, what hope is there for meaningful change? Accountability must be real – not performative. And those of us who've been in this field long enough know the cost of getting it wrong. Children pay the price. Always.

I've watched this unfold firsthand. Coming back to social work after the pub years, things felt different – better, in some ways. New policies and initiatives had taken hold, and the language was full of optimism and intent: *Every Child Matters, Education, Education, Education.* It felt as though change wasn't just being promised – it was happening.

Private sector children's homes were starting to appear, but the bigger picture wasn't yet visible to the naked eye. Over time, though, I began to realise that something had shifted – quietly, but decisively. The focus was moving away from care and towards a business model built around profit.

It was like slowly discovering that Father Christmas wasn't real. At first, you believe in the magic. But then one small detail after another makes you question it. The more I looked, the clearer it became: the system was no longer grounded in compassion or long-term care. It had become a service like any other – focused on costs, targets, tick-boxes, and market forces.

In 2017, after stepping away from the world of private equity childcare I was looking for closure. The personal impact had been profound and I was searching for answers when I came across *Ethical Business Practice and Regulation* by Professor Chris Hodges and Ruth Steinholtz. Their work introduced me to Ethical Business Regulation (EBR) – a framework that brings regulators and businesses together through shared values. It immediately resonated with me.

Though I was familiar with the Regulators' Code, I couldn't reconcile it with my own experience. The UK government had endorsed EBR in its 2017 *Regulatory Futures Review* – a model that encourages trust, transparency, and a focus on long-term outcomes, rather than box-ticking and blame. It promotes collaboration over punishment and values ethical intent above rigid compliance. But in children's services – particularly under Ofsted – that spirit felt completely absent. The focus remained fixed on inspections, ratings, and managing risk, often shaped more by media scrutiny than by what actually helps children thrive.

The more I read of Hodges' work, the more I understood that the problems in children's social care weren't just about practice – they were structural. His writing championed a values-led approach to regulation: one that places relationships and ethical judgement at its core, rather than efficiency and control. For me, it gave language to something I had long felt but hadn't quite been able to name – how performance metrics had come to matter more than people, and how the essence of care had been displaced by the machinery of systems.

When Pete and I returned to the world of regulated childcare a couple of years later, we came back with a renewed sense of purpose. After rescuing a small company from financial ruin, we linked the children's homes we had taken over with our supported accommodation to create a through-care service. The idea was simple but powerful: young people could transition to independent living without losing the support network they had come to trust. Seamless care – from childhood to adulthood – was what we believed they needed.

We set out to address how care changes so abruptly for many young people at 16. It doesn't end – not officially – but for many, it starts to feel like it does. Moving from a regulated children's home to supported accommodation often meant a sudden drop in oversight, structure, and emotional security. One day they were surrounded by professionals; the next, they were expected to manage far more alone, in settings never designed to offer the same level of care.

Our idea was different. We weren't just offering supported accommodation – we were offering a supported transition. A model that preserved relationships, ensured continuity, and allowed care to move forward with the young person, not away from them. It was shaped by trust, paced to their readiness, and grounded in the belief that independence should never mean disconnection.

While primarily designed for young people leaving our own children's homes, we also supported those moving on from foster placements, other residential settings, and a growing number entering the system late – often following family breakdown, including adoption breakdowns. For these young people, the need for relational consistency was even more urgent. Many had passed through multiple homes in a short time. What they needed wasn't another service – it was stability.

But as we worked to deliver that continuity, the world around us was shifting – and we could feel it. What began as a clear and purposeful mission was becoming entangled in bureaucracy, and growing operational complexity.

Our vision has remained steady. We still believe in a pathway that allows young people to grow into adulthood with the same trusted adults beside them. But the broader environment was changing. The rise of large corporate providers, increasing financial pressure on local authorities, and a surge in critical media attention were starting to obscure the work itself.

At first, we were still able to hold our ground. The noise was growing louder, but it hadn't yet drowned out the work we were doing day to day. We focused on relationships, stability, and the kind of quiet, steady presence that makes a difference over time – not on rigid rules and control.

But a new pressure was building – one rooted not in what young people needed, but in how their care was being portrayed.

The campaign to regulate supported accommodation had gained momentum, fuelled by media coverage that suggested regulation alone could resolve the system's problems.

Although our goal was to protect children and help them thrive, it became increasingly clear that the system was more focused on ticking regulatory boxes than on truly meeting young people's needs – or managing the fallout from the next media scandal. The political and media-driven desire for regulation seemed to overshadow the importance of investing in real, relational care.

Yet the evidence had been there all along.

Too many decisions were made in response to political or media pressure, not in the best interests of children. Policies became more risk-averse – designed to avoid blame, not solve problems. Crisis management took the place of long-term thinking. Even the Department for Education has acknowledged that a blame culture leads to systems more concerned with covering faults than fixing them.

Regulation offered the appearance of action without addressing the deeper, systemic failures. Instead of asking why the system was struggling to meet young people's needs, supported accommodation became a convenient scapegoat— easier to target than to confront the policy failures at the heart of the system.

Meanwhile, the promise of care – of preparation for adulthood, of stability, of hope – was slipping further away. For those of us trying to provide care that was age-appropriate and relationship-led, it felt like we were swimming against the tide. Policy, politics, and public perception were taking precedence over the lives of children.

And alongside all this, an even more disturbing trend was quietly unfolding: the rise of unregistered children's homes operating outside legal frameworks and without the necessary safeguards. It was never lawful to place a 13-year-old in an unregistered setting. But it was happening – on Ofsted's watch. And they knew it.

Supported accommodation – known as a sixteen-plus unit when I worked in the public sector, and later as semi-independent living for care leavers – was never meant to be a children's home. It was designed specifically for 16- and 17-year-olds, serving as a bridge to independence. The goal was to provide support, guidance, and a gradual reduction in supervision to help young people develop the life skills they needed to transition into adulthood.

This type of accommodation was never intended for younger children, yet, over time, the lines became increasingly blurred. What was supposed to be a stepping stone toward independence began to be used for a wider range of needs. As a result, it started to house young people who were not yet ready for that level of independence, further highlighting the gaps and challenges in the system that should have been addressed.

In the mid-2000s, the Commission for Social Care Inspection (CSCI) visited Brighter Futures – the service Mark and I had set up in our own home – and approved the model for this very purpose. At the time, this was seen as a lawful and practical solution grounded in both legislation and lived reality.

The Children (Leaving Care) Act 2000 placed a duty on local authorities to provide accommodation that promoted independence, while Section 20 of the Children Act 1989 allowed such placements for older looked-after children. In practice, it offered a humane alternative to what was happening elsewhere – where too many young people were moved into rundown B&Bs in coastal towns, isolated and unsupported.

CSCI's recognition of our model reflected a shared understanding: that supported accommodation could offer a vital middle ground for those who didn't require the intensity of a children's home but still needed support. It was a proactive, legitimate response to the real needs of care leavers. But that understanding didn't last.

Over time, the same system that once endorsed supported accommodation as progressive and appropriate began to frame it as a policy failure and regulatory blind spot. Without any real shift in purpose or legal foundation, it was recast by the media as a problem to be fixed. What had been encouraged was suddenly rebranded as unsafe, unregulated, and out of control.

Twenty years on, supported accommodation had become the subject of growing controversy – labelled *'Britain's hidden children's homes.'* Media headlines focused on poor housing, profiteering landlords, and young people being placed in unsafe settings. Public outrage followed, as did calls for stricter regulation.

Yet much of the coverage failed to interrogate the real drivers of the crisis. It rarely acknowledged the chronic underfunding, the desperation of local authorities, or Ofsted's failure to act – even when the law was clearly being broken.

The pressure had been building for years. A 2009 court ruling extended housing responsibilities to all homeless 16- and 17-year-olds, just as austerity was gutting the support infrastructure – Sure Start centres closed, youth services vanished, and families were left with less and less.

Supported accommodation was never intended as a default for all older children in care. Yvette Stanley, Ofsted's National Director for Social Care, admitted as much in a 2025 accountability hearing. The problem was misuse – not the model itself.

There were, without doubt, rogue providers who entered the market to make money. But they weren't the only ones operating. Many ethical providers – some of whom had pioneered the model – were swept into the same narrative, as public attention focused on the worst-case scenarios.

The explanation offered was that there were no other placements, or that the child had been placed under a Deprivation of Liberty Safeguards (DoL's) order. Even though government data showed that only twelve percent of children in unregistered settings were covered by such orders. So why were the rest left in unlawful care?

When the facts are known, when public statements admit to delay, and when the vast majority of placements fall outside any legal safeguard – it becomes impossible to argue that this was an unforeseen crisis. It wasn't. It was tolerated.

And in that tolerance, a shift occurred. Regulation became the political solution, the tool to soothe public concern. But the rush to regulate didn't acknowledge the years of failure that preceded it.

Larger providers, with their legal teams and compliance departments, welcomed this. Not because it would improve care – but because it raised the barriers to entry. Regulation became a moat around a market they already dominated.

Writers like Tim Worstall have noted how big business doesn't fear regulation – it often depends on it. Complexity protects incumbents. And smaller, values-led providers? They struggle to keep up or get pushed out entirely.

I struggle to see the point of creating laws if the people tasked with enforcing them can ignore them without consequence. What's worse is when there's no meaningful mechanism for challenge. The silence that follows isn't just frustrating – it's dangerous. It signals that some rules are optional, and some voices don't matter.

Over time, that silence becomes part of the structure. A system that protects itself instead of the children it was built to serve.

And as market thinking continues to dominate children's care, so does the commodification of children's lives. Personal stories become marketing assets. Lived experience becomes a branding tool. Children's pain becomes promotional copy.

Real care is quiet. It's built on relationships, not slogans. When the people we're meant to protect become the product, that's not just a distortion – it's a betrayal.

The crisis in supported accommodation didn't come out of nowhere. It was the product of political decisions, regulatory drift, and a refusal to acknowledge long-term consequences. While attention stayed fixed on headlines and individual providers, the deeper system failings were ignored.

The result? A system reshaped by blame, not by learning – and one where the people most affected have been consistently shut out.

The MacAlister review was meant to address this. But in reality, it repeated the same mistakes.

Hundreds of people with lived and professional care experience were excluded from the Experts by Experience panel without clear explanation.

Instead of reforming care, the review called for more regulation without reflecting on how regulation had helped create the current problems in the first place.

In doing so, it missed the point. And the chance for real change slipped by again.

23

REBUILDING CARE

From Compliance to Compassion

The Independent Review of Children's Social Care was presented as a once-in-a-generation opportunity for a radical reset – a chance to fix a failing system. But, when the government responded with the 'Stable Homes, Built on Love' strategy, it became clear that this wasn't a true reset, but just another political illusion. Rather than confronting the failures of past policy, the response recycled the same approach launched in 2016—just under a new slogan. A true reset would have required an honest reckoning with what had gone wrong. Instead, the MacAlister Review avoided any real critique of the 2016 reforms.

Far from offering a fresh perspective, it reaffirmed a familiar hierarchy: adoption, fostering, and kinship care were prioritised, while residential care was once again relegated to a last resort. Though the 2016 review endorsed 'corporate parenting' principles in law, it offered no serious investment to make them meaningful.

The result? A care system pushed deeper into crisis—early intervention services underfunded, complexity ignored, and the same structural pressures left intact.

The review also failed to assess the long-term impact of accelerating adoption or address the "fostering first" policy—despite high placement breakdown rates and limited evidence of improved outcomes. It also overlooked Ofsted's regulatory framework, rather than ensuring safety, became a driving force behind placement instability.

Contrary to what some campaigners and media outlets would have you believe, the crisis wasn't caused by supported accomodation providers or a lack of regulation. The real issue was local authorities struggled to meet demand with finite budgets. Faced with rising numbers of children, particularly teenagers, authorities increasingly opted for cheaper alternatives that fell short in providing the essential support required.

As far back as the 1989 Children Act, legislation had emphasised the importance of preparing young people for leaving care, ensuring they had the life skills and support needed for adulthood. This was strengthened by the 2000 Children (Leaving Care) Act, designed to address gaps in support for older young people.

However, many authorities began to overlook services aligned with the spirit of the legislation, turning instead to less supportive and cheaper alternatives, such as unsuitable housing and minimal floating support. These options lacked 24-hour on-site support and consistent guidance essential for navigating adult life. Research by The Children's Society in 2019 highlighted the consequences, finding that young people in unsupported accommodation were sixty percent more likely to be at risk of criminal exploitation compared to those in regulated children's homes.

Blaming private providers for this crisis was both convenient and misleading—an oversimplification that ignored the deeper, systemic issues driving instability. While some unethical landlords undoubtedly capitalised on the situation, the real issue lies with the decisions made by local authorities. Those who knowingly allowed substandard placements to persist by opting for cheaper services instead of those better equipped to support young people.

This was highlighted in the Children's Commissioner's 2017 report, which showed how financial pressures led local authorities to compromise on care quality, ultimately failing in their duty to safeguard vulnerable young people.

Despite knowing the risks, many social workers, constrained by systemic pressures, were forced to leave young people to remain in environments lacking essential support.

In reality, the crisis wasn't caused by the greed of private providers or a lack of regulation. It stemmed from a systemic failure to prioritise the needs of young people – driven by cost-saving decisions rather than a commitment to reliable, legally compliant services. Ofsted's overemphasis on teenage neglect only made things worse, pushing local authorities to focus on managing risk rather than providing long-term, meaningful support.

Already burdened by the 2009 court ruling on homeless teenagers, which revealed the lack of adequate housing, local authorities continued to make decisions that left vulnerable young people exposed to harm. This wasn't a new issue – it was a recurring failure, with each decision compounding the risks and instability these young people faced.

The truth is that care cannot undo the long-term effects of neglect and poor parenting in short timescales. The work required to heal these deep wounds is long-term, and governments have failed to provide the necessary funding and resources. Instead, these children remain trapped in a failing care system, often becoming over-represented in vulnerable adult groups later in life.

Despite years of reviews, reports, and recommendations, little has changed. The same systemic issues – insufficient support, financial pressures, the failure to learn from past mistakes and the blame culture persist. These problems keep resurfacing, with the same errors being repeated. More regulation won't fix this; it's part of the problem, reinforcing a system that focuses on process and cost, rather than implementing real, sustainable solutions for vulnerable young people.

When the government announced in December 2020 that Ofsted would regulate supported accommodation for looked-after children aged 16 and 17, my heart sank. This came just weeks before the care review was announced - so why make a decision ahead of its findings. From the outset, it was clear that this wasn't about real reform. It felt like another decision made under pressure to appease media fuelled public opinion, rather than a genuine attempt at meaningful change.

The thought of Ofsted's compliance-driven regulatory approach filled me with dread. This approach has not consistently ensured safety and basic care standards as promised. Instead of prioritising the genuine support, growth, and care young people need to thrive, it focuses too heavily on meeting regulatory requirements.

From my perspective, this rigid, tick box system failed to address the deeper, more complex challenges many young people face. Many who had struggled in children's homes thrived in the supported accommodation we provided because we could offer the flexibility and experiential support that the regulatory framework stifled.

The thought of applying the same approach to supported accommodation left me with little doubt: it would not lead to meaningful change. Box-ticking would remain the focus, while the root causes of struggle went unaddressed—perpetuating a system that hinders growth rather than supports it.

My greatest fear was that supported accommodation would be turned into an extended children's home— repeating the very failures the Children Act 1989 sought to correct. That Act recognised the lack of preparation for adult life; yet, decades later, we risk sliding back.. The care system cannot change the reality that childhood officially ends at eighteen. If supported accommodation becomes overregulated and institutionalised, I fear it will create dependency, not independence—undermining young people's ability to transition confidently into adulthood.

One moment that stands out to me: in a children's home, six weeks before her 18th birthday, a young woman was still having her underarms shaved by staff – not because she asked, but because someone decided she couldn't be trusted with a razor. She was about to become an adult, expected to manage rent, bills, and work. Yet, here she was, treated like a child, stripped of control over her own body.

This wasn't about care or protection; it was about minimising risk at all costs. Driven by fear, the provider was more concerned about what an Ofsted inspector might say if something went wrong. This had nothing to do with preparation for adult life. It was about ticking a box, managing risk on paper, not supporting her reality.

If staff felt she was in such distress that she couldn't be trusted with a razor, shouldn't they have asked a bigger question? Was she actually ready for independence? And if she was genuinely at risk of self-harm, what had been done to help her before that point? Taking away the razor wouldn't stop her self-harming. Just like turning 18 doesn't magically prepare someone for adulthood. The system's response shattered her trust in herself. The message wasn't just, 'we don't trust you'; it was, 'you shouldn't trust yourself.'

Every time a decision is made for them, every time they're told what they can't do, every time a risk is managed instead of discussed, young people absorb one message: they're not capable. Instead of being supported to build the skills, confidence, and resilience they need, they're taught to doubt themselves, fear mistakes, and rely on others to make decisions for them. If we can't trust someone with a razor, how can we expect them to manage a tenancy, hold a job, or deal with a crisis?

By prioritising risk management over preparation, the system robs young people of the experiences needed to grow into capable adults. They don't learn to navigate challenges – they learn to avoid responsibility, fear failure, and second-guess every step. So, when they leave care, they're not confident – they're stuck, afraid to ask for help, and convinced they're not capable of coping alone.

This is what the system gets so wrong. True safety doesn't come from eliminating every risk – it comes from helping young people believe they can handle what life throws at them. The contrast is clear. For most young people, adulthood is a gradual process. They have a safety net – parents who offer advice, help with mistakes, or a place to retreat when life gets tough. If they mess up, someone's there to help figure out the next step.

There's always a place at the dinner table – a meal they don't have to plan, cook, or budget for. A moment of comfort away from pressure, without fear or expectation, where they don't have to prove they're coping.

But for many care leavers, that doesn't exist. No home to return to when things fall apart. No financial cushion to soften the blow of a missed bill or lost job. No one reassuring them they'll work it out. Just the cold, unforgiving reality: no food if they don't shop. No roof if they don't pay rent. No job if they don't show up. There's no second chance.

Adulthood arrives whether they're ready or not – and too often, they're not. Not because they lack potential, but because no one ever gave them the chance to fail safely, to make mistakes and learn, to build resilience with support instead of punishment.

While most children still have a lifeline. Care leavers are expected to leap into independence without practice. And when they struggle, the system doesn't support them – it asks why they're not coping, as if they were ever given a fair chance.

As many care-experienced adults will tell you, life beyond the 'care cliff' can be unforgiving. The sudden shift from a sheltered environment to independent living often leaves young people isolated, unsupported, and unprepared. Without proper preparation, they're not set up to thrive – they're set adrift.

I left home at sixteen. I had a lot to learn, but motivation and self-sufficiency were on my side. For me, the goal has always been clear: to equip young people with the skills, confidence, and knowledge they need to stand on their own. Help them believe in themselves, face the world, and take control of their futures. This means understanding their rights and responsibilities – and facing the tough realities of life beyond children's social care. Even before regulation, their transition was hindered by layers of unnecessary bureaucracy. Now, with another layer of complexity, the barriers are even higher.

Rather than fostering self-determination, too many young people are tied up in red tape, delaying the confidence and autonomy they need. Regulations meant to protect them stifle their growth – prioritising stability over development. In managing every possible risk, we risk managing away their future.

System failures don't just affect the moment – they echo for a lifetime. Teenagers entering care face worse outcomes than younger children. They're more likely to bounce between placements, struggle in school, and develop mental health problems. Many find themselves criminalised, with trauma-driven behaviours treated as delinquency rather than cries for help.

And the problems don't end in childhood. The issues young people face in care follow them into adulthood – unemployment, homelessness, addiction, mental health struggles, and unstable relationships. Some survive but carry lifelong health challenges, as research into Adverse Childhood Experiences shows. Early trauma, neglect, and instability don't disappear at eighteen – they shape futures, affecting everything from physical health to life expectancy.

Even those who follow a more stable path often carry invisible scars – struggles with trust, relationships, and belonging. Many care-experienced adults succeed on the surface but live with anxiety, imposter syndrome, or a constant fear of instability. Some thrive – but many do so despite the system, not because of it. The contrast between those who thrive and those who struggle reveals a painful truth: survival is not success.

A truly effective system wouldn't leave young people to rely on wit alone. It would provide stability, support, and long-term care – not just to help them survive, but to thrive. The disconnect between policy and lived experience is where the system is broken.

Rather than ask how best to support young people into independence, we build systems that prioritise risk management over growth. And that mindset – efficiency, compliance, and process over people – runs through every layer of social care, including how we recruit and train the professionals responsible for supporting them.

For too long, we've relied on the least trained and least experienced individuals to care for our most vulnerable children. Entry into residential care requires no qualifications, yet these workers are expected to handle complex, emotional, and often dangerous situations. When mistakes happen, the system sacrifices these workers.

Rather than addressing this fundamental problem, policymakers have doubled down on flawed thinking. Fast-track social work programmes exemplify this logic – assuming that complex, relationship-based work can be reduced to a crash course and a *computer says* approach, in which decisions are driven by data, processes, and rules rather than the individual's needs.

And yet, while ill-prepared frontline workers are held to impossible standards, some providers face little meaningful scrutiny. Behind the scenes, exemptions under the General Data Protection Regulation (GDPR) keep much of this from public view. Laws designed to protect individual privacy are now used to shield systems, decisions, and organisations from accountability.

Even more troubling, the failures we see may be only the tip of the iceberg. These are just the cases brought to public attention – those exposed by investigative journalists or whistleblowers. We don't know how many others follow the same hidden path: registration granted, children placed, serious failings uncovered, homes quietly closed or, worse still, allowed to continue operating by Ofsted.

Behind the scenes, General Data Protection Regulations (GDPR) exemptions keep much of this from public scrutiny. Laws meant to protect personal data are now used to shield decisions, systems, and organisations from accountability. The public remains largely unaware of the full extent of these failures, allowing indefensible actions to remain hidden. When safeguarding concerns arise in services previously approved by regulators, we should urgently question not only what went wrong, but what else is occurring beyond public view.

These troubling exemptions were not in the original draft legislation. They were added later at the request of regulators who claimed they needed protection in decision-making. In practice, these additions have allowed serious failings to escape scrutiny, enabling systems to hide their mistakes rather than be held accountable. Regulators pushed for these powers, and now we see the consequences: a system that hides failures rather than confronting them.

In early 2021, shocking revelations emerged about a group of children's homes where young people with complex needs – including learning disabilities and autism – were subjected to sustained harm and abuse. These children had been placed in specialist settings intended to offer therapeutic care and protection. Instead, they endured mistreatment, physical abuse, neglect, and inappropriate restraint by staff.

The situation was made even worse by the regulator's failure to act. Ofsted had received over 50 serious reports about these homes but continued rating them as 'Good.' Despite protected disclosures from whistleblowers, complaints from parents, and concerns raised by local authorities, no decisive action was taken. Children remained in placements where harm persisted unchecked.

Only after media scrutiny was an independent investigation launched, revealing multiple missed opportunities – not only by Ofsted but by local authorities and safeguarding partners. The review highlighted a culture prioritising compliance and paperwork over the safety and wellbeing of children. Following the investigation, these homes were closed, yet the provider continues to operate.

This was no isolated incident. That same year, another home – operated by a provider with no background in children's social care – was suspended by Ofsted due to serious leadership and safeguarding failures. Despite these issues, the provider had been registered, suspended soon after, then reopened, and then ultimately closed. In 2022, a similar scenario occurred elsewhere, with a newly registered home declared unsafe within months. Each time, homes were approved, childrenwere placed, and serious concerns emerged

These are not unfortunate one-offs; they highlight a system that repeatedly approves unsafe services, responding only after the damage is done. When patterns persist despite multiple reports, reviews, and inquiries, it reveals a deeper truth: this is not merely a series of failures but systemic resistance to accountability.

When regulators approve homes that later prove unsafe – or knowingly allow children to be placed without proper registration – it is more than an error of judgement. It is a fundamental failure of process. When these failures go unchallenged, the system protects itself at the expense of vulnerable children.

Even more troubling is the unequal treatment providers experience. Smaller services, frequently operating on tight margins and primarily driven by care rather than profit, often bear the brunt of regulatory interventions. Without the legal or financial resources to effectively challenge adverse Ofsted decisions, many are forced to close – not necessarily because they failed to safeguard children, but because they simply cannot withstand regulatory pressures. Conversely, larger companies, possessing greater resources to navigate or contest regulatory scrutiny, are often able to sustain operations and even expand.

Ofsted's power is rarely contested. To date, there has been no legal test case challenging its refusal to release decisions under the Freedom of Information Act. GDPR exemptions, designed to protect personal data, are now used to shield processes from transparency. This has created a culture where scrutiny flows in only one direction – leaving providers in the dark and children vulnerable.

As the Competition and Markets Authority (CMA) has warned, the care market is consolidating around large providers. Their 2022 market study found that smaller services struggle under the weight of regulation, even when the care they deliver is strong. The system doesn't support them – it filters them out.

So, homes close quietly. Some are sold to bigger providers. And those that disappear are often not the worst, but the most ethical – those built on trust, continuity, and care. Meanwhile, the system favours those best equipped to navigate bureaucracy – not those best equipped to care for children.

Without scrutiny, the pattern continues unchecked. Ofsted routinely relies on broad exemptions – especially those tied to safeguarding and internal decisions – which are difficult to challenge without significant legal support. In the absence of challenge, transparency quietly disappears.

But Ofsted isn't an outlier – it's a mirror. The patterns seen in its regulatory practices reflect a deeper culture across the care system: one that resists scrutiny, protects institutions over individuals, and silences those it fails.

The system cannot admit when it's wrong. It hides behind procedures, avoids accountability, and privileges institutional interests over the needs of individuals. GDPR – intended to protect personal data – is now frequently misused to block legitimate access, including by care-experienced adults seeking their own case files.

What they often receive are heavily redacted documents – pages blacked out under vague references to third-party data or safeguarding. What remains is not a full record, but a fragmented and often distressing account of their lives: stripped of context, riddled with gaps, and raising painful questions without answers. This isn't protection. It's dispossession.

This is a regulator that insists, *'If it's not written down, it didn't happen.'* Yet when people ask to see what was written down about them, they're denied access. That contradiction is hard to defend. It reveals a system that demands written proof from others, yet hides behind documentation when the truth is owed to those it has failed.

And when access is finally granted, another truth emerges: what's written down isn't always reliable. Many records are filled with inaccuracies, assumptions, and professional judgments presented as fact. Lives are reduced to risk categories, behaviours to labels, and entire relationships left undocumented. The voices of children – their fears, strengths, and perspectives – are often absent.

For care-experienced adults, reading their files can feel like reading someone else's version of their life. It's not just what's redacted that harms – it's what was never recorded, or recorded wrongly. When official records distort the truth, they claim to preserve, they cease to be safeguards. They become instruments of harm.

It denies people the right to understand their own lives. It prevents healing. And it repeats the message many absorbed in care: you're not allowed to know, you don't get to ask, your story doesn't belong to you.

The truth is, it's simply not possible to write everything down. No log, report, or case note can fully capture the complexity of a child's life or the depth of a relationship. Moments of care, fear, connection, or harm often happen outside formal processes – quietly, instinctively, and in between the paperwork.

What gets recorded is a selective snapshot, filtered through the lens of professional judgment, time pressure, and institutional priorities.

For care-experienced people, that gap between lived experience and written account can be disorienting – even traumatising. You remember what happened. The file doesn't. But it's the file the system believes – not what can be read between the lines.

24

A JOURNEY OF CARE
Honouring the Past, Building the Future

It should never have taken the tragic death of a dedicated headteacher – and her family's tireless fight for justice – to shine a light on the serious flaws in our regulatory system. Ruth Perry's story is complex, but what it reveals is painfully clear: we urgently need real reform in how we oversee education and children's social care.

This isn't just about one case. Ruth's story reflects something much bigger – a system that's become overly focused on compliance, rules, and public judgments, rather than the real needs of children and the people who care for them. Too often, the system rewards box-ticking over understanding. It's designed more to catch people out than to support them.

That kind of culture creates fear. It leaves dedicated professionals second-guessing themselves, unable to work with confidence or flexibility. Instead of helping them grow, it holds them back. Instead of encouraging innovation, it discourages it. Worst of all, it makes it harder to truly meet the individual needs of each child.

We need to stop and ask ourselves: what are we really

expecting from teachers and care workers? Because right now, it seems like we're more focused on whether they've met the standards on a checklist than whether they're being given the time, space, and trust to actually support children.

This has to change. Not just for the professionals in the system – but for every child who depends on it. And nowhere is this more urgent than in our children's social care system.

The truth is the care system should be about far more than just meeting a list of prescriptive standards. At its heart, it should be a system designed to heal, nurture, and guide children who have faced unbearable challenges. The real question isn't whether the system ticks the right boxes – it's whether it truly meets the needs of the children who rely on it.

To do that, we first need to understand the lasting impact of trauma. Abuse, neglect, and instability don't just threaten a child's immediate safety – they reshape how a child sees the world, others, and themselves. These experiences can deeply disrupt emotional regulation, trust-building, and social development. If we don't understand this, we can't begin to provide the right support.

Children in care often display behaviours that are difficult to manage and even harder to understand. Too often, these are misinterpreted as defiance or bad behaviour. In reality, they are often trauma responses. Experiences like abandonment, neglect, or abuse shape how children trust others – or not – and how they respond to the world around them. Recognising these responses for what they are is key to helping children heal.

One of the most profound challenges is forming relationships. Many children in care struggle to develop secure attachments because their earliest emotional bonds were broken. When shown affection or consistency, they may withdraw or become overly clingy – both are expressions of fear and past hurt. These behaviours are not inconvenient; they are protective instincts formed in response to deep emotional wounds.

Emotional dysregulation is another common trauma response. Children may experience sudden outbursts, meltdowns, or periods of numbness. These are not signs of poor discipline but symptoms of a nervous system that is constantly on alert. Their brains have been conditioned to expect danger, making it difficult to manage emotions or trust that they are safe.

Some children live in a state of hypervigilance – always scanning for threats, even in safe environments. They may startle easily or seem anxious without cause. This is not paranoia; it is survival instinct honed through lived experience. It makes it hard to relax, to trust, and to fully engage with others.

Aggression, too, can be a trauma response. It may be the only way a child has learned to protect themselves or assert control. These actions are often misunderstood as malice, but they are more often about fear and survival.

Others withdraw completely. When trust has been repeatedly broken, it can feel safer to shut down than to risk further hurt. These children may seem distant or unresponsive, but their silence is often a shield.

Some children turn their pain inward. Self-harm or risk-taking behaviours are desperate attempts to feel something, to regain control, or to express emotions that have no outlet. These actions may be difficult to witness, but they are signals of profound internal struggle.

Distrust of authority is another legacy of trauma. Children who have been let down by adults find it hard to believe that those in power have their best interests at heart. Teachers, social workers, and caregivers may all be viewed with suspicion, regardless of their intentions. Pushing people away becomes a defence mechanism.

Many children display inconsistent behaviour – moments of calm followed by sudden distress. These shifts reflect internal chaos, not manipulation. The nervous system reacts unpredictably when shaped by fear.

Poor impulse control is also common. When a child is stuck in fight-or-flight mode, it is nearly impossible to pause and think before acting. Impulsive behaviour is often a reflex, not a choice.

And social withdrawal can persist long after the trauma. After years of betrayal or neglect, isolation can feel safer than connection. Rebuilding trust takes time, patience, and deep understanding.

All of these behaviours are cries for help. They are not signs of defiance or rebellion, but evidence of hurt children doing their best to survive. Too often, systems punish these behaviours instead of addressing their root causes.

And if we fail to recognise and respond to these behaviours in childhood, we don't just fail children now – we risk carrying that failure forward. Trauma that goes unaddressed in care does not simply disappear with age. It evolves. It can shape the adults these children become, influencing their ability to form relationships, hold down employment, manage emotions, and trust others.

Often, the public only sees the consequences of that trauma years later – in adults who struggle, who lash out, or who withdraw. And without knowing their history, society is quick to judge. We ask why an adult can't regulate their emotions, but we rarely ask who helped them learn. We question why they can't trust others, without asking who first broke that trust.

This is why prevention matters. It's not just about supporting children in the moment – it's about changing the trajectory of their lives.

Children in care need more than a roof over their heads. They need skilled, compassionate adults who understand trauma and are trained to respond to it. And crucially, they need care that is real, not perfect. The pursuit of perfect care often burdens caregivers with unrealistic expectations and leaves little room for humanity. But care doesn't have to be flawless to be transformative. What matters most is being present, consistent, and emotionally available. When mistakes happen – as they inevitably will – what counts is the ability to repair, reflect, and reconnect. This kind of responsive care, grounded in empathy and humility, is where real healing begins. They need a system that offers patience, empathy, and pathways to recovery.

We need a care system that sees beyond behaviour to the pain beneath. One that does not shame children for their coping mechanisms, but helps them build new ones. A system that is built on healing, not compliance.

A truly effective care system prioritises children's wellbeing above all else. It empowers professionals to build trust-based relationships, and gives children the stability and support they need to heal. Physical safety is just the baseline. Children must also feel seen, heard, and valued. They need spaces that support emotional healing and social growth, where they can begin to trust again.

And the system must prepare them for life beyond care. It's not enough to protect them in childhood – we must equip them for adulthood. That means life skills, emotional literacy, and consistent long-term support to help them understand their past and build a future.

Yet what's happening right now falls far short of what we know is needed. Instead of nurturing and supporting caregivers, the system burdens them with relentless scrutiny. When things inevitably go wrong, it is the caregivers who are blamed – their actions too often framed as personal failings, when in reality they are operating within a system that is broken at its core.

This fear-driven culture suffocates the very trust and connection that children so desperately need in order to heal. Both children and caregivers are stuck in a system that punishes mistakes instead of learning from them. This culture of fear and blame doesn't exist in isolation – it is mirrored and magnified by how care is portrayed in the media.

The media has a powerful role to play in shaping how society understands care. And too often, that role is misused. Care scandals make headlines – they generate outrage, fear, and digital clicks. But in focusing on dramatic failures, the media rarely explores the deeper systemic issues that lead to breakdowns in care. Instead, individual caregivers or professionals are scapegoated, reinforcing a culture of blame. This kind of coverage distorts public understanding, stigmatises children in care, and discourages those who work to support them. It sells stories – but it silences truth.

We need a different kind of storytelling – one that reflects the complexity, the courage, and the connection at the heart of real care. When we share stories of compassion, growth, and resilience, we remind the public that care is not about perfection but about presence. We show that healing is possible – not through quick fixes or headlines, but through sustained, supported relationships. And we help build the empathy needed to turn policy into progress.

In the 1970s, family placements – foster care, kinship care, and adoption – emerged as the ideal solution for children in care. The belief was simple: children would thrive in a family environment, surrounded by love and care that institutional settings couldn't provide. For many, this approach worked. But for some, it didn't.

At the time, family placements were also seen as a more affordable alternative to residential care. The high cost of residential care made family placements the financially palatable choice for policymakers and budget holders. However, this focus on cost efficiency ignored the complex trauma many children carried. The policy became rooted in the belief that family placements were the ideal solution, even though they didn't always meet the needs of every child.

The real issue is that the limitations of family placements have never been fully acknowledged. For children with severe trauma, even a loving family home can be an inadequate setting. Trauma doesn't simply disappear when a child enters a family environment. In fact, when family placements fail, trauma deepens, and each failure compounds the emotional wounds. Children begin to lose trust in the very structures meant to protect them. Yet the system continues to push family placements as the default solution, disregarding the reality that setting is not suited for every child.

What's troubling is that we don't even track unsuccessful placements. Data on these failures is scarce, making it difficult to assess the level of success. But what we do know is that each failed placement adds another layer of trauma. By the time these children are placed in residential care, they have often been through multiple unsuccessful placements, and the damage done makes it even harder to begin the healing process. Children arrive in residential care carrying the compounded trauma of failed placements, each one deepening their emotional wounds. They've already been failed by a system that insisted family placements were the answer, despite the reality that these placements were not always suitable.

Residential care, when done right, can offer needs-led care specifically tailored to meet the unique needs of these children. But too often, it continues to be seen as the last resort – a place to send children when everything else has failed. As a result, children are often left for far too long with their emotional needs unmet until it's too late for meaningful intervention.

The system persists in positioning family placements as the gold standard, despite clear evidence that what these children need is specialised care in an environment designed to meet their complex needs. This focus on family placements, with all their limitations, only perpetuates the cycle of trauma and delayed healing. What these children truly need is not simply a return to family care, but a shift in how we think about and deliver care. Specialised residential care, with the right support and resources, can provide a crucial opportunity for healing. But when it is treated as an afterthought or a last resort after a tour of foster homes, it is too often too little, too late.

At the same time, the system failed to address the increasing number of teenagers entering care later in life, many of whom carried years of unresolved trauma. Unlike younger children, these teenagers didn't have the time to heal gradually. Their emotional scars ran deep, and their healing journey became more urgent. The real failure wasn't just in placing them in environments ill-equipped to meet their needs; it was in rushing them toward adulthood before they were ready. Their transition into independence came too quickly, leaving them unprepared for the challenges of adult life.

Children entering care at a young age had time to build trust, receive support, and heal before adulthood. But for these teenagers, the system didn't offer that luxury. Instead, they entered care with unresolved trauma and had little time to heal before they were expected to transition into independence.

In many cases, they are moved into supported accommodation at age 16 or 17, where they are meant to learn to live independently. The system assumed that they ready for this leap – ready to manage their finances, hold down a job, and live alone. But for a child who has spent years in neglect or abuse, these skills cannot be learned overnight. The trauma they've endured doesn't just disappear because they've reached a certain age.

In an ideal world, the transition to adulthood is gradual, supported, and carefully planned. But for many children in care, that transition is abrupt and overwhelming. The trauma they've experienced has left deep emotional scars that impact their ability to thrive in adulthood. They may struggle with relationships, managing emotions, and understanding how to navigate the complexities of the world around them. Instead of having time to heal and gain the necessary life skills, they are pushed out into an adult world that they are not prepared for.

The use of supported accommodation as a solution for children in care, particularly teenagers, originally had its merits. Designed as a way to help young people transition from residential care into independent living, it was a model intended to offer more autonomy while still providing the necessary support to manage the complexities of life after care. In its early forms, supported accommodation provided tailored assistance with a focus on helping young people build the life skills necessary for adulthood, while offering 24-hour support from trained professionals in a stable environment. It was designed to bridge the gap between care and independence.

However, the crisis in supported accommodation today is rooted in how this once effective model was gradually misused, largely due to financial pressures and misguided policy decisions. As demand for placements increased, local authorities, under pressure from tightening budgets, sought out cheaper alternatives to residential care, which had higher costs. The appeal of supported accommodation was clear: it offered an affordable way to house children without the expensive overheads of traditional residential settings. The system's financial priorities led to a shift away from the model of well-resourced 24-hour support, instead opting for floating support – where a child would be placed in a rental property, often with minimal supervision and care.

If the rise of unregistered services and sky-high fees isn't enough to force a rethink in how we care for vulnerable children, then nothing will. It's time to stop treating these children as financial burdens and start recognising them as individuals with complex, unmet needs. We cannot continue pushing young people into adulthood without giving them the skills, support, and care they need to thrive. The misuse of supported accommodation highlights the systemic failures that, unless addressed, will persist.

More regulation won't fix a fundamentally broken system. The problem isn't the lack of rules; it's the failure to create policies that truly meet the evolving needs of children in care. For too long, we've focused on compliance and cost-cutting instead of addressing the deep trauma these children face. The system has failed them – no amount of inspections can change that.

There is a growing conversation about the care system, but too often, the voices of care-experienced adults – those still living with the long-term effects of their time in care – are missing. It's not enough for a few privileged individuals to speak on behalf of the many who continue to struggle with the system's impact. Success stories cannot represent the entire care-experienced community. The idea that a handful of voices speak for all who've been through the system is a dangerous misconception. While these stories are valuable, they don't reflect the reality for everyone. True change requires recognising that each experience is unique, and the system must listen to all voices – especially those who challenge the status quo and those who bear witness to their journey.

Some argue that the reintroduction of semi-secure units might offer a solution to the challenges faced by children in care. But this view risks ignoring the deeper, systemic issues and the individual needs of these children. More restrictive environments are not the answer if we don't first address the root causes of trauma and instability.

Without challenge, there is no progress – only the risk of repeating past mistakes. We owe these children more than containment – we owe them care that heals, relationships that last, and futures that feel possible.

If only the system truly listened to the voices of lived experience, it would know this is not the solution.

It would know that these were the very places that caused so much harm in the past – and that regulation alone cannot provide the assurance needed to stop history from repeating itself.

On loss and grief

We once were the same,
We looked like one another,
Living in just one place
With a sister or a brother.

From the outside looking in,
There was no difference,
In my life and in yours
Family, home and picket fence.

I'm not presuming as I write,
Your Life was tinted rose,
I'm taking a run up with my words,
An explanation, I suppose.

To talk about life lessons,
As they don't all look the same,
Behind the doors, closed where I lived,
The ones I loved brought nowt but pain.

A life of fear immeasurable,
No light of day nor play,
Hunger till I ached no more,
Hurt till I had no voice to say.

The years went passed so slowly,
it was all I ever knew,
The ones I loved, they wronged me,
Loved innocence till black and blue.

Then light came as a chink,
Quiet a journey through care tunnel
Police and social ever near
My family into trouble.

Then one fine day within the courts
A light that shone so bright
Took me away from greatest harm
The last time in their sight.

The only way to have my life,
Was to lose everything and everyone,
The family, friends, the school, the place
In a blink lost one by one.

So please forgive my silence
Please forgive my tears and shrugs,
As loss takes hold, consumes me,
The loss like detoxing off of drugs.

It may not look like loss to you,
As loss to most is sadly death,
But as I know loss in both ways
I can say it takes same breath!

So could you take my words and hold them?
In your mind and in your heart,
For our children who are in care,
They could've had a similar start.

And go curiously gentle,
With your gifts within your mind,
And support them with their life of loss,
With all your love and all that's kind.

By Rachel W

Epilogue:

IN HINDSIGHT

Lessons from a Very Broken System

There are moments when everything shifts – when you realise the system isn't just broken but designed in a way that perpetuates harm. I remember the day I understood that this wasn't about individual failings, but about a structure that protects power while failing the most vulnerable. And yet, amidst all the failures, I still hold on to one thing: hope.

As I reflect on this journey, I am struck by the profound lessons it has taught me – lessons about survival, the power of connection, and the responsibility to speak out for those who cannot. These lessons converge on a simple but undeniable truth: division has no place in a system designed to nurture and protect. Division fractures both systems and people, undermining our ability to create compassionate, effective care – the kind of care every child and young person deserves.

Throughout my work in children's social care, one guiding principle has remained constant: children learn what they live. This truth, beautifully captured in Dorothy Law Nolte's timeless poem, reminds us that the environments we create for children shape not only their childhoods but also the adults they become.

I first encountered Nolte's words on a poster in a children's home 49 years ago. It was my first lesson in childcare, and its wisdom has stayed with me ever since. Her poem – and later, her 1998 book *Children Learn What They Live: Parenting to Inspire Values* – offered more than inspiration. It provided a roadmap for creating nurturing relationships and environments where children can begin to heal and thrive.

A copy of the book still sits on my shelf, a quiet but constant reminder of the values that have guided my practice. '*If children live with criticism, they learn to condemn.*' I've seen this time and again in the lives of children who arrived in care after being relentlessly judged or blamed. They often came carrying the weight of those early experiences, learning to distrust others – and sometimes, even themselves. But I've also seen what's possible. '*If children live with encouragement, they learn confidence.*'

These words are more than a sentiment – they're a truth I've seen lived out, especially in trauma-informed care. Encouragement builds confidence. Fairness teaches justice. Kindness fosters respect. These are the values that matter – and they are learned through experience.

Yet all too often, those ideals clash with the realities of our current care system. The children who enter care do so carrying the scars of a world that failed to nurture them. Their pain is not only the result of individual harm but also of systemic neglect – a compliance-driven system that too often values procedures over people, and policies over connection.

These words remind us of what is possible when we embrace trauma-informed care. They call us to create environments that heal, that reassure children of their inherent worth, and that teach them to trust again. But systemic challenges demand urgent and fundamental action. The current system cannot simply be tweaked; it must be rebuilt to break cycles of harm and prioritise healing, stability, and growth.

This means providing trauma-informed support for children and young people, integrating services that address the complexities of family life, and ensuring care leavers have the resources they need to build stable and fulfilling futures. It means reforming inspections to focus on meaningful outcomes, not mere compliance. Most importantly, it requires dismantling the barriers of division and recognising that we are stronger when we work together toward a shared vision of care and justice.

I have seen firsthand what becomes possible when connection replaces division and action triumphs over indifference. I have witnessed the unwavering dedication of caregivers who work tirelessly to create stability and healing for children, despite immense obstacles. I have felt it in the shared stories of survival and courage at events like YLYS, where voices are lifted, truths are shared, and connections are forged. And I have seen it in the lives of children who, with the right support, overcome unimaginable odds to thrive.

But survival alone is not enough. Every child deserves the opportunity to heal, to grow, and to thrive. True care goes beyond ensuring physical safety; it is about cultivating spaces where children feel a deep sense of worth and belonging. Whether through trauma-informed care or integrated support systems, our work must rise above compliance and bureaucracy, ensuring that every child and young person has the chance to flourish.

The consequences of systemic failures reach far beyond childhood. Care-experienced individuals face disproportionate challenges in every aspect of their lives. Research shows they are 70 percent more likely to die prematurely, with many deaths resulting from preventable causes such as mental health struggles and substance misuse. For care-experienced mothers, the cycle of harm often continues, with 40 percent involved in recurrent care proceedings – trapped in a system that isolates them instead of supporting their healing.

These statistics are not just numbers; they represent real people whose lives have been shaped by a system that stepped in too late – or not well enough when it did. Regulation, although meant to safeguard standards, often exacerbates the problem. Standardised thresholds and rigid frameworks disregard individual complexities, delaying interventions or resulting in unnecessary removals. Yet regulation itself is not the enemy. When thoughtfully implemented, it can guide practice and empower caregivers to make informed, compassionate decisions.

Children and young people require more than physical safety. They need emotional healing, stability, and the assurance that they are valued. Trauma-informed care must become the standard at every level of the system. We must also address the silos created by the structural separation of children's and adult services, prioritising integrated approaches that support families.

Furthermore, care must not end when a child turns eighteen. From mental health services to housing and employment opportunities, care leavers need robust resources to build stable, meaningful lives. This is not just a call for policy reform – it is a call to action.

Policymakers, social care professionals, educators, and community leaders must unite to demand systemic change. Together, we can advocate for reforms that prioritise care over compliance, support trauma-informed practices, hold institutions accountable for harm, and elevate the voices of care-experienced individuals to shape policies that reflect their lived realities. This is not the end of the story, nor is it mine alone.

Imagine a care system where no child is treated as a last resort, where trauma-informed support isn't just a buzzword but the foundation of everything we do. A system where inspections uplift rather than punish, and were turning eighteen doesn't mean being cast adrift – but stepping into adulthood with stability, guidance, and purpose. This isn't just an ideal – it's a future we must strive for.

Together, we can build a system rooted in connection, compassion, and hope – a future where division has no place, and where every child and young person is given the opportunity to heal, grow, and reach their full potential.

At the heart of this vision is the need for care that is truly therapeutic grounded in deep understanding, emotional connection, and a commitment to healing.

One person whose work embodies this is Christine Bradley. Her contributions have the potential to shape modern therapeutic practice, offering an approach that integrates psychoanalytic insight with contemporary neuroscience to support traumatised children.

Christine's work, rooted in the pioneering traditions of the Cotswold Community, builds upon the legacies of Donald Winnicott and Barbara Dockar-Drysdale, who helped redefine therapeutic care for children with complex emotional needs. Her teachings reinforce what many of us have long known: children's behaviours are not isolated problems, but expressions of unmet needs and unresolved trauma.

Her book, *Trauma in Children and Young People: Reaching the Heart of the Matter*, along with her subsequent publication, *Developing a Therapeutic Treatment Programme for Traumatised Children and Young People: A Needs-Led Assessment Model* – serve as invaluable resources for shaping the future of care.

Together, we can create a future where every child and young person receives the care, understanding, and support they deserve. A future where the system is not defined by compliance, but by compassion – where every child has the opportunity to heal, grow, and reach their full potential.

The time for change is now, and it begins with us – all of us.

ACKNOWLEDGEMENTS

Your Life Your Story is a community of people who have lived and worked in the care system over five decades – a collective of voices and experiences, and a testament to resilience, truth-telling, and the power of connection. This memoir would not exist without the strength and contributions of this extraordinary community.

When people come together to speak openly – about struggle, survival, and hope – change becomes possible. We've built a powerful network of connection, one that insists on using our collective voice to challenge injustice and champion humanity.

To my fellow Your Life Your Story Directors – past and present. Yusuf, sadly no longer with us but not forgotten, Tasmin, David, Saira-Jayne, and Jackie – thank you for your steadfast support and shared purpose. To the poets and authors whose words deepen these pages – thank you.

As I near the end of five decades in children's social care, I honour the influence of Christine Bradley. Her legacy shaped my understanding of trauma-informed care and continues to guide my practice.

To the children and young people I've cared for – and the remarkable adults you've become – thank you. Your courage and honesty have shaped everything I do.

To those who stood with us – attending events, offering time, resources, and belief – thank you. To Pete, my business partner, for your unwavering support and vision. To Lisa, who's walked this journey beside me – your strength and loyalty have been vital. To Dr George – thank you for your steady, thoughtful guidance.

To my husband – my rock – and to my daughters, whose passion and purpose inspire me every day, thank you for grounding me in love and giving me the courage to keep going.

This is not the end of the journey. The work continues. The hope endures. I move forward with deep gratitude – for the roots we've planted, the community that has grown, and the belief that compassion, care, and connection will always find a way.

To everyone who has been part of this story – caregiver, care-experienced, ally, professional, or quiet supporter – thank you. There are too many of you to name, but none of you are forgotten. You belong here. Your voice matters. This community is stronger because of you.

All net proceeds from this book will go to YLYS.

*(Should YLYS cease to operate, the rights and proceeds will
revert to my grandchildren, or as directed by my estate,
for their benefit or for the benefit of the care-experienced
community, as deemed appropriate at that time, including but
not limited to their education and well-being.)*